AUTOCOURSE

Hartmut Lehbrink/Jörg-Thomas Födisch

Faces of Formula 1

The Sixties – Photos Dr. Benno Müller

Forewords by Bernie Ecclestone & Richard Attwood

icon PUBLISHING LIMITED

Credits

This English-language edition is published by:
Icon Publishing Limited,
2 Redesdale House, 85 The Park,
Cheltenham, GL50 2RP, United Kingdom.
Tel: +44 (0)1242 245329

Editorial office: Park Farm Barn, New Street,
Deddington OX15 0SS, United Kingdom.
Tel: +44 (0)1869 361940

Publisher: Steve Small
Commercial Director: Bryn Williams

© Icon Publishing Limited 2024
All rights reserved. No part of this publication may be reproduced, stored in a retrieval system or transmitted, in any form or by any means, electronic, mechanical, photocopying, recording or otherwise, without prior permission in writing from the publisher and the authors.

ISBN: 9781 910584-60-6

© Design & layout:
Rainer Rossbach, www.magazinmacher.de

Text: © Hartmut Lehbrink
Photos: © Jörg-Thomas Födisch/Archiv Födisch
English translation: David Nash, Sally Bald
Text editor for Icon Publishing: Ian Penberthy

Printed in China through World Print Ltd.

Contents

5		Foreword by Bernie Ecclestone
6		Foreword by Richard Attwood
8		Foreword by Hartmut Lehbrink
11		Introduction by Steve Small
13		Dr. Benno Müller
14		Letters from Dr Müller
17		Letter from Stirling Moss
18		Maurice Trintignant
20		Harry Schell
22		Stirling Moss
24		Roy Salvadori
26		Edgar Barth
28		Wolfgang Seidel
30		Hans Herrmann
32		Jack Brabham
34		Olivier Gendebien
36		Henry Taylor
38		Tony Brooks
40		Joakim Bonnier
42		Wolfgang Graf Berghe von Trips
44		Masten Gregory
46		Carel Godin de Beaufort
48		Giulio Cabianca
50		Graham Hill
52		Cliff Allison
54		Phil Hill
56		Alan Stacey
58		Bruce McLaren
60		Lucien Bianchi
62		Innes Ireland
64		Dan Gurney
66		Chris Bristow
68		Richie Ginther
70		John Surtees
72		Jim Clark
74		Lance Reventlow
76		Willy Mairesse
78		Jim Hall
80		Trevor Taylor
82		Jack Lewis
84		Nino Vaccarella
86		Lorenzo Bandini
88		Giancarlo Baghetti
90		Tony Maggs
92		Ricardo Rodrìguez
94		Roger Penske
96		Tim Mayer
98		Neville Lederle
100		Jo Siffert
102		Tony Settember
104		Chris Amon
106		Ludovico Scarfiotti
108		Gerhard Mitter
110		Bob Anderson
112		Mike Hailwood
114		John Taylor
116		Mike Spence
118		Pedro Rodrìguez
120		Moisés Solana
122		Peter Arundell
124		Richard Attwood
126		John Love
128		Ronnie Bucknum
130		Walt Hansgen
132		Jochen Rindt
134		Paul Hawkins
136		Jackie Stewart
138		Denis Hulme
140		Bob Bondurant
142		Guy Ligier
144		Chris Irwin
146		Mike Parkes
148		Alan Rees
150		Jo Schlesser
152		Hubert Hahne
154		Jean-Pierre Beltoise
156		Kurt Ahrens
158		Silvio Moser
160		Piers Courage
162		Jacky Ickx
164		Johnny Servoz-Gavin
166		David Hobbs
168		Jackie Oliver
170		Brian Redman
172		Vic Elford
174		Derek Bell
176		Henri Pescarolo
178		Mario Andretti
180		Credits

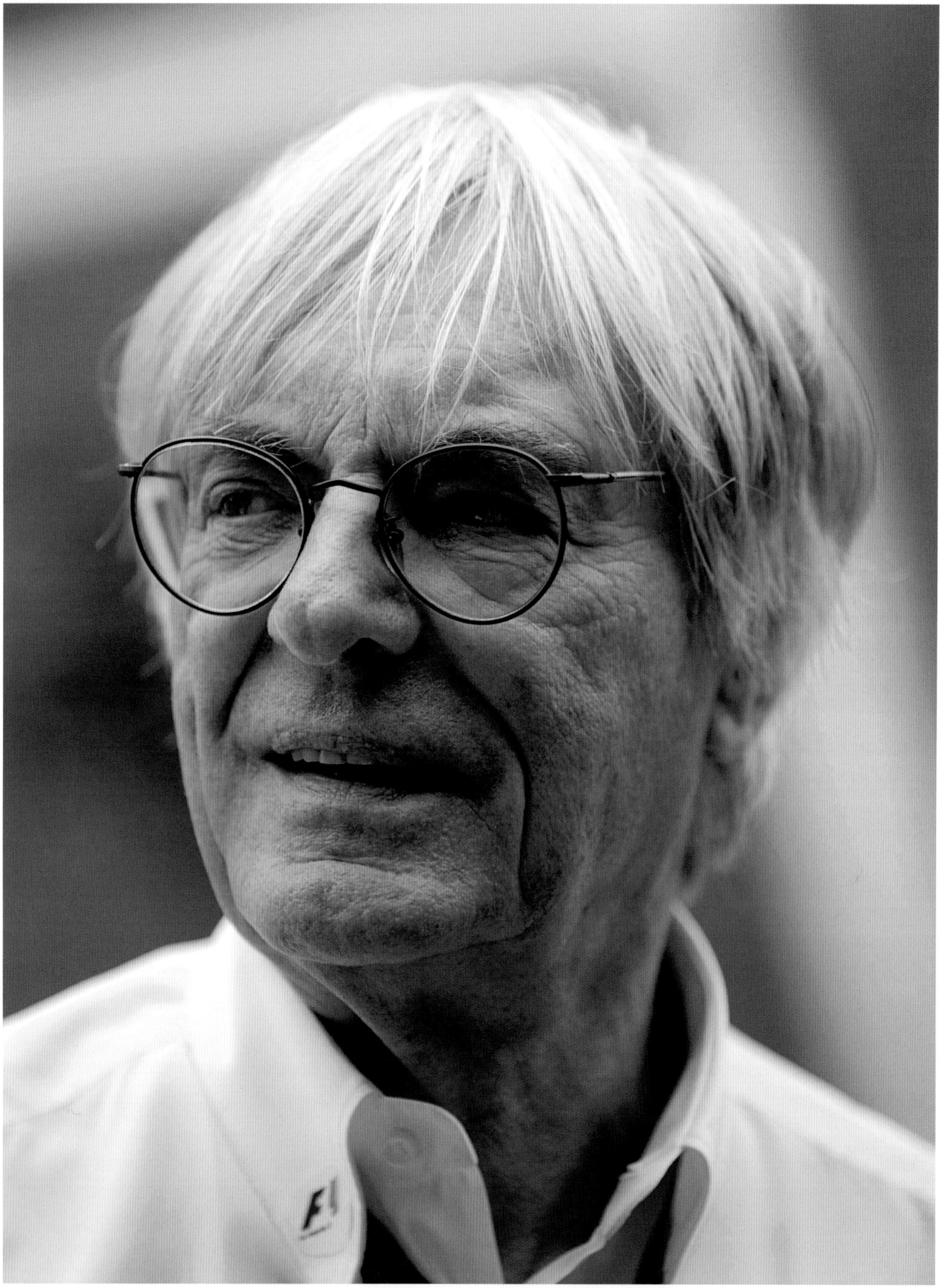

Bernie Ecclestone Foreword

▶ F1 racing in the sixties – that mere handful of words evokes a lot of mixed feelings: perhaps the most romantic phase of the sport; fragile machinery run on shoestring budgets; incredibly dangerous venues like the old Nürburgring and Belgian Spa circuits; the loss of many good drivers.

My own role in racing during those years was fairly modest. After my close friend Stuart Lewis-Evans had been killed driving a Vanwall at Casablanca in 1958, I retired from competition altogether.

Meeting Jochen Rindt, who was then driving in both Formula 1 and Formula 2, reignited my passion, and Jochen became a close mate, as did Graham Hill, whose business matters I looked after. When Roy Winkelmann Racing withdrew from F2 at the end of the decade, I formed a partnership with Rindt, whom I lost in September, 1970, when he died at Monza. Then I became a major shareholder of the Brabham racing car business a year later.

But, of course, I knew them all, the fabulous drivers included in this book, most of them unjustly long since forgotten. Dr Müller's portraits are so much more than just pictures, radiating much of these men's characters and personalities.

I wish the book and its authors the plaudits and success that they deserve.

Richard Attwood Foreword

▶ *Faces of Formula 1, The Sixties* is an amazing new motor racing book. There are no action pictures because it depicts only the drivers of that era, the protagonists of what is seen by many enthusiasts as the most glamorous of all sports. It was also a very dangerous time when the survival rate was not good. Safety was of a very low standard, as the cars were utterly deformable and the circuits very unforgiving. This was because essentially a lot of circuits were based on normal roads that had been adapted to race on – like Reims, Rouen, Le Mans, Spa and Monte Carlo – rather like it was in the earliest days of GP racing.

For me, it is sad to see so many great friends in this book who died unnecessarily in circumstances that were primitive by today's standards. Ultimately, it was Jackie Stewart who made a move to make racing safer. He was the first driver to address this terrible situation, and as far as I remember, he was alone in his quest to start a very real safety campaign. This was after his 1966 accident at Spa in the rain, when he was trapped in his BRM and needed outside assistance to escape. I had a similar crash in 1965, again at Spa, where two spectators came to my aid. Otherwise, I would have become another statistic.

Those were very different times in a completely different era, when mostly we stayed in the same hotels, travelling together, racing together and partying together.

Today, it is difficult to believe that we were so close and lived our racing lives together. This is why the modern racing world can never really understand how life was back then.

I still have two lovely pictures of myself at the Nürburgring taken around 1964–68 by Müller, quite an impressive character. He had a lovely smile and a softness not seen very often. He enjoyed people more than racing. That is all I know about the man behind the lens.

But, I'm sure that this book will ensure that his work will be remembered for ever.

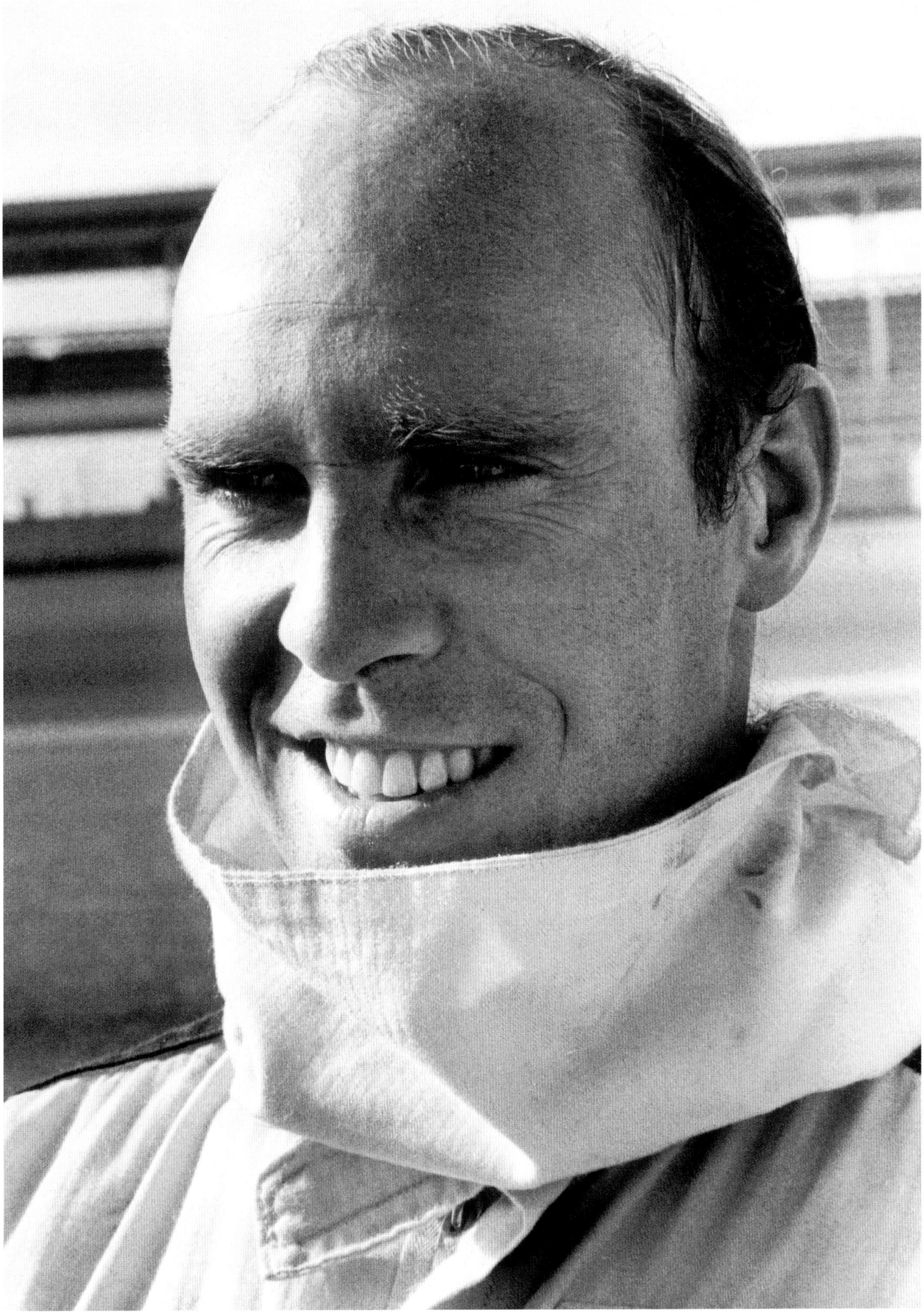

Author's introduction

Hartmut Lehbrink

▶ Strictly speaking, the change from yesterday to tomorrow, from the past to the future of grand prix racing, took place in 1961 rather than 11 years earlier, when Formula 1 had been invented. From the first year of the rapid and nimble 1.5-litre single-seaters onwards, the new architecture, with the engine sitting behind the driver, had become imperative, and that has remained the case to the present day.

In the following nine years, the evolution of the top tier of motor sport brought forth ever newer offspring, such as Colin Chapman's trailblazing Lotus 25 with its light and strong monocoque. And the potent and compact discounter V8 Cosworth DFV, from the 1967 Dutch GP onwards, which provided access to podium places even for have-nots like the young Frank Williams.

With his triumph in the Ferrari Dino 246, chassis 0007, in September, 1960 at Monza (where else?), Phil Hill had left a final exclamation mark behind the conventional arrangement. The F1 cars of the fifties still featured the unmistakable genes of their predecessors from 20 years earlier, although refined to the latest state of the art, and epitomised by the Mercedes-Benz Silver Arrows in 1954 and '55. The rear-engined principle was not even a novelty, given that Auto Union had created grand prix oddities that only Mozarts of the wheel – like Bernd Rosemeyer and Tazio Nuvolari – could tame. Four metres of engine bay plus one emergency seat at the front was the common description, and there was certainly truth in that.

At the same time, Formula 1 moved to Britain as its new home, spiritual as well as material. Four of the six leading manufacturers and teams (Cooper, BRM, Lotus and MRD, aka Brabham) resided on the island, with just two on the Continental side of the Channel: Matra, the French state-owned group, and Ferrari. Watching from his splendid isolation at Maranello, the *Commendatore* grudgingly had to accept the rapid growth of the *garagisti*, those tinkerers and assemblers, as he contemptuously put it. The year of supremacy, 1961, was succeeded by a painful slump for the *cavallino rampante*, which lasted until the mid-seventies, interrupted only by the two Ferrari championships in 1964, courtesy of John Surtees, and then only by a hair's breadth.

One of the aspects of that decade, appreciated far too little, is that the glamorous grand prix could be competed for on a shoestring. Roy Salvadori once told me that his Cooper-Maserati outfit in 1966 and '67 was run with little more than a handful of staff, thanks to elaborate and extremely efficient multi-tasking.

Nino Farina, Alberto Ascari, and Juan Manuel Fangio – between them, holders of all eight titles between 1950 and '57 – were not prepared to answer you in English, nor were they able to. But now, the idiom of Cooper, Lotus, and Vanwall quickly began to spread as the lingua franca of the circuits. English, in a great variety of colours, was spoken by the seven world champions of the sixties: Jack Brabham, Phil Hill, Graham Hill, Jim Clark, John Surtees, Denny Hulme and Jackie Stewart. That also applied to the key protagonists of Formula 1, such as Colin Chapman, Ken Tyrrell and Rob Walker, who for quite a while ran a very successful private racing stable. Curiously, the sixties was also the decade of the Scots, above all the two world champions, Clark and Stewart, and the laid-back whisky heir Walker.

A word that cautiously began to make its presence felt in racing's dictionary towards the end of the decade was 'safety'. Up to that point, danger had threatened everywhere – from trees, walls, kerbstones, marshals' posts and bunkers – you name it. As late as 1969, at the newly-opened Österreichring, in a worst-case scenario, a car that had left the track at the fast Bosch Kurve might have hit a small Baroque chapel. The drivers just had to live with the smirk of the Grim Reaper beside Burnenville, Fuchsröhre, Lesmo and Peraltada. Peril was part and parcel of their occupational profile, like the imperative for others to show up in the office punctually, with shirt and tie and clean fingernails. But it couldn't be eradicated from their subconscious, and the same went for the haunting images of their comrades' deaths, which they would witness time and time again.

Men like Stirling Moss and Maurice Trintignant, not unlike Mercedes pre-war star Manfred von Brauchitsch, even made it clear that the very challenge of their sport was formed by the ultimate risk they were taking. Of course, first you have to survive to utter such pithy lines, unlike so many of that era.

Even the fragility of their cars played its part in that thrill. Graham Hill, in his later years heavily stigmatised by numerous crashes, bore it with grim humour. "Whenever I'm overtaken by a wheel of my own car," he would say, "I know that I'm sitting in a Lotus." Or just, "A wheel fell off." Four little words after yet another dramatic shunt.

A couple of words on behalf of the author. To a certain extent, I seem to be qualified to recount something of that far-away era, and do so from the heart. Admittedly, such a claim smacks of an empty boast and a blatant conceit, but in my case it is a fact, not a merit, just a unique feature that just continued as time went by. It is due solely and exclusively to the irresistible fascination of this sport, and maybe also to the fact that the writer of these lines seems to be a particularly hard-core specimen among its disciples.

Strange as it may seem, I'm telling my own story.

I watched them all driving, knew many of them personally and had – still have – the immense pleasure to be friends with some of them. Beyond my professional aims, I've always been keen on getting in touch with, or even being close to, the people who occupy my mind so much. That was much easier when they were not being chased and besieged by hundreds of journalists and other supplicants, only to vanish as quickly as possible into the well-tempered seclusion of the residential sections of the team hospitality areas.

Only as this book came into being did I begin to realise how lucky I have been. Comfortably equipped with a lifetime FIA Honorary Pass, with more than 550 GPs in my CV, I am indeed probably the only person in F1's paddock and media centre to have witnessed the complete history of Formula 1, from Ascari, Farina, Fangio, Villoresi, de Graffenried, and company, through to the third era of the Silver Arrows, with the serial victories of Lewis Hamilton and the Mercedes-AMG Petronas Formula One Team, under the expert guidance of Toto Wolff, and into F1's postmodern age, which will be shaped by the likes of Max Verstappen, Charles Leclerc and Lando Norris.

At first, I was there as a fan, gatecrashing into the sites of my dreams with the help of painstaking local knowledge and sheer brashness. In the sixties, more and more owing to friendships, good relations and the odd little job, then from 1971 onwards, as a reporter and author. Teddy Yip, the legendary wealthy Hong Kong-based entrepreneur and supporter of racing greats like Patrick Tambay, Vern Schuppan and Keke Rosberg, once told me, "If you really want something, you will get it." Racing stable owner Walter Wolf used to voice the same message.

They were right.

Leading and supporting actors in the great grand prix drama: To the fore, from the left, are: Wolfgang von Trips, Joakim Bonnier, John Surtees, Stirling Moss, Jim Clark, Tony Brooks and Phil Hill. The stage is Spa-Francorchamps in 1961 at the Belgian Grand Prix driver briefing. Scepticism prevails...

Publisher's Introduction

As an avid fan of motor racing since my teenage years in the 1960s, F1 gladiators such as Brabham, Clark, Hill, Stewart, *et al*, were captured by evocative photos in books bought at the start of my early motor-racing library. Both *Automobile Year* and AUTOCOURSE were in the vanguard of quality motor racing publications, with modern layouts and often daringly cropped photos taken by the leading lensmen of the time, such as Horst Baumann, Julius Weitmann, David Phipps, Rainer Schlegelmilch and, of course, Dr Benno Müller.

II was fortunate to purchase a copy of his *Race Drivers* (published in 1963), a large-format book that dramatically captured portraits of the drivers of the day. Since then, there have been a couple of further books of more modest size, but in the German language only, to showcase the Doctor's work.

At last, this English-language book from AUTOCOURSE brings together in one volume all of the major drivers of the sixties, Müller's stunning photos being complemented superbly by Hartmut Lehbrink's succinct and highly personal portraits. Together, they provide a vivid and moving document of a long-lost era, when triumph and tragedy so often went hand in hand.

Steve Small
Icon Publishing Limited
2024

Copyright: Dr. Benno Müller
Kirchhofen/Brsg.
Veröffentlichung nur mit ausdrücklicher Genehmigung des Autors.

Dr. Benno Müller

* 1912 – † 1997

▶ Quite unjustly, the terms 'amateur' and 'dilettante' are fraught with negative connotations. From an etymological view, both encompass the type who would lovingly tend a rose garden, without having to earn their keep from so doing.

Dr Benno Müller, a country doctor from Kirchhofen, not far from Freiburg im Breisgau, in the Black Forest, was just such an amateur or dilettante, in the best (original) sense of the words. In 1957, his friend Heinz-Ulrich Wieselmann, bustling editor-in-chief of the specialist magazine *Auto Motor und Sport*, took him to the 1,000km at the Nürburgring. Müller was blown away by what he saw. He was fascinated by the facial characteristics of the drivers. To his mind, they were landscapes depicting their souls, not unlike the faces of his patients in which he read both diagnoses and therapies. In the drivers' cases, he had no doubt at all: incurable, but in an intriguing way.

The medium he used to record and render his impressions was the camera: his Leica, his Hasselblad, his Rolleiflex. Always, as he tried to explain his profoundly psychological art, he took his photos from the point of view of a doctor, and quite soon was doing so professionally.

Four books, primarily in the sixties, as well as countless contributions to magazines and exhibitions, bore witness to that. His pictures spoke volumes, with black and white his preferred medium, boiling down the complex into the essential. It was helpful, indeed, that Müller was capable of relieving the photographic moment of all tension, capturing the very essence of a personality in one of his masterpieces.

Racing cars and the races themselves left him cold. Long before the flag dropped, Müller would disappear in the direction of the Black Forest. He would have been unable to bear it if something had happened to one of his heroes, worse still to somebody with whom he had just held one of his close conversations.

The racing cosmos of the sixties was a man's world, a historical gauntlet, as it were, flung down before the agitated feminists, 60 years later. Dr Benno Müller counterbalanced this elsewhere, at the Iffezheim horse races halfway between Freiburg and Hockenheim, his camera in hand as usual. What appealed to him most of all was the elegance, grace and style of the women – but also the failed attempts to create that impact.

Dr. Benno Müller
Arzt für Allgemeinmedizin
Kirchplatz 5
D-7801 Kirchhofen

Kirchhofen 1.III.90

Dear Misters

Your address I recieved from Mr. Max Mosley and he wrote, that You are Book-publishing Specialists.

Please excuse my bad English. I learnt a little as a prisoner of war.

I am medicine Doctor but as hobby I learned (but I had no teacher) 1956 to make photos and because I was always a motorsport fan (as a young Doctor I drove 1936 - 1938 a used Grand Prix Bugatti (two liters without compressor) And from 1957 to 1980) was nearly every year on a Grand-Prix race or on the 1000 km race at the Nürburgring.

1961 appeared my first book „Race car driver" 1970 the second and 1976 a book over motorcycle races. In the first years I maked many portraits from car-drivers, later too, but often I maked photos from the atmosphere on the boxes, the ladies, the fitters, the cars the motors and the details of cars and motors.

A real rarity are my photos from drivers with ladies together and drivers in conversation. Today the drivers don't speach together! I know Clark very good and my collection of pictures is 80 Blak and White (Portraits and Living in the boxes and cars) and 25 Color Dias (6×6 Hasselblad-Camera) In this context it is interesting that my Hasselblad Dias from 1957 til 1962 are so very good in color like the Leicaflex Dias from the next years.

I had a other manner to make photos the the professionell photographers. I never made photos for money and worked exclusive because enthusiasms and just for fun. Not only the faces from the drivers and ladies were interesting for me also the beauty from the cars and details and the game of light and shadow. Enclosed is a list from my photos. If you are interested to make a book or more I would send a collection from photos in Black and White and Color.

With best wishes

Are you interested on motorcycle-races? I have 1700 pictures from the best car drivers I have respective 5 til 20 pictures

Yours sincerly
Benno Müller

BENNO MÜLLER

RACEDRIVERS

Stirling Moss Limited

16th January, 1990.

SM/SP

Dr. Benno Muller,
Kirchplatz 5,
D-7801 Kirchhofen,
Germany.

Dear Dr. Muller,

What wonderful pictures!

I am so grateful to you for sending me such magnificent shots of so many friends in my racing career. Each one of them is absolutely superb.

I don't know if I shall ever write another book relative to my racing career but if I should, can you tell me what your position is concerning copyright.

I do hope you are keeping well and look forward to receiving your reply when you have a moment.

All the best,

Ciao,

46 SHEPHERD STREET LONDON W1Y 8JN   TEL 01-499 7967 & 3272   CABLES ESSEMM LONDON W1
Directors: STIRLING MOSS, O.B.E., F.I.E.   V. K. PIRIE   R. L. GINSWICK   S. PAINE

Maurice Trintignant

* 1917 – † 2005

▶ Amid the sixties generation, Maurice Trintignant occupied a unique position: robbed of his best racing driver's years by the Second World War, the man with the woollen cap, the caravan behind the pits and the finely-trimmed moustache had already been active in the thirties, taking on the likes of Tazio Nuvolari and Rudolf Caracciola, as well as Juan Manuel Fangio, Stirling Moss, Jim Clark and Graham Hill. "Racing is a lifelong passion," he used to say. "Whoever wants to do this for eight or ten years only should leave it altogether."

Somehow, Trintignant's career on either side of the interface between the epochs is mirrored by his two GP victories, both at Monaco: in 1955, aboard a Ferrari 625/555 as an exponent of the doomed front-engined giants, then in 1958, driving Rob Walker's nimble little Cooper T45, the second triumph for the British lightweight, with its Climax 4 engine mounted in the rear, following Stirling Moss's momentous first that year at Buenos Aires.

The way he did it says a lot about him. Almost a local, as a citizen of neighbouring southern France, Trintignant was anything but a charger. In the roaring roulette around the Casino, he drove intelligently, using the bad luck of others to his advantage, with a cool head and precision. That also went for his 1954 Le Mans win, in a Ferrari 375 Plus, partnered by 'Pampas Bull' Froilan González.

Since the outbreak of the war, Maurice Trintignant had lived not far from Vergèze, a picturesque little town on the border between Provence and Languedoc. After finally pulling the plug on racing in 1965, he continued to live in his beautiful hacienda, 'Mas d'Arnaud', surrounded by 52 hectares of grapes over which the mistral brushed in summer. The wine he produced, which filled neat bulbous bottles, was called 'Le Pétoulet', which once had been his own nickname.

How that came about is a long story – and not necessarily one to make your mouth water.

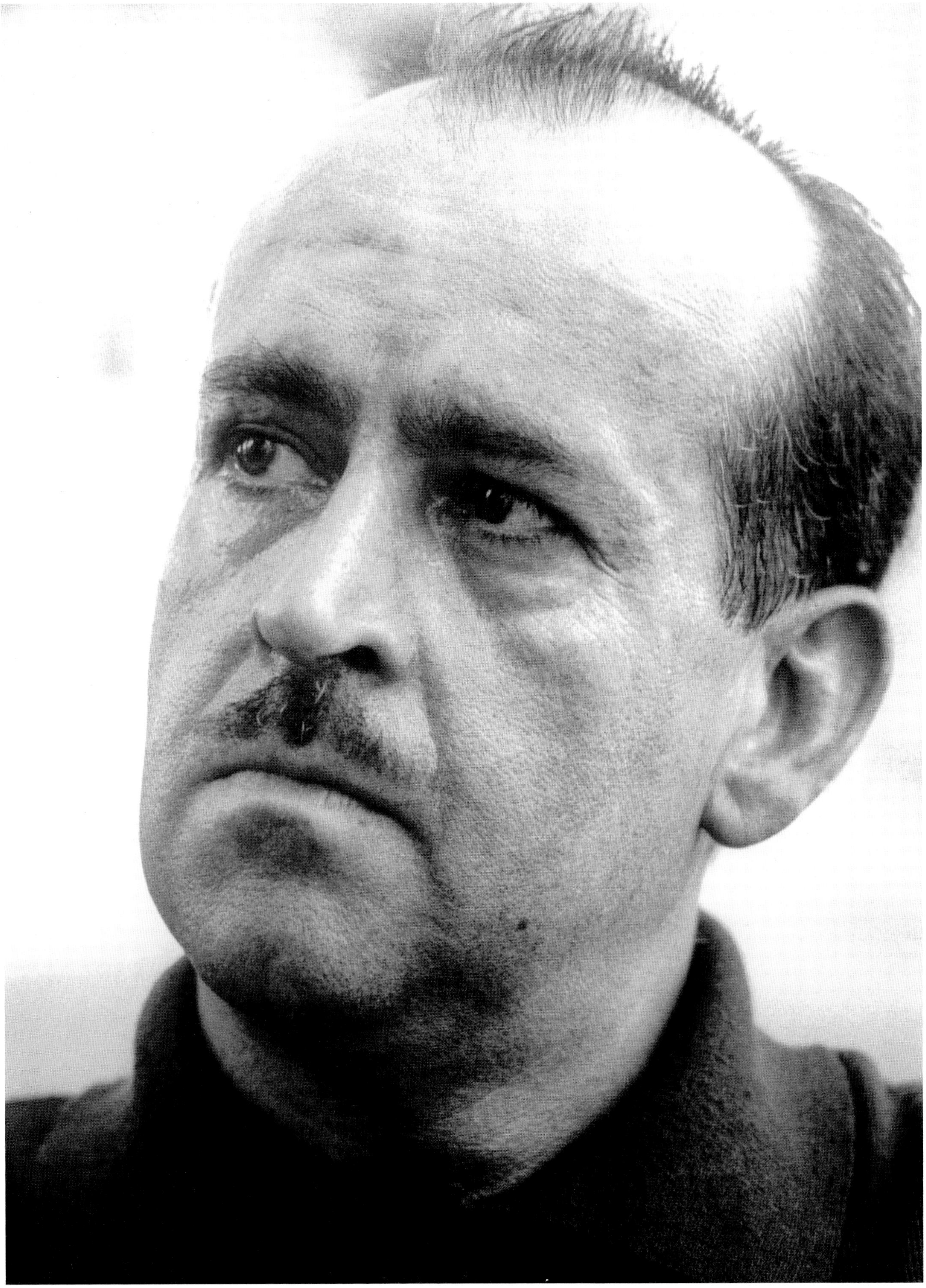

Harry Schell * 1921 – † 1960

▶ In the fifties, Harry Schell was ranked among the great driver personalities, as they might have been called during that time, but certainly not because of the 30 points he gathered in 56 grands prix between 1950 and 1960. Also not because he contested his maiden GP, the second altogether in the brand-new Formula 1 format, in a rear-engined car, a premiere in Monaco in 1950, aboard the minuscule F3 Cooper T12-JAP.

Instead, or rather in addition to his ability on the tracks, he caused a stir as a vivacious complete 'work of art', of which his racing was only one facet, being an 'American in Paris', where he had been born. His mother, Lucy, was of Irish extraction, while his father, Laury, had Native American ancestors. Together, they founded and ran the Écurie Bleue team, not least to give their bustling and talented son an opportunity to race.

Harry liked women, wine and song, in that order, and was one of the founding members of a respected group of playboys. With friends 'Fon' de Portago and Porfirio Rubirosa, he ran in Paris an immensely popular sporting bar named 'L'Action Automobile', not unlike London's Steering Wheel Club. Its prices were horrendous. He was a great one for practical jokes of all sorts, and if you heard a loud mooing behind you in the French traffic, you could be sure that Schell's Lancia would be in your mirrors, Harry, grinning, honking the very unusual horn that had been specially made for him.

Like de Portago and Rubirosa, Schell died in a car, on 13th May, 1960. Practising with the British Racing Partnership's Cooper T51 at Silverstone, he ran off the damp track and that was it. BRP manager Ken Gregory had the macabre task of identifying his friend, the first dead person he had ever seen. Time and again, he would say that Harry Schell had been smiling.

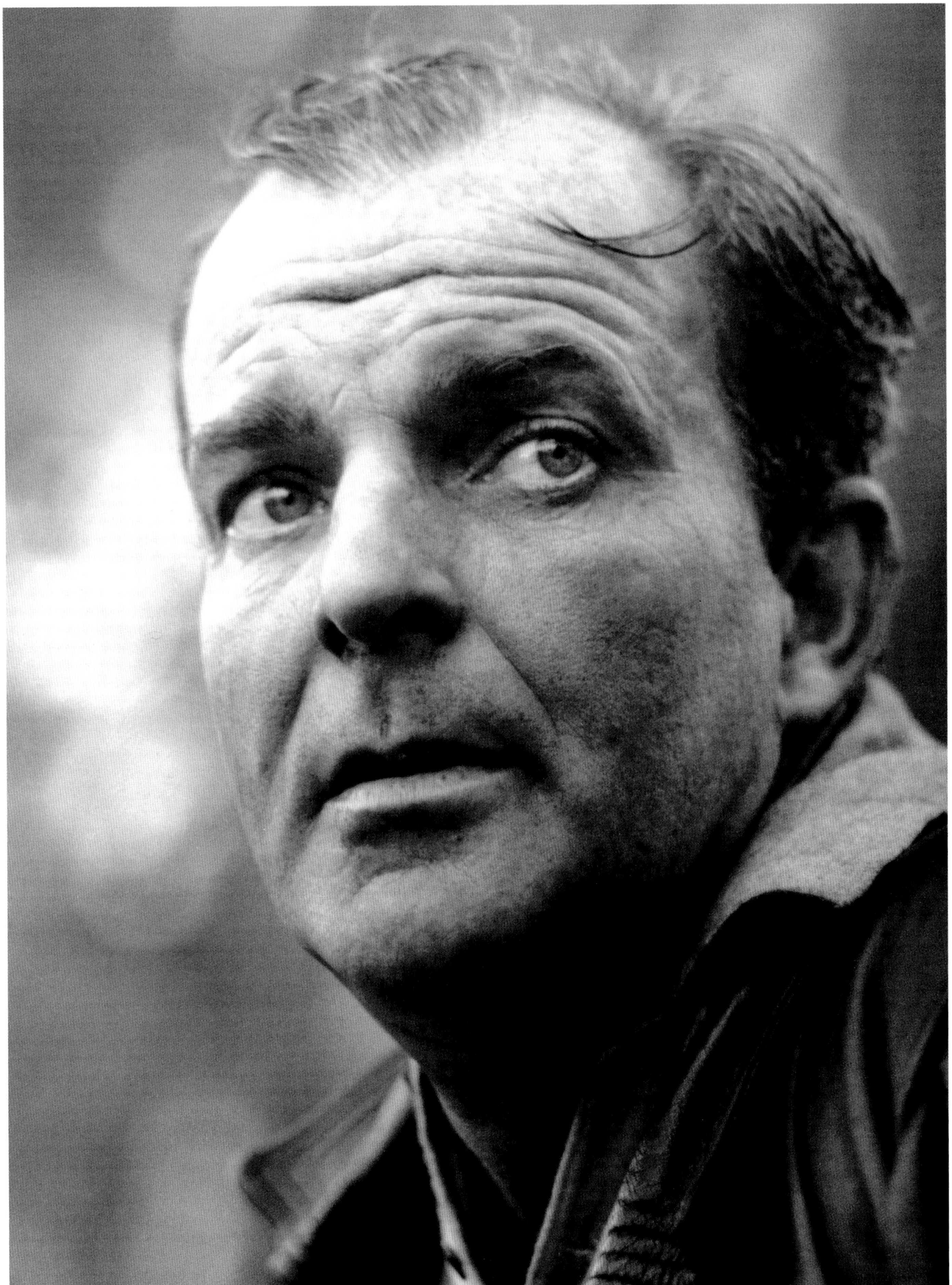

Stirling Moss

*1929 – †2020

▶ For quite some time, an ominous silence had shrouded the condition of Stirling Moss, OBE. Rumour had it that he was still living in his London house, a haven of peace in the long shadow of the Hilton on Park Lane, lovingly cared for by his charming wife, Susie. Occasionally, it leaked out that Sir Stirling, knighted in 2000 for his services to Queen and country, was not faring well.

The Moss myth lay dormant. With his death on 12th April, 2020, however, it suddenly re-emerged, and hence the saga of the hero who had won the Mille Miglia in the mighty Mercedes-Benz 300 SLR, and the blue-riband grands prix of Monaco (twice!) and Germany in Rob Walker's minuscule Lotus 18. He who had gone down in history as the best driver never to have become world champion. With the 90-year-old's late crossing of the finish line, the chequered flag had been waved, ending an era whose eloquent spokesman Moss had always been. His message: no challenge without danger, no ultimate satisfaction without risk of death.

Moss definitely knew what he was talking about. His 14 years of racing were peppered with terrible accidents. One of them, on 23rd April, 1962, at Goodwood, put an end to his career and very nearly his existence. Moss was a massive all-round talent, a genius at any wheel. However, the big titles escaped him for two basic reasons. In the fifties, the racing gods had thrust the untouchable fivefold champion Juan Manuel Fangio under his nose, but eventually Stirling's fervent patriotism turned out to be his worst foe.

Moss considered himself a dyed-in-the-wool son of his country, whose very soul was wrapped in British Racing Green, as it were. In the private racing stable of the laid-back 'Gentleman' Walker, he finally found the warmth and security in which he flourished best. The underdog who constantly manages to work wonders with inferior material is, after all, one of the most attractive facets motor sport has to offer.

Stirling Moss was the ideal fit.

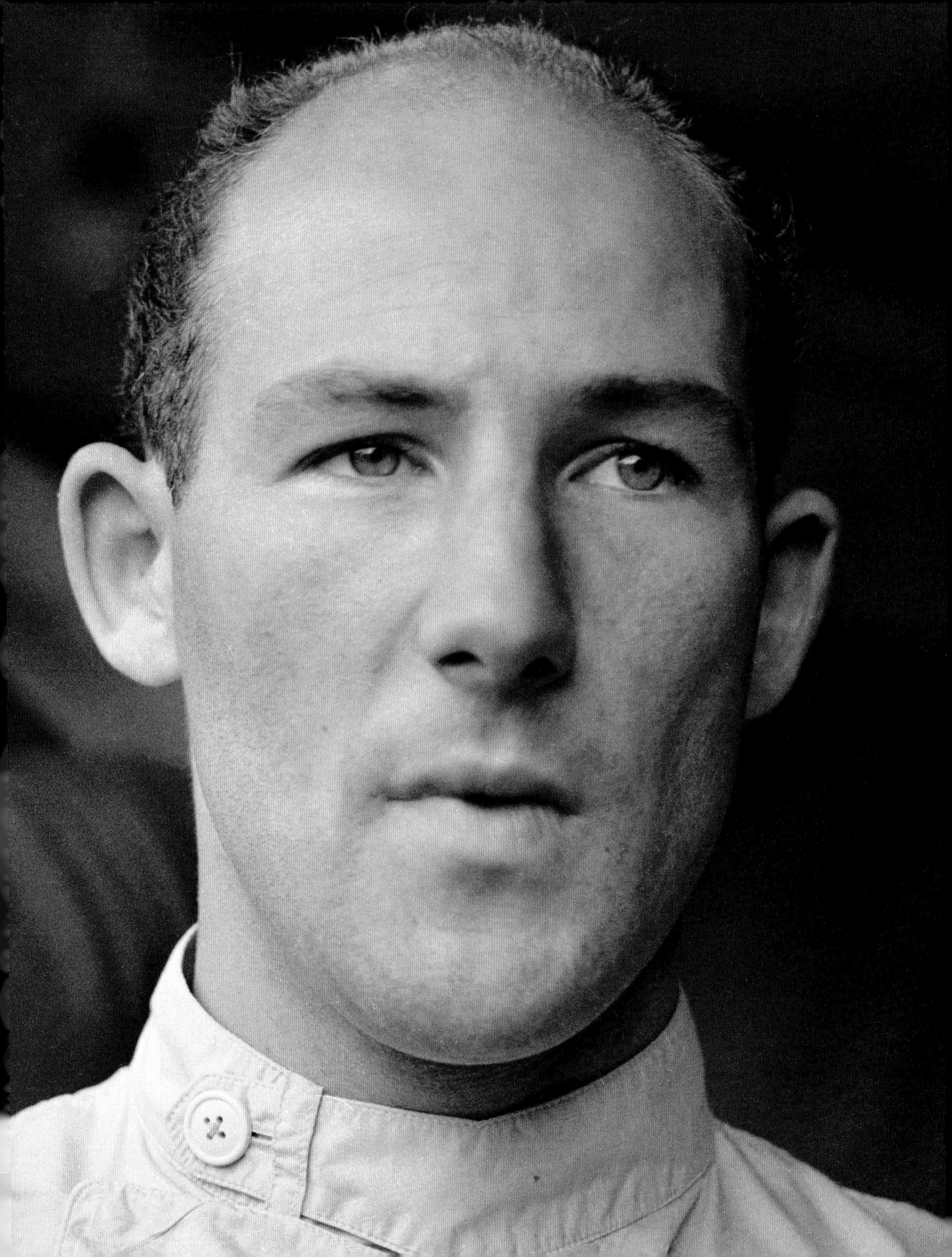

Roy Salvadori * 1922 – † 2012

Roy Francesco Salvadori certainly didn't conquer the Formula 1 world in a daring surprise coup, having a second, a third and a fourth as his best results over 47 races, between 1952 and 1962. Victory had seemed within reach when, during 1961, in his Cooper at Watkins Glen and full of hope, he appeared in the rear-view mirrors of Innes Ireland's Lotus. But then Ireland won, and Salvadori was left in the lurch, ignominiously, by his Climax four-cylinder engine.

At that time, he was already outshone by such new British icons as Graham Hill, Jim Clark and John Surtees. All the same, he enriched the sport with his 1959 Le Mans triumph in an Aston Martin, and his two years in 1966 and '67 as boss of the Cooper-Maserati outfit, which had a total of six employees. More importantly, though, he contributed his charm and personality.

Eventually, Salvadori, like the protagonist of a Somerset Maugham novel, realised the dream of so many affluent Englishmen and moved to Monaco. On the balcony of his noble abode in the Shangri-La apartment block, he enjoyed a wonderful view: the finishing straight of the most exclusive racing circuit in the world below him and out across the gorgeous billionaires' yachts, gently bobbing in the Principality's harbour, to the horizon, where the azure blue of the Mediterranean and the sky melt into one another seamlessly. There, in the golden depths of prevailingly Scottish spirits, the blurring memories of the good old days were shared with his numerous visitors, in particular when, every two years and a fortnight before the actual grand prix, the GP Historique was run.

Eventually, Salvadori's retirement seat morphed into a haven of cost-free hospitality, sometimes for an extensive two weeks. His amiable wife, Sue, indefatigably dished out finger food, sandwiches and even more substantial hot meals. One day, however, the couple had had enough and thereafter regularly retired to some remote place on that spring weekend.

In the meantime, though, their balcony was at the disposal of solvent friends, a vantage point indeed, though rather noisy.

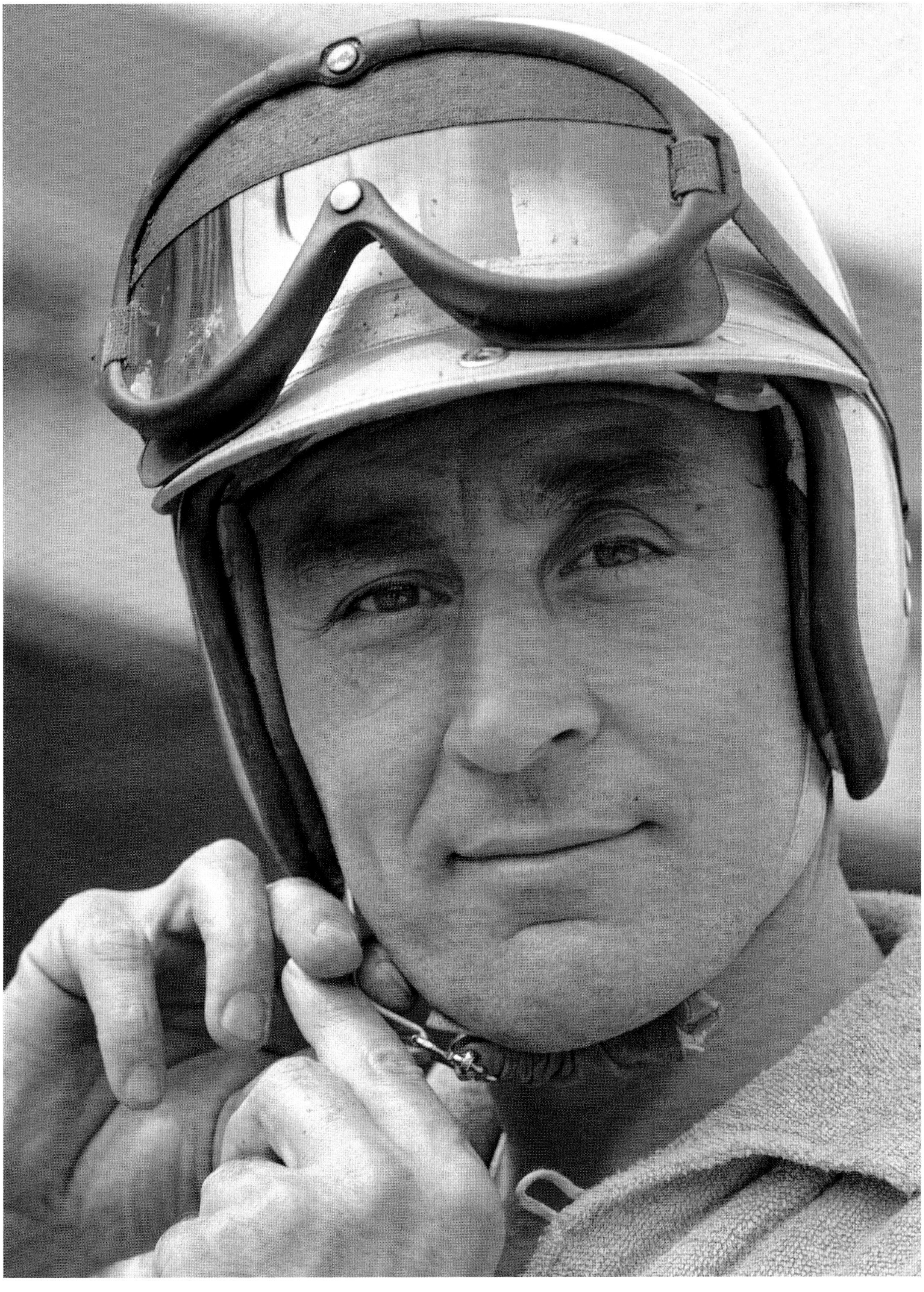

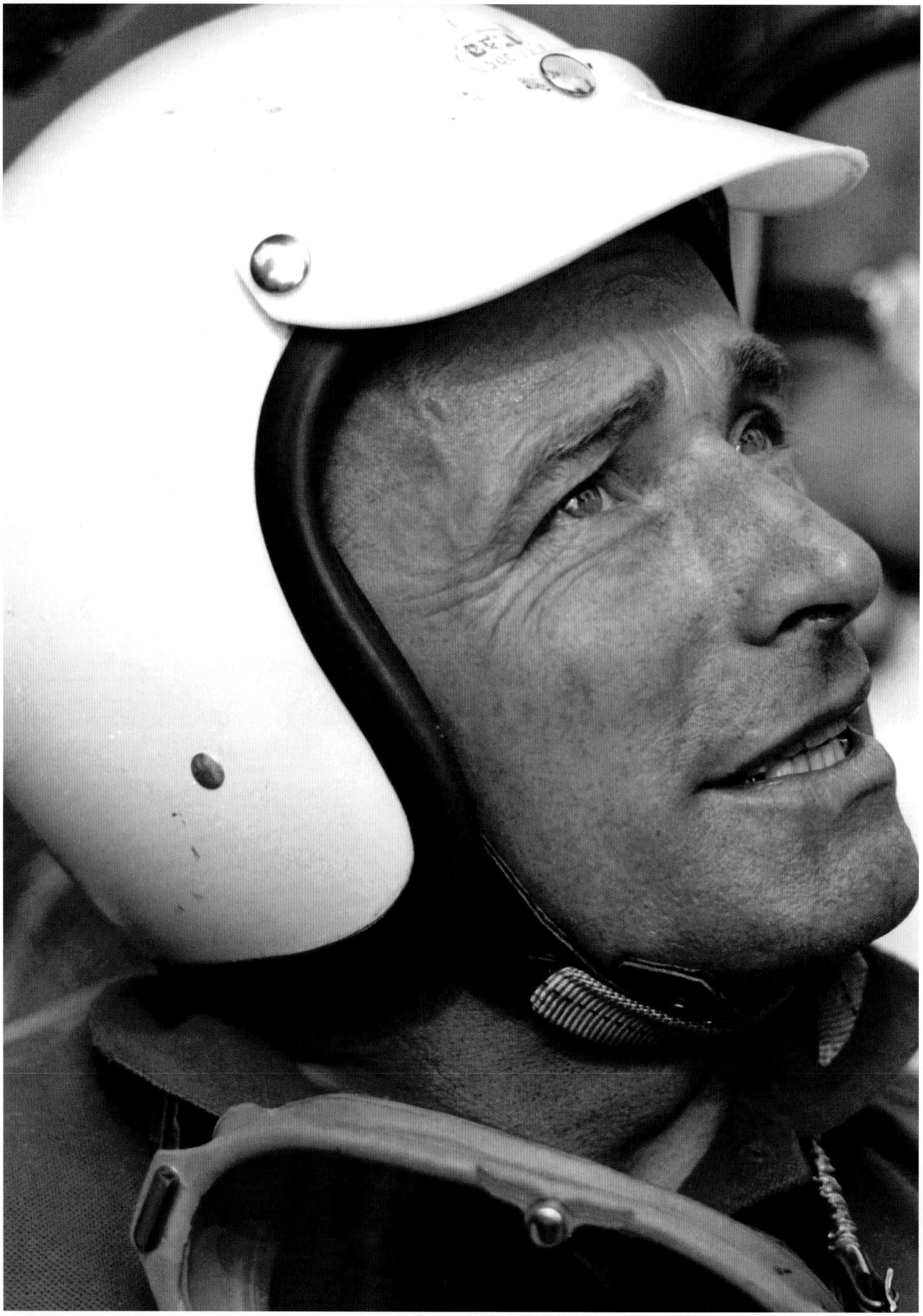

Edgar Barth

* 1917 – † 1965

▶ Edgar Barth is all about a singular CV that unfolds across a stage comprising no fewer than five Germanys. Having been born in the last year of the German Empire and grown up in the Weimar Republic, he was a witness to the Third Reich, the post-war so-called German Democratic Republic (DDR) and also the German Federal Republic in its early stages. A power slide, as it were, through the recent past.

Three systems with one constant, Barth's passion for motor racing, which began on two wheels in 1933, the year in which Hitler seized power. Two years later, he was a DKW works driver, but then the Second World War sidelined his career, as it did for so many.

The DDR potentates encouraged racing, though it was not necessarily a socialist sport. Barth rode a Norton and later drove the nimble EMW silver arrows from Eisenach, and was even permitted to travel to the capitalist West. He was fifth in the 1953 Eifelrennen for the EMW Rennkollektiv, only to retire in that year's German Grand Prix at the Nürburgring after a midfield run in 12th position. Twice he was the DDR's Formula 2 champion, but in 1957, he succumbed to the siren calls of the country's more attractive western neighbour, turning his back on the 'workers and peasants' state', and taking with him his talent and the Saxon tinge to his dialect.

The tight-knit Porsche community received him with open arms. Edgar Barth and the Stuttgart marque became almost synonymous, even more so after he had won the 1959 Targa Florio, in a 718 RSK, with Wolfgang Seidel.

At the 1960 Gran Premio d'Italia at Monza, he extracted the utmost from his chubby Porsche 718 F4 with a seventh place. Only at the German GP, three years later, did he sit in a 'real' F1 car, Rob Walker's Cooper T66-Climax (F1-2-63), but he was sidelined with clutch failure.

Ten months later, Edgar Barth, wanderer between the worlds, died of cancer.

Wolfgang Seidel

* 1926 – † 1987

▶ In December, 1962, the respected weekly *Der Spiegel* referred to Wolfgang Seidel as "the most highly decorated among the active German racing drivers". That certainly sounded good.

Indeed, Seidel already had had a most eventful career, featuring a trio of highlights, primarily in sports cars: second place at the 1957 Reims 12 hours, in his own Ferrari 250 GT LWB, with Phil Hill; third at the Sebring 12 hours a year later, driving a Porsche 718 RSK, with Harry Schell; and, above all, his Targa Florio victory in 1959 aboard another 718 RSK, with Edgar Barth.

The tall Düsseldorfer's ten grand prix starts were spread across the decade from 1953 to '62, with a long break between his debut at the German GP in a Veritas, four laps behind winner Nino Farina, and his race retirement at Spa in 1958 with the Maserati 250F of Scuderia Centro Sud. In the course of his sporadic appearances, Seidel drove a strange variety of cars, either to lowly placings or breakdowns of every imaginable kind, ranging from his private Veritas RS6 to an F1 rarity, the Emeryson 1006, built in a small workshop in the London district of Hammersmith by ingenious Brit Paul Emery.

During his last year in Formula 1, Seidel opened a can of worms when he took up the fight against the omnipotent ONS, the highest national motor sport commission in Germany. The wardens of the self-invented rules took away his racing licence for life, a measure that was soon reduced to two almost equally devastating years.

Seidel had protested furiously when, in practice for that year's German GP, he had completed only four instead of the five laps stipulated by the regulations and, as a result, was excluded from the race on the Sunday.

Followed by scornful laughter, and not only from the media, he asked, in his own words, for "sporting asylum" in Mexico and defiantly drove an F1 Lotus 24 at the Circuit Magdalena Mixhuca without the correct papers. After that, silence descended upon Wolfgang Seidel, who died far too early, poverty stricken.

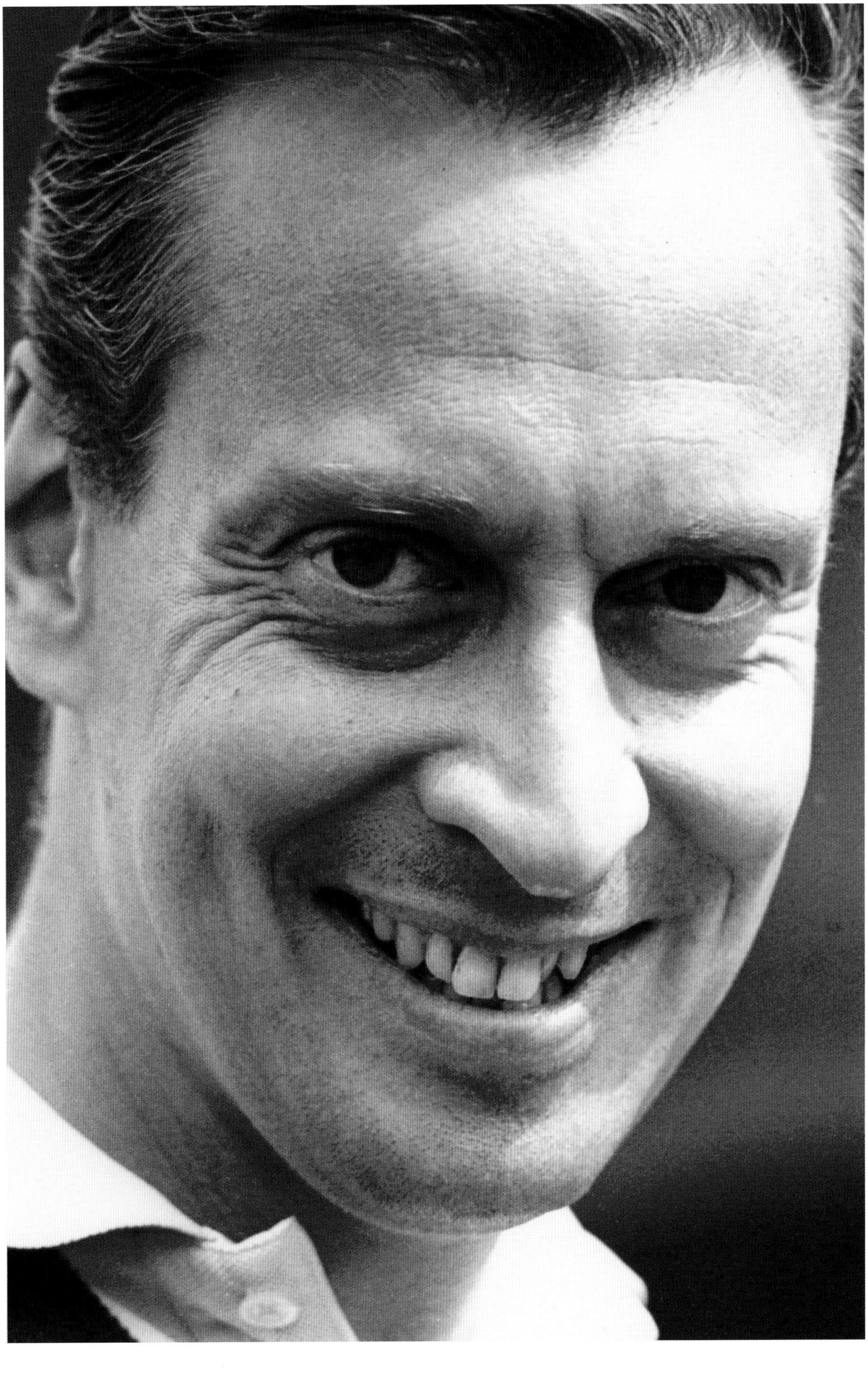

Hans Herrmann *1928

▶ Hans Herrmann certainly drew attention, again and again, but on three occasions, his name was on everyone's lips. Once soon after the beginning of his career, again in the middle of it, and finally at the very end, with real gems from the treasure trove of motor racing.

The Mille Miglia, 2nd May, 1954, somewhere not far from Pescara: The Hans Herrmann/Herbert Linge pairing hurtles around a fast right-hander at full throttle in their Porsche 550 Spyder, only to find a closed railway-crossing barrier in their way. Herrmann doesn't hesitate: he smacks his co-driver on the head, then ducks down into the cockpit with Linge for a second or so, passing under the obstacle without a scratch.

The German GP, AVUS, 2nd August, 1959: Herrmann slams on the brake pedal of his BRM P25 at 280km/h, some 250m before the tight Südkehre. But nothing happens. Seconds later, car and driver loop around one another in a macabre *pas de deux*. Herrmann gets away with a few knocks and scratches, and an hour later is flirting with a pretty nurse in a Berlin hospital.

Le Mans, 14th June, 1970, around 4 pm: together with Dickie Attwood, Herrmann wins the 24 Hours in a 917K, the first really big victory for Porsche. After that, he calls it quits, honouring a promise he had made to his wife, Magdalena, before his departure.

For 18 years, from 'Küken' ('the Kid') to veteran driver, the friendly Swabian served many masters: Abarth, Borgward, Brabham, BRM, Cooper, Ferrari, Lola, Lotus, Maserati, Veritas, even the legendary Mercedes-Benz team in 1954 and '55. His F1 appearances were sporadic, though, numbering 18 races altogether, spread over 14 years.

The be all and end all of Hans Herrmann's racing life were his Porsche engagements, from Winterfahrt Hessen in February, 1952, aboard a 356 Coupé, through to his Le Mans triumph. He would have loved to win one more race, the 1955 Mille Miglia in the Mercedes-Benz 300 SLR. He remains quite convinced that only a jamming fuel cap prevented him from doing so.

But that, again, is a different story. And Moss fans wouldn't like it.

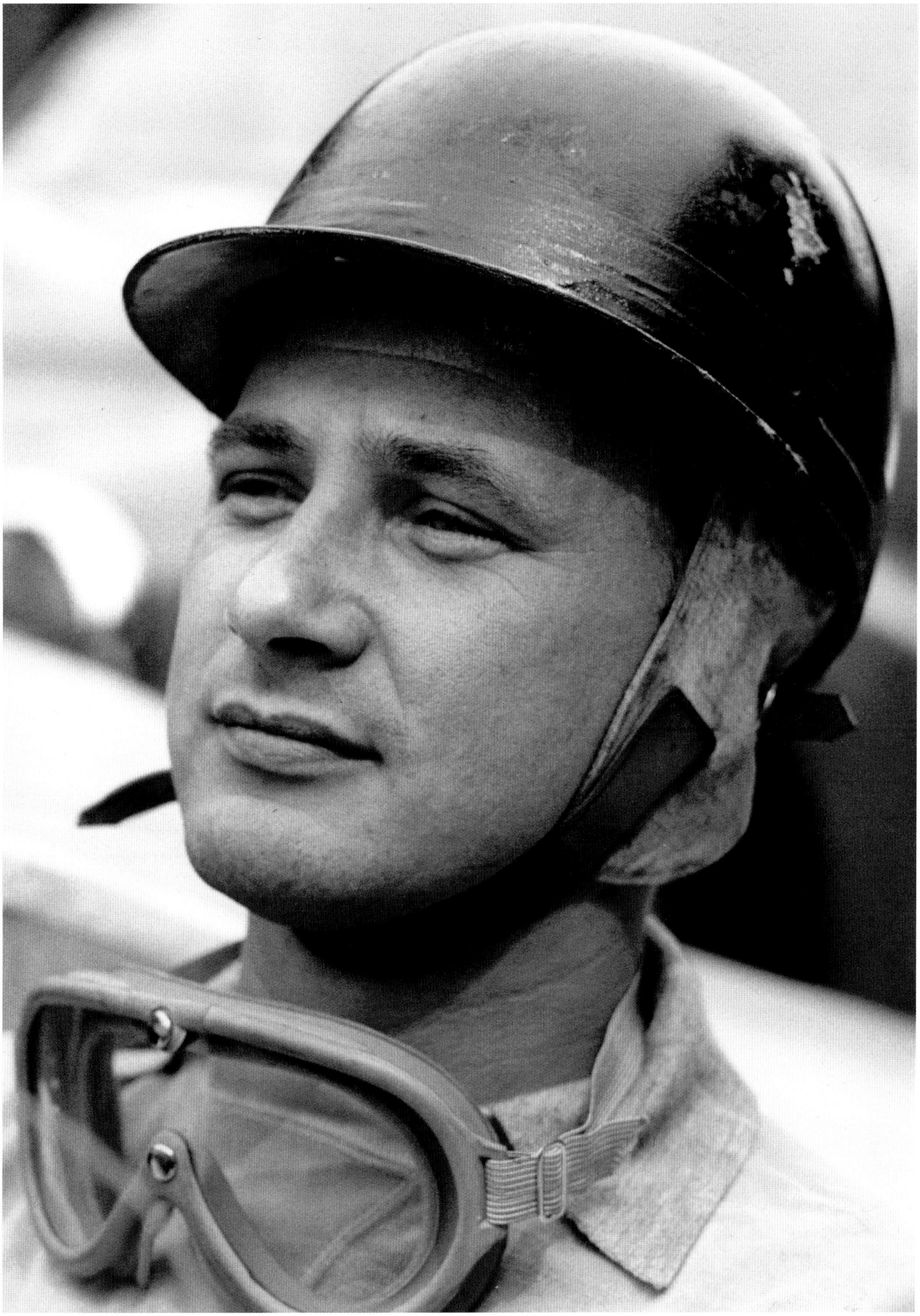

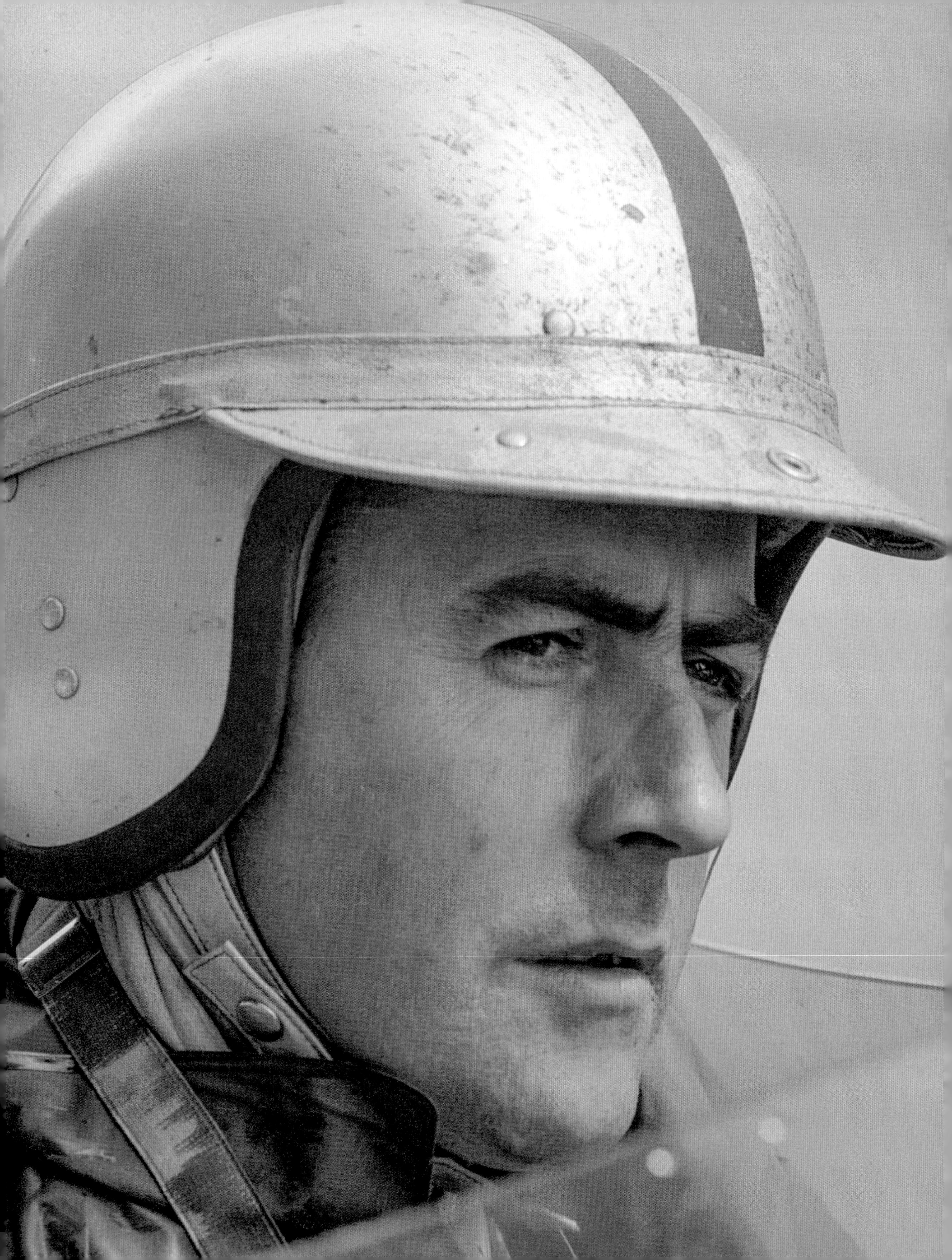

Jack Brabham

* 1926 – † 2014

▶ Zandvoort, 1966: an elderly man with a crutch hobbles across to the car on pole position. To general amazement, he suddenly throws away a false beard and jack handle, swings himself into the cockpit and wins the Dutch Grand Prix. Jack Brabham had just flung down the gauntlet to all those who had consigned him, at the ripe 'old age' of 40, to history.

They called him 'Black Jack', or 'The Quiet Australian', but that's only half the truth. The triple champion spoke only when he felt like it, even less so during the second half of his life, as the screaming V8s at his back had made him deaf. On the occasion of Brabham's farewell banquet, on 30th November, 1970, in London's Savoy hotel, Ford had prepared a documentary about him, reserving a minute or so for the final words of the taciturn pensioner. But then he stood up and surprised everybody with a brilliant 50-minute impromptu speech about his life and career.

Wit and eloquence are also the hallmarks of his autobiography, *When the Flag Drops*. The title is the first half of a self-quotation. Together with the second, "the bullshit stops", it captures Black Jack's philosophy in a nutshell. As the race gets under way, all the monkey business and ballyhoo come to an end. Even so, Brabham could flash the smile of a 'Hollywood soap' GP winner like nobody else.

To squeeze oneself into a racing car is a matter of trust. But you can only trust yourself. That's why Jack Brabham took things into his own hands in 1962, building his own cars and being the first to win a grand prix in his own product, at Reims in 1966, the launch year of the 3-litre Formula 1. The thing was built like a tank, its Repco V8 a bit feeble, but also as robust as a chrome vanadium wrench.

At the end of that season, Jack Brabham and the Brabham team had secured both world titles – another novelty in the business.

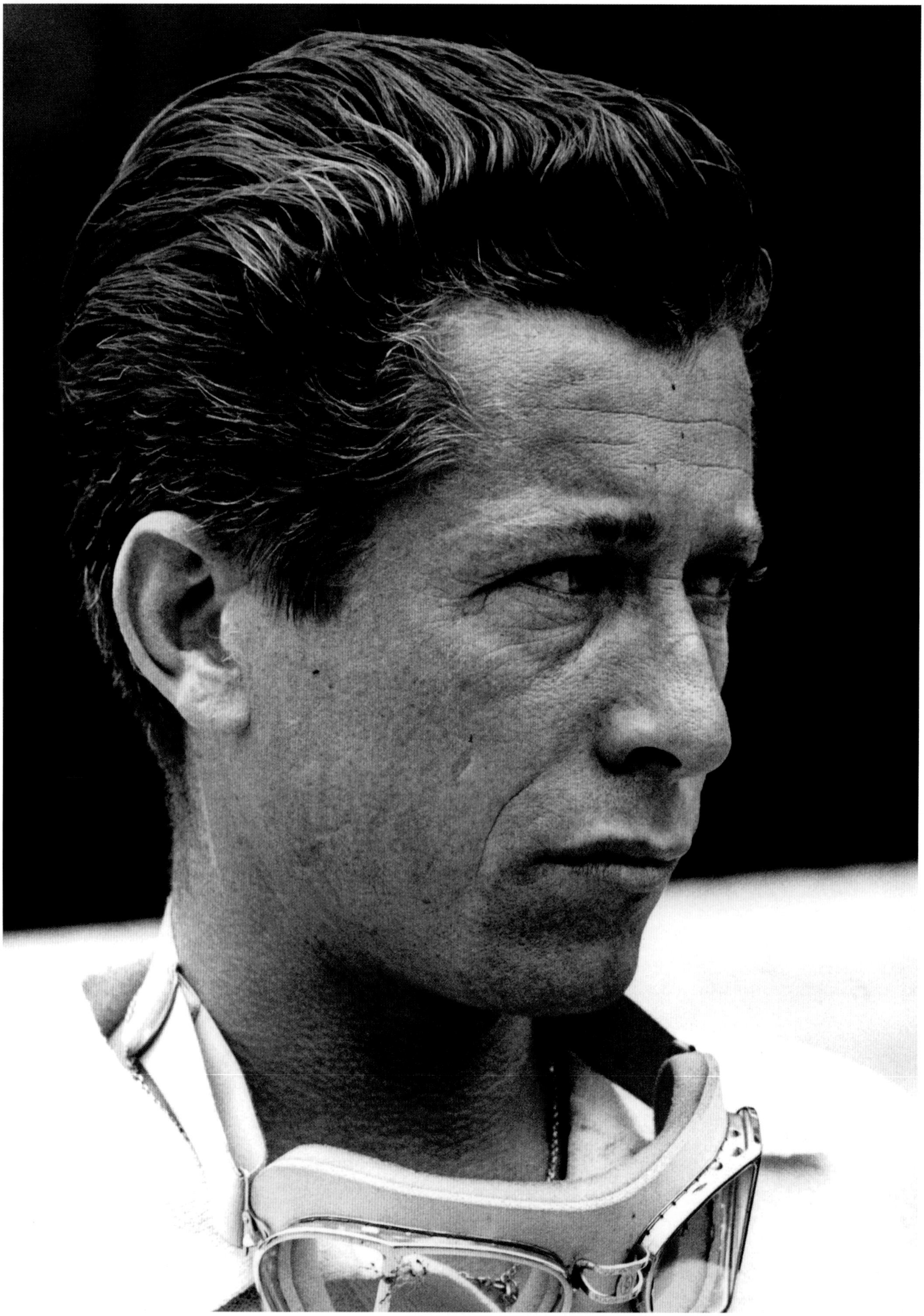

Olivier Gendebien

* 1924 – † 1998

▶ On the 50th anniversary of Ferrari's move into the production of road cars, on 31st May, 1997, guarded by colossal marble statues of nude athletes, the most valuable vehicle fleet of all time – more than 200 racing, prototype and street sports cars of the red marque – was assembled in the Roman Stadio dei Marmi.

Belgian legend Olivier Gendebien sunbathed in a Testa Rossa, majestic, but completely motionless and almost a monument in himself, smiling as he answered the questions of fans and journalists. That was arguably the last public appearance of one of the best sports car drivers in history.

Gendebien passed away a year later in Tarascon, not far from Les Baux-de-Provence, his home in the southern French Alpilles. An untypical legacy he left behind was that a disease had been named after him, the neurovegetative ailment that was already apparent at the Roman event. His late suffering was perhaps an act of retributive justice of fate, because he had definitely spent a major part of his life on its sunny side.

The good years: certainly the late fifties and early sixties, when Gendebien amassed, among others, four victories at Le Mans, three respectively at Sebring, the Targa Florio, and the Tour de France, and one at the Nürburgring 1,000km, often in a dream team with Phil Hill. His vision of similar success in F1 never materialised, despite eight GP starts for Ferrari between 1956 and '59.

From the slipstreaming game of musical chairs played by the four Ferrari drivers at Spa in 1961, his 'Sharknose' Tipo 156 in Belgian racing yellow, Gendebien emerged as a member of the threesome in row one, leading for three glorious laps (totalling 42km) and ending in fourth position. Instead of giving him the seat in the works team that he had hoped for, the Maranello Machiavelli dismissed him to F1's reserve bank.

In 1962, he gave up racing altogether because his wife and mother of three, Marie-Claire, had implored him to do so. Shortly afterwards, she died of cancer – a cruel twist of fate.

Henry Taylor * 1938 – † 2013

▶ The common English name Taylor was unusually widespread in Formula 1 in the sixties: in the cockpits of GP single-seaters, Henry, John, Mike and Trevor Taylor strove for fame and honour, or whatever was left for them, in the shadow of the greats – Clark, Hill, Surtees, Brabham, Gurney and company.

In the Formula Junior race at the Monaco GP in June, 1962, Dennis Taylor died a few days before his 41st birthday, one of the surprisingly few motor racing deaths in the Principality. And on the British touring car scene, Anita Taylor made a name for herself with speed and pretty looks.

Her brother, Trevor, undoubtedly went furthest, while Henry Taylor, a farmer's son from Shefford, in Bedfordshire, hardly ever made it into the headlines. A fourth place in the Yeoman Credit Racing Team's Cooper T51 at the 1960 French GP was the best of his eight GP starts, between Silverstone in 1959 and Monza in 1961, but the three points at Reims were well deserved. However, they also testified to the superiority of the Cooper-Climax T53s and T51s, which took the first four places of that slipstreaming skirmish on the Champagne circuit, the other three in the hands of Jack Brabham, Olivier Gendebien and Bruce McLaren.

What was particularly remarkable about Henry Taylor was his versatility. For example, his two English F3 championships in 1955 and '56, with 17 victories in the tiny motorbike-engine-powered racing cars of the time; his third place in the Jaguar D-Type, behind Tony Brooks and Roy Salvadori in the supporting race for the Belgian GP in 1957; or a brief appearance in the 1,000km at the Nürburgring in the same year. He had rally successes and good placings in the ground-breaking Lotus Cortina, later becoming competition manager for Ford.

He was also a regular on the cresta run and various bobsleigh tracks. In 1964, the seemingly incompatible came together when Taylor was one of 19 daredevils who careered down the Cortina d'Ampezzo bobsleigh run in a Ford Cortina.

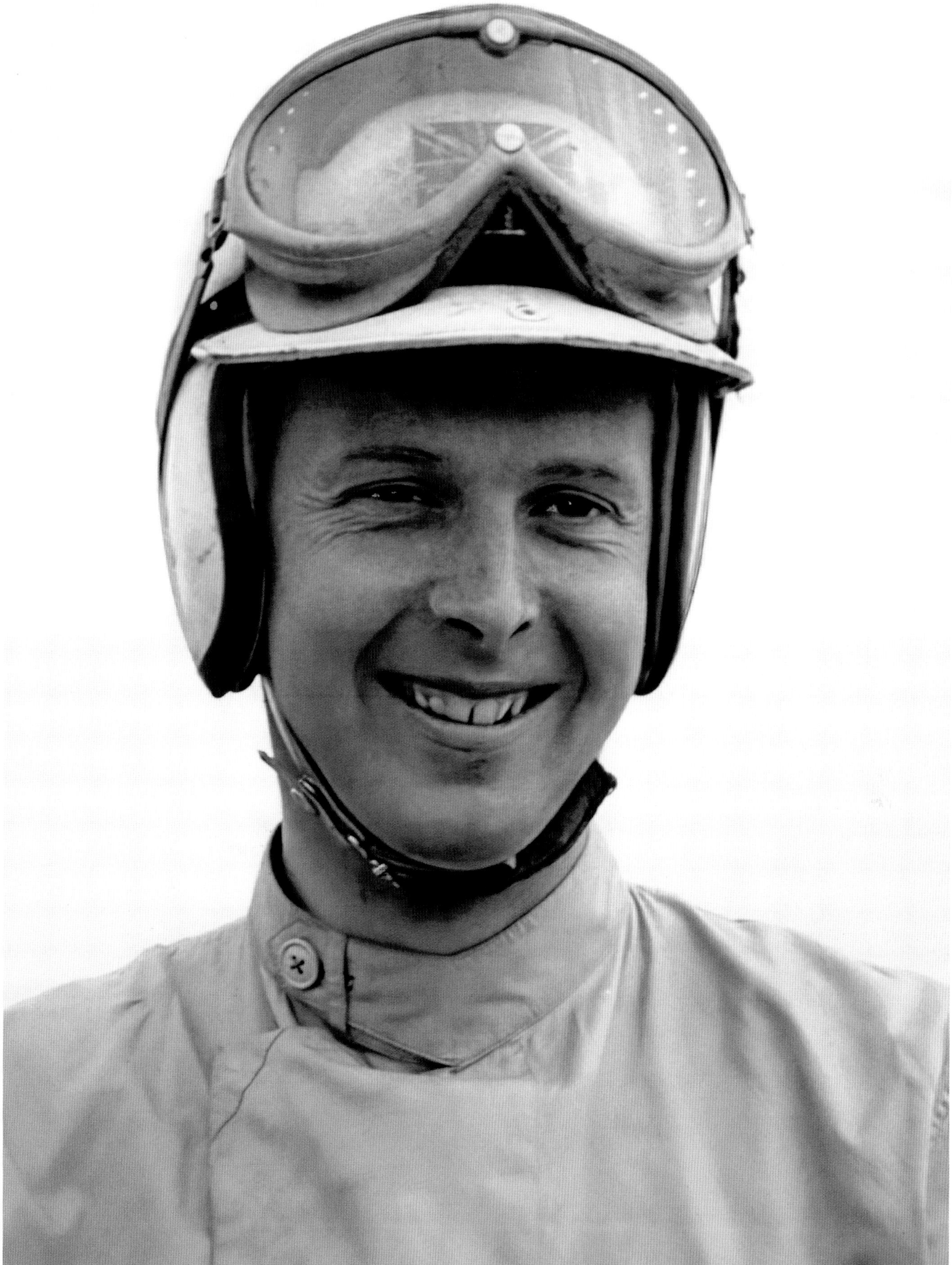

Tony Brooks

*1932 – †2022

▶ "The greatest little-known driver of all time," that's how Stirling Moss described Tony Brooks, on many occasions his team-mate in F1 and sports car racing, and not without a twinkle in his eyes. But also, seriously: "If I was going to have a team, I would put Tony Brooks at No.1, with Jim Clark alongside him. He was careful with the car and very, very fast."

The title of his biography *Poetry in Motion*, sounds a bit precious in the noisy and reckless world of racing, but it was fitting for the man himself and for his virtuosic way of driving. Racing as a gentle art form: Brooks, praised by John Wyer, Aston Martin team boss in the fifties, showed grace and style at the steering-wheel and justifiably took great pride in doing everything correctly.

Tony Brooks' name became etched into the German fans' souls through three impressive victories in their country: at the 1957 Nürburgring 1,000km driving an Aston Martin, with his congenial partner Noël Cunningham-Reid; at the GP again at the Ring a year later in a Vanwall; and at the 1959 German Grand Prix, which had been relocated to the Berlin AVUS circuit, in a Ferrari.

Media and track commentators referred to him as "The Racing Dentist", resorting to customary pithy simplification. Brooks actually had a diploma in dentistry, in the family tradition, but freely admitted that he had not ever inserted an amalgam tooth filling. Instead, he was "mechanically *simpatico* and nursed the machinery or retired before the damage was too excessive," as Ted Cutting, the designer of the Aston Martin DBR1, put it.

Unlike many others in the polygamous Formula 1 whirlpool, Tony Brooks was a family man. He and his wife, Pina, were racing's dream couple. Pina, a pretty doctoral student, had met Tony during a sports car racing weekend at Rouen, while staying in the Alizay Château de Rouville, and thereafter they became inseparable. They had five children.

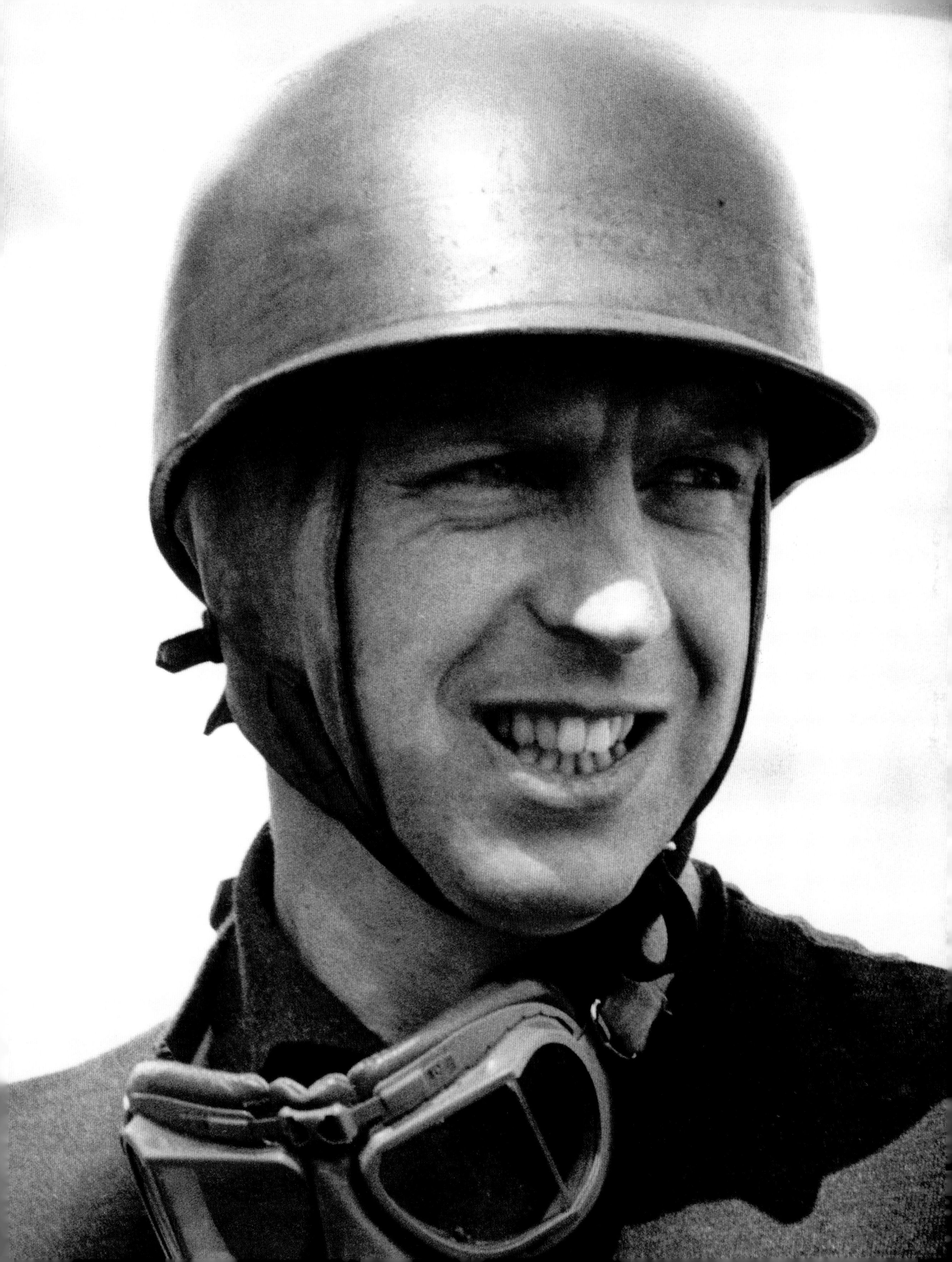

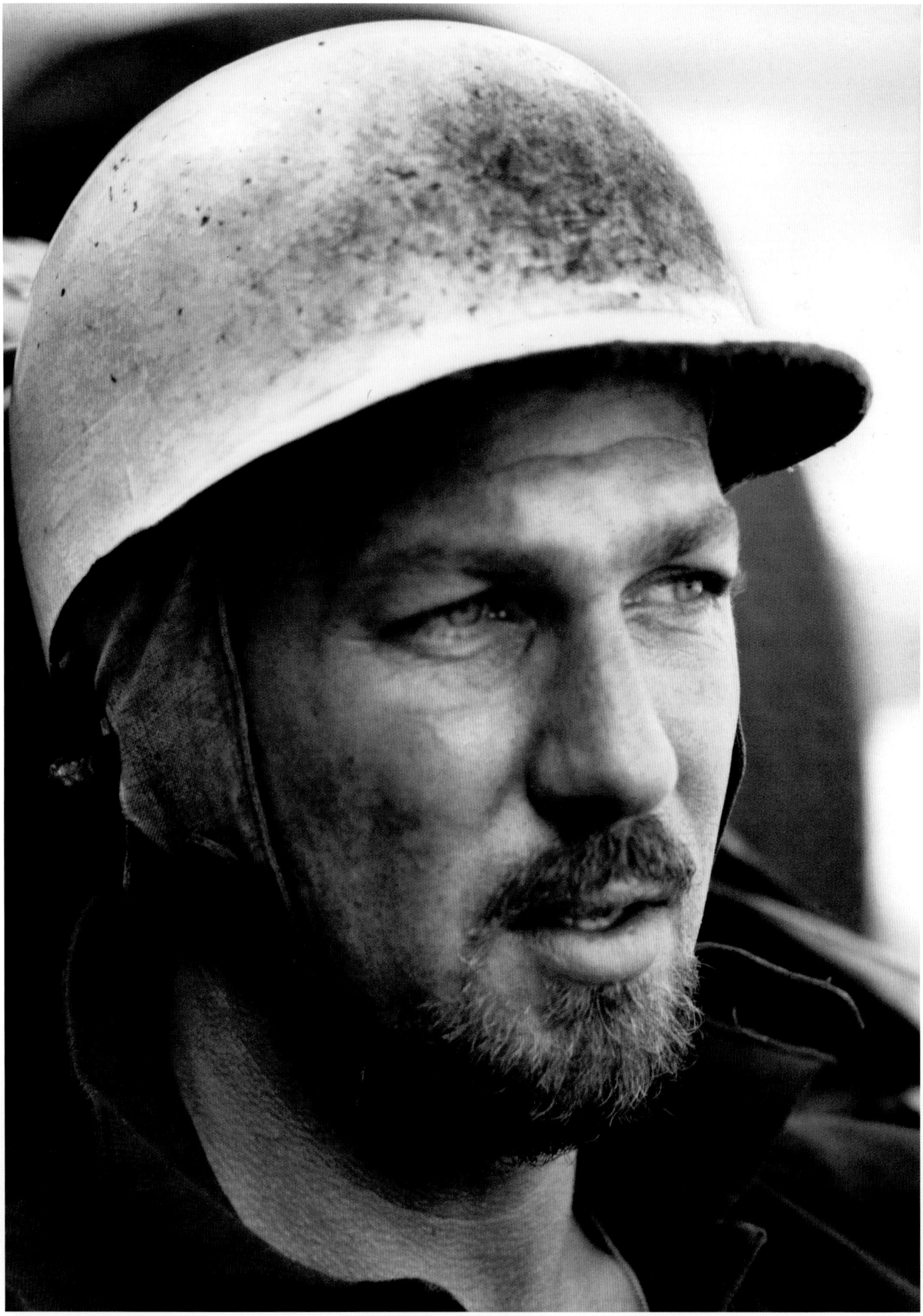

Joakim Bonnier

*1930 – †1972

▶ Not even a handful of GP drivers continued to race from the late fifties to the early seventies, from the swan song of the front-engined single-seaters to the first heyday of the 3-litre cars. Three of them, Jack Brabham, Graham Hill and Bruce McLaren were famously destined for higher glory.

Swede Joakim Bonnier caused a splash when he won the 1959 Dutch GP, his 16th grand prix, in a conventionally conceived BRM P25. But from then on, it was downhill all the way for F1 driver Bonnier, mockingly called 'JoBo' by some. Already, his team-mate at Porsche, Dan Gurney, had shown him his limits: in 1961, with the chubby little 787 F4, and in 1962, with the marque's steely sounding purpose-built 804 F1 car.

So it was symbolic when eventually JoBo not only hung up his helmet, but also a whole racing car. The yellow McLaren M5A-BRM V12, which had accompanied him through the 1968 season, an immobile sculpture of mesmerising beauty, decorated a wall in his Lausanne home.

Bonnier maintained his presence in the F1 paddocks, however, as one of the founding fathers of the Grand Prix Drivers' Association (GPDA), which he had helped to form in 1961. Its mission, above all, was safety. Jo was the ideal choice for that job, a cosmopolitan polyglot with a certain aloof dignity, interpreted by some as arrogance, by others as a product of his former career as an officer, but by his racing mechanic, Heini Mader, as a protective shield for his shyness.

In sports cars, JoBo remained world class, for instance with his two Porsche victories, in 1960 and '63 at the Targa Florio, and his win in the 1966 Nürburgring 1,000km, with Phil Hill, in the white automatic monster Chaparral 2D-Chevrolet.

It was in a sports car that Jo Bonnier, top advocate of drivers' safety, met his death in the 1972 Le Mans 24 Hours, when his Lola T260 hit the rear of a backmarker and was thrown sky-high into the trees. Many said that Jo had been very tired.

Wolfgang Graf Berghe von Trips

* 1928 – † 1961

▶ The plot seemed custom-made for a fairy-tale, light novel or Hollywood film: a young aristocrat, living in a real castle, handsome, dashing and with an engaging personality, dreams of being Formula 1 world champion. We are in the fifties – for the sake of historical patina.

And indeed, he makes a name for himself in the best racing cars of his country, let's say Porsche and Mercedes. Eventually, he gains access to the most famous racing stable of them all, Ferrari. Everything goes according to plan. But as he is about to grab the crown of his sport in the early sixties, the Grim Reaper intervenes, at Monza, where death has always been an option and will continue to be so.

However, there is so much more to Count von Trips than just being the subject matter for a script. They've called him 'The Last Knight', an errant character from a medieval cloak-and-dagger piece. And, in fact, he would say, "My ancestors were robber barons. All of them were beaten to death."

But then a process of refinement must have taken place over the centuries. Von Trips had all the makings of an idol, far beyond his lifespan and generation, right up to the present day, although that description has become questionable, or is projected on to the wrong people. A surprising number of entries in his diary, as such the mirror of his soul, bear witness to that, betraying something deeply humane, decent and, well, chivalrous about him. No sheet of paper would fit between von Trips the man and the image.

'Taffy', as they called him, was the perfect answer to some deeply rooted longings of post-war Germans for a true hero of motor racing, which still suffered from the aftermath of the 1955 Le Mans tragedy. A shining light to inspire courage and confidence.

When Count von Trips was killed at Monza on 10th September, 1961, a whole nation was in tears.

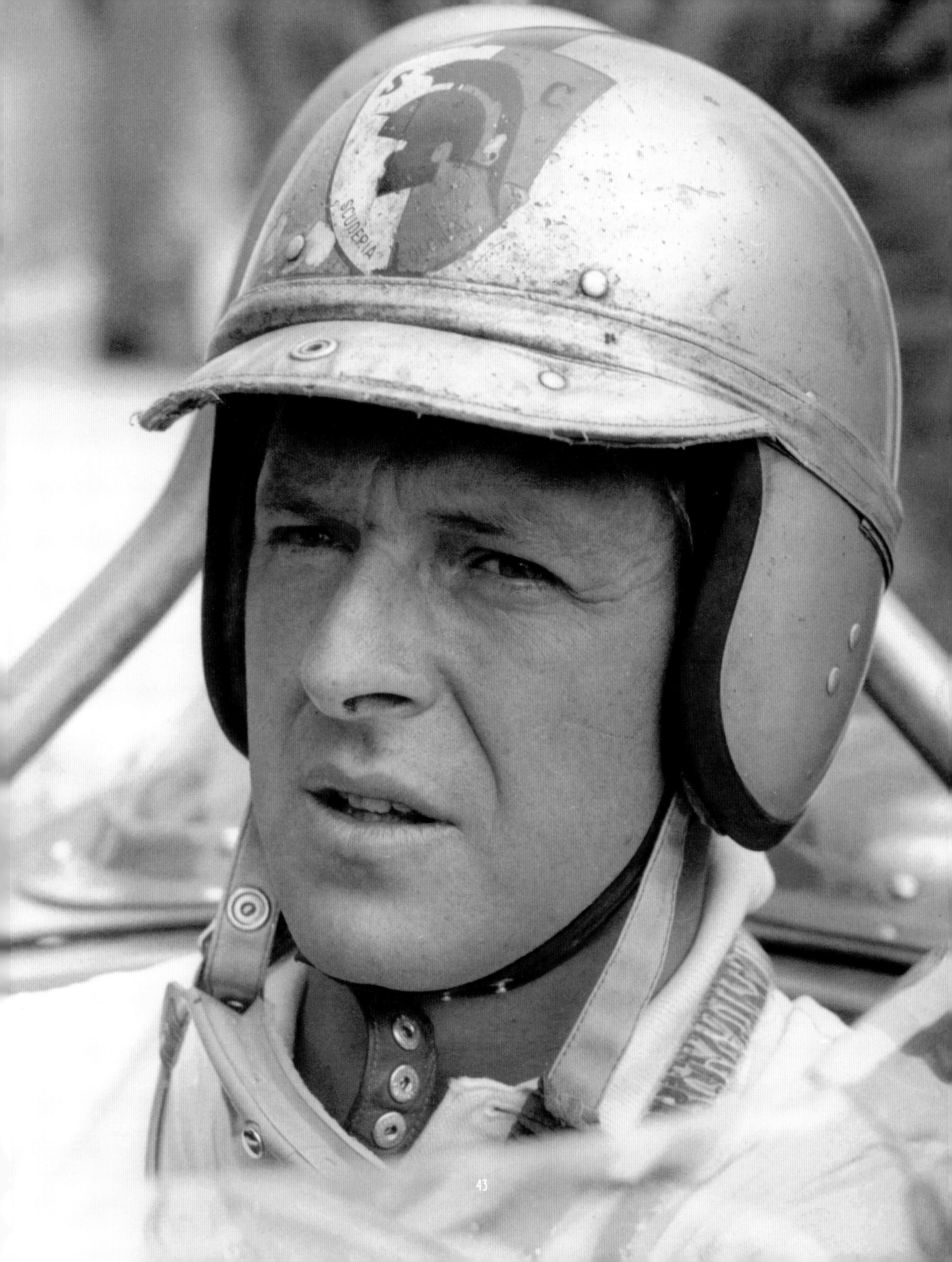
SCUDERIA

Masten Gregory *1932 – †1985

▶ Until the sixties and seventies, wearers of glasses inevitably faced massive prejudice. Common wisdom had it that they were meditatively minded, dreamers or even stay-at-homes.

Some of these characteristics probably applied to Masten Gregory, born in February, 1932, in Kansas City. He was a music lover, ballet fan and gourmet, as well as a mild-mannered and pleasant person to meet and talk with, as long as nothing provoked him.

But appearances were deceptive. They began with his heavy Missouri cowboy accent, which had not been softened by several years of living in the finer quarters of Rome and Paris. He was barely 1.70m tall and weighed only 64kg, but his voice was a booming double bass, and in a crowd sometimes he was overlooked as those around him wondered where that rumbling noise had come from.

But, above all, there was Masten Gregory the racing driver – a tough customer indeed. From 1952, he was part of the racing inventory of the circuits for 20 years, winning the 1957 Buenos Aires 1,000km in a Ferrari 290MM, the 1961 Nürburgring 1,000km in a 'Birdcage' Maserati of the Camoradi Team and, above all, the 1965 Le Mans 24 Hours in a Ferrari 250LM of the North American Racing Team, with rising star Jochen Rindt.

Gregory was not really destined for grand prix stardom, however, with 17 retirements in his 38 races between 1957 and '65, and a meagre total of 21 championship points, topped by a second place in a Cooper T51 at the 1959 Portuguese GP at Monsanto.

He emerged unshaken from horrendous accidents that destroyed his cars, like the sad remains spat out by a scrapyard crusher. He suffered severe burns and broke a plethora of bones. Three times, he simply stood up and bailed out of cars that had gone out of control at 100mph, to be sucked off by the airflow. Such incidents didn't worry him at all. For a long time, he thought that he wouldn't live to be 30.

Masten Gregory did die young, although at 53, after a heart attack – the death of a chain smoker.

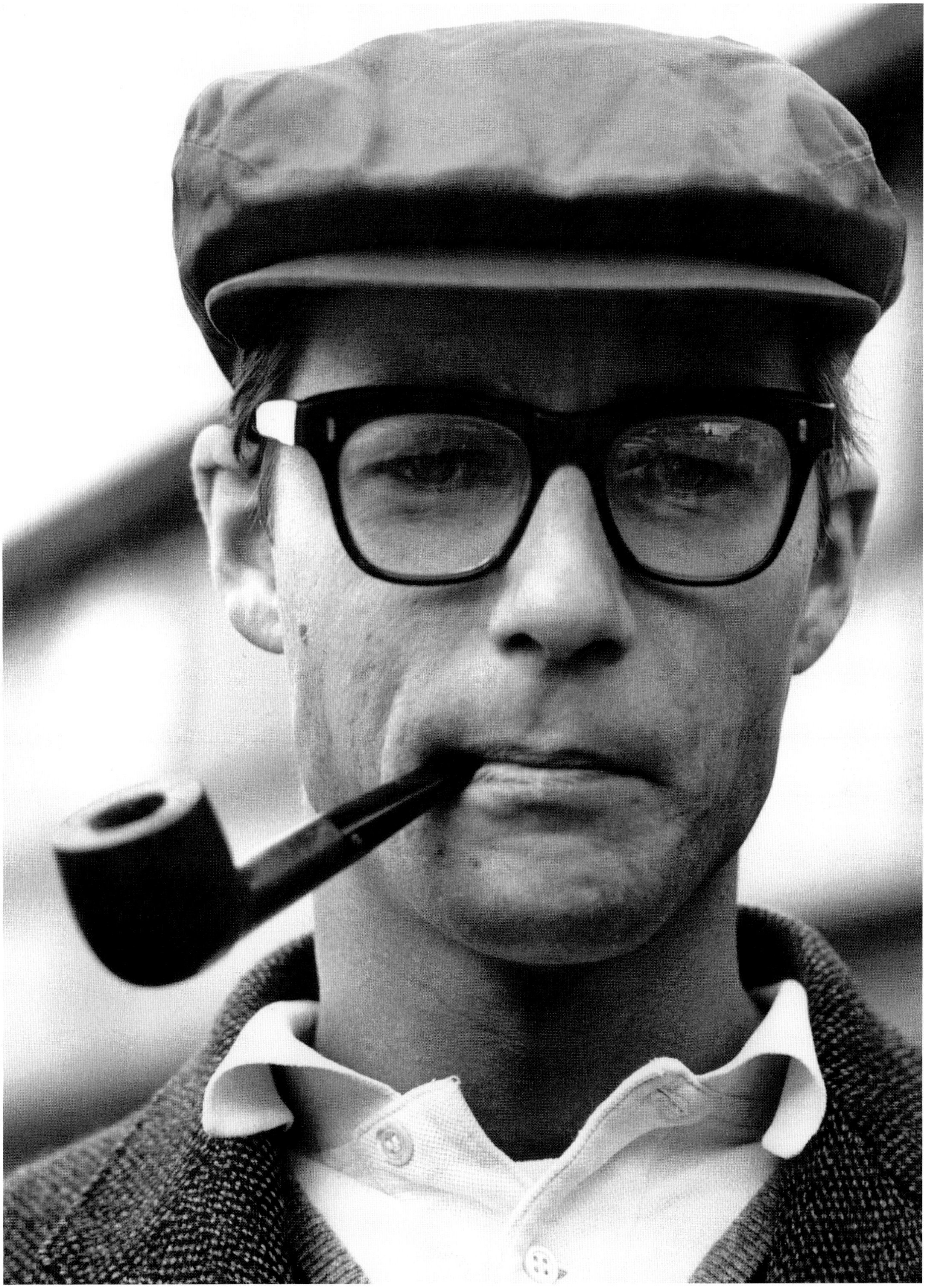

Carel Godin de Beaufort

* 1934 – † 1964

▶ During a sports car race in the supporting programme of the 1959 German Grand Prix, on the AVUS circuit, Dutchman Jonkheer Carel Godin de Beaufort slid over the edge of the wet banked Nordkurve in his Porsche RSK, plummeting 10m into the unknown on the other side. The anxious question as to what had happened to the driver was answered a short time later, when the heavily damaged Spyder suddenly came limping on to the circuit again.

De Beaufort even tried to insert himself into the race anew, until he was black-flagged. Living in Castle Maarsbergen, near Utrecht, he was a cheerful character, completely fearless, with a strong affinity for practical jokes and an excessive party life. Fun was his motto.

It led him into the serious world of grand prix racing, though. He was big and broad-shouldered, so the delicate single-seaters of the 1.5-litre era didn't suit him. De Beaufort was the last real amateur in this sport, in the proper sense of the word, and somebody who loved what he was doing. The important thing was the taking part, quite in keeping with the Olympic ideal.

When, in 1961, he bought Rob Walker's Porsche 718/2, which so far had been busy in Formula 2, a bond for life developed. The plump little Porsche, in the blue-and-white colour scheme of the whisky heir, already had had a fruitful racing life. De Beaufort, however, added another 57 races to its CV. Painted in Dutch racing orange and dubbed 'Old Fatty Porsche', the veteran car became a legend itself, admired, belittled – and respected.

During Saturday's practice for the 1964 German GP, however, de Beaufort's guardian angel glanced away from him for a second or so and, at the Bergwerk passage of the Nürburgring, he was seriously injured.

He died a day later. He had been black-flagged off the AVUS by a marshal, but now the black flag was held out by Death itself.

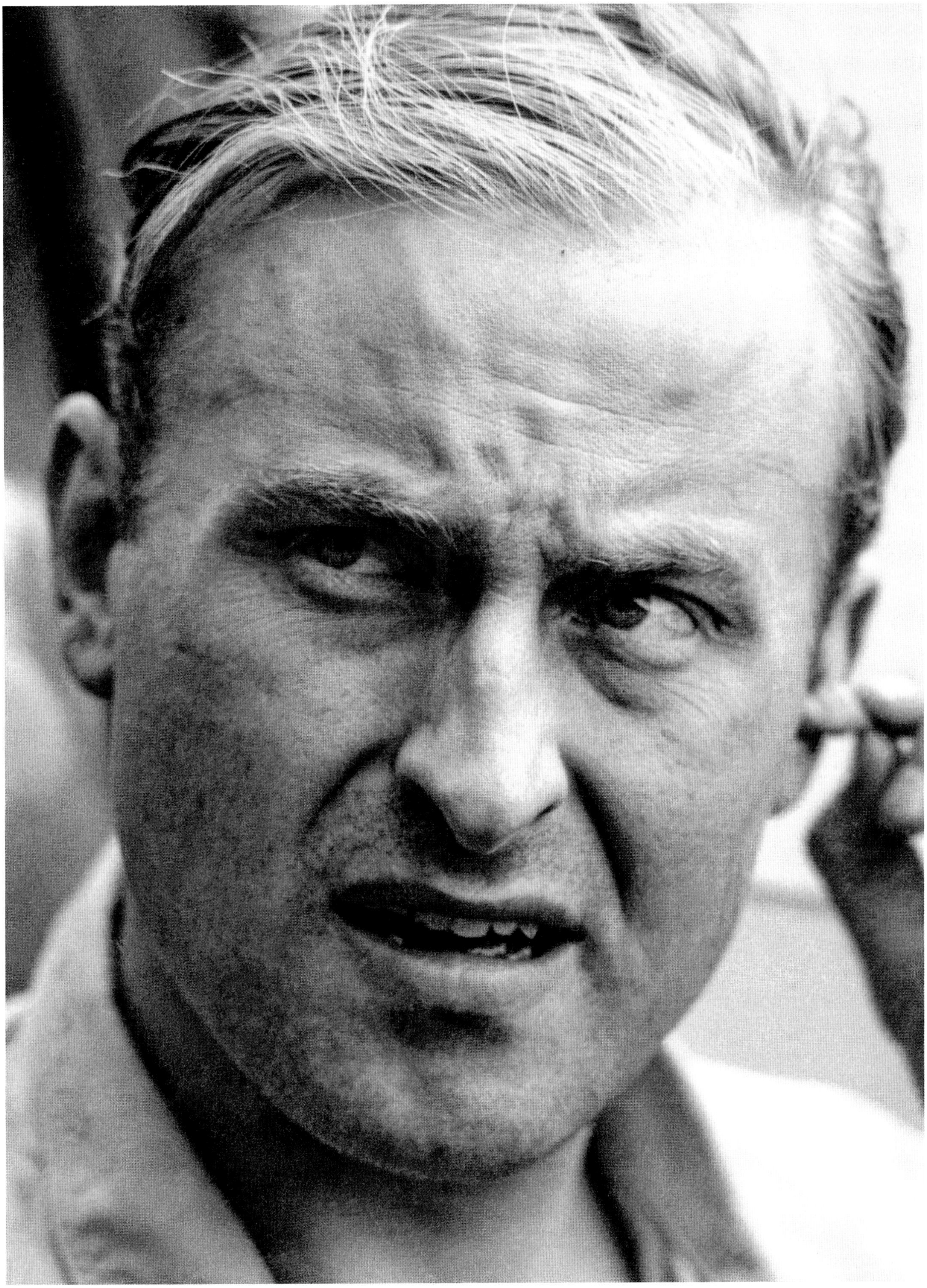

Giulio Cabianca * 1923 – † 1961

▶ Cabianca in an OSCA – in the fifties, that was a common combination. It also epitomised the not-un-attractive role of the Veronese in motor racing: the David valiantly fighting the Goliaths. He wallowed in that role, with, for instance, class victories in the Mille Miglia (1952, '56 and '57) and the Targa Florio (1955).

A member of the Ferrari sports car équipe since 1959, never did Cabianca come closer to the top three on the Piccolo Circuito delle Madonie than in 1960. In the closing stages, team manager Romolo Tavoni tasked him and his Dino 246S with wresting third place from Porsche driver Hans Herrmann. The mission was hopeless, and it failed.

In Formula 1, the outlook was rather poor for Giulia Cabianca, just three outings in the Gran Premio d'Italia aboard venerable secondhand machinery: Jo Bonnier's Maserati 250F in 1958, and another 250F that belonged to Swiss privateer Ottorino Volonterio in 1959.

His fourth place at Monza a year later, in a Cooper T51-Ferrari of the Scuderia Castellotti, practically fell into his lap. The British teams had stayed at home, as the organisers had reactivated at short notice the historic circuit with its fearsome uneven bankings. That was the only chance the robust front-engined Ferraris stood against their nimble opponents from Britain, whose engines had long since performed their work behind the drivers – the way to go in the future.

Essentially, the Cooper T51-Ferrari was a synthesis of the entirely incongruous. The wily *Commendatore* was even said to have outsourced the development of the mid-engine principle to the Scuderia Castellotti. In a way, Giulio Cabianca fell victim to this experiment. During the late afternoon of 15th June, 1961, he was testing the hybrid on the Modena Autodromo. Suddenly, the accelerator became stuck, and Cabianca raced through an open gate and on to the busy Via Emilia, killing three unsuspecting road users.

Seriously injured himself, he passed away before the day was out.

Peter Kurze

Graham Hill

*1929 – †1975

▶ The mien as the mirror of a human soul – our face, they say, is our calling card. Graham Hill's expressive traits were particularly revealing, although the world champion of 1962 and 1968 could also put on a poker-face like nobody else.

The early Hill: fully focused and determined, his moustache neatly trimmed. But his iron discipline also left room for humour and charming David Niven-like slapstick. The victory of Jean-Pierre Sarti, aka Yves Montand, at the 1966 Belgian GP in John Frankenheimer's epic racing movie *Grand Prix* is feted in a wild party. Pros like Hill, Jo Bonnier and ubiquitous journalist Bernard Cahier grace the MGM frolic with their presence, exchanging comments and telltale glances. Suddenly, champagne sloshes in Hill's eye. The hilarious dignity with which he bears this speaks volumes.

Unforgettable: his return to the Nürburgring paddock in 1962 in a marshal's car, after an enormous practice shunt. His BRM had hit a camera, shed by de Beaufort's Porsche, and he was wrapped in the film like the mythological Laocoön with the serpents, livid, but with comic reproach.

The late Hill: stigmatised by his many accidents, which he shrugs off nonchalantly, hair and sideburns run wild. His detractors begin to call him 'Auntie Hill', though he has secured an impressive statistical one-off, the 'Triple Crown', with victories at the Monaco Grand Prix (in 1963, '64, '65, '68 and '69), The Indianapolis 500 (1966) and the Le Mans 24-hour race (1972), the three most iconic battlefields in racing. Long since, he has become an ambassador of his sport, switching his charm and eloquence on and off as the cameras and microphones are directed at him. In 1973, he founds his own team, Embassy Hill Racing, while the calls for his retirement as a driver become more frequent.

That happens, with effect as of July, 1975, at the British Grand Prix at Silverstone, where else? In an irony of fate, Hill dies, a few months later, in a plane crash, like Carlos Pace, Harald Ertl and so many protagonists of the US racing scene, on 29th November that year, in the debris of his Piper Aztec after trying to land on the foggy Elstree airfield. Onboard with him are his gifted charge and protégé, Tony Brise, and four other members of the team.

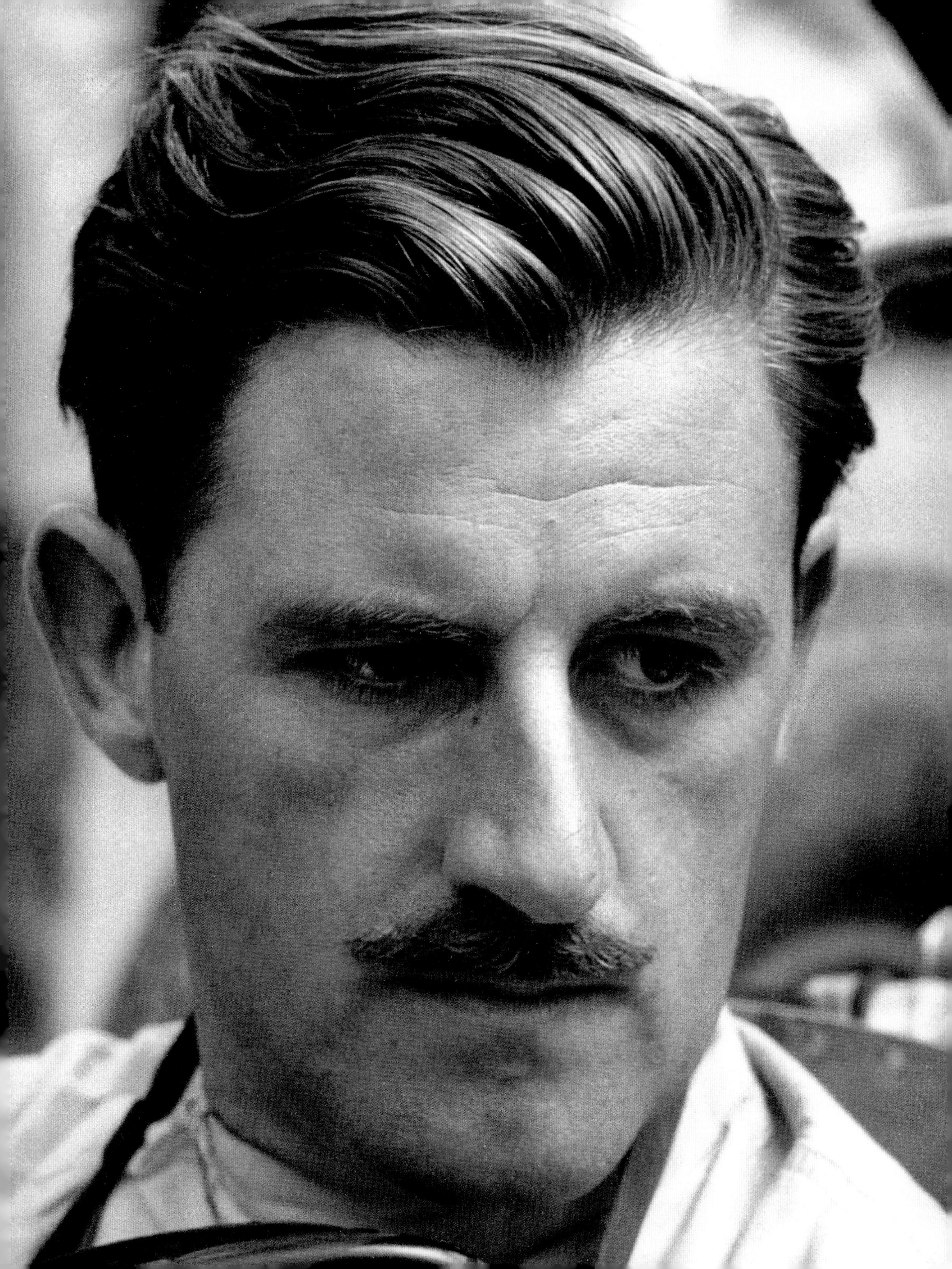

Cliff Allison

*1932 – †2005

▶ "Britain's forgotten F1 ace", as top grand prix journalist Mark Hughes headlined his *Motor Sport* profile of Allison in 2019.

Indeed, the cheerful resident of the county of Cumbria, in the northwest of England, made it to the motor racing pinnacle step by step during the fifties, until he became a member of the illustrious Ferrari équipe. Up to then, he had been closely involved with Colin Chapman and his up-and-coming Lotus venture.

In 1959, with the help of influential friends, like Mike Hawthorn, Allison found himself in the red elite squad, teamed with Tony Brooks, Phil Hill, Jean Behra, Dan Gurney and Olivier Gendebien.

But Allison was different. Born in the market town of Brough and looking more like a tractor driver than a single-seater pilot, he spoke with the heavy accent of his native region and was a dyed-in-the-wool Cumbrian. Moving to Emilia-Romagna with his wife, Mabel, and their four children was no option, so business trips such as going to a test session at Modena, then back to Britain, were made by bus, train, underground, plane and taxi.

He got on well with the *Commendatore*, enjoying excursions with the boss to the finest restaurants of the region. But Ferrari could also be a nuisance. Once, in 1960, he kept asking Allison why he had not put more pressure on the leader, Bruce McLaren, in the Cooper at Buenos Aires, in spite of his worn tyres. He might have won, he insisted, spoiling Cliff's pasta and Sangiovese. After all, Allison had gained a triumphant victory in the 1,000km race at the same venue a week earlier, with Phil Hill in a Testa Rossa.

Three terrible accidents – 1958 at Oporto, 1960 at Monaco and 1961 at Spa – were difficult to shrug off. After the last one, in the ultra-fast Blanchimont corner, Allison gave up racing, though with a heavy heart.

In later years, he drove the Brough school bus, taking turns with Mabel. Few of his wards knew that the man behind the wheel was a former British hero.

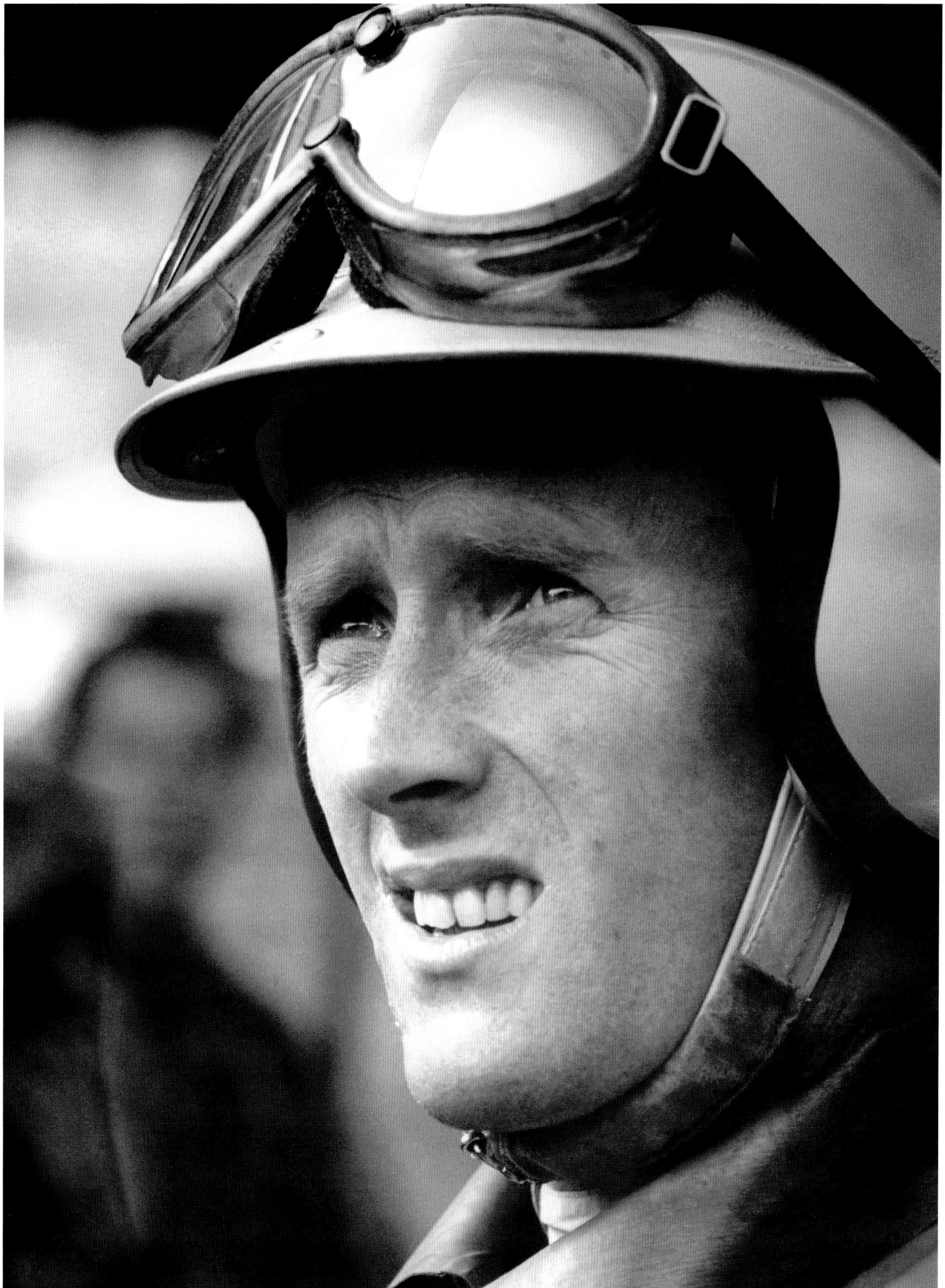

Phil Hill

* 1927 – † 2008

▶ Somehow, Philip Toll Hill was in league with Luck and Death, the two often being rather closely related to one another. And, as he was no tough customer, but introverted and musical, that dubious coalition gave him the creeps again and again.

Only after the Grim Reaper had wrought havoc among the Ferrari drivers in the second half of the fifties, in 1958, did a seat become vacant in the Scuderia's GP team for the affable Californian-by-choice. And it was the death of his friend and closest competitor, Wolfgang von Trips, that finally opened the door for Hill's world championship three years later.

A soloist rather than a man of the collective, Phil seemed cut out for the absolute solitude of the single-seater. But appearances were deceptive. Apart from Mike Hawthorn, he scored the fewest victories of all F1 champions, just three. He achieved his greatest successes as a team player, reliably world class even in the view of that great taskmaster, Enzo Ferrari.

In a modest racing machine, an MG TC, he had left his first skid marks in 1950. In a sophisicated sports car, the mighty winged Chaparral 2F, he called it quits in 1967.

In the meantime, Hill had gathered an impressive number of successes, with victories at Le Mans in 1958, '61 and '62, always for Ferrari, and at the Nürburgring 1,000km in 1962 and 1966. In the latter, Phil no longer drove for the red Scuderia, but tamed, together with Jo Bonnier, the white high-tech coupé Chaparral 2D, introduced to the world by his compatriots, Jim Hall and Hap Sharp.

Many say that after the Ferrari hegemony in 1961 and his title, things went downhill for the American. But that is only half the truth. And with his victory in the Chaparral 2F in the BOAC 500, at Brands Hatch in July, 1967, he certainly ended his long and distinguished career on a high note.

His parting words a day later, however, were plain indeed: "Until yesterday, I was Phil Hill, the racing driver. As of today, I'm Phil Hill, the non-racing driver."

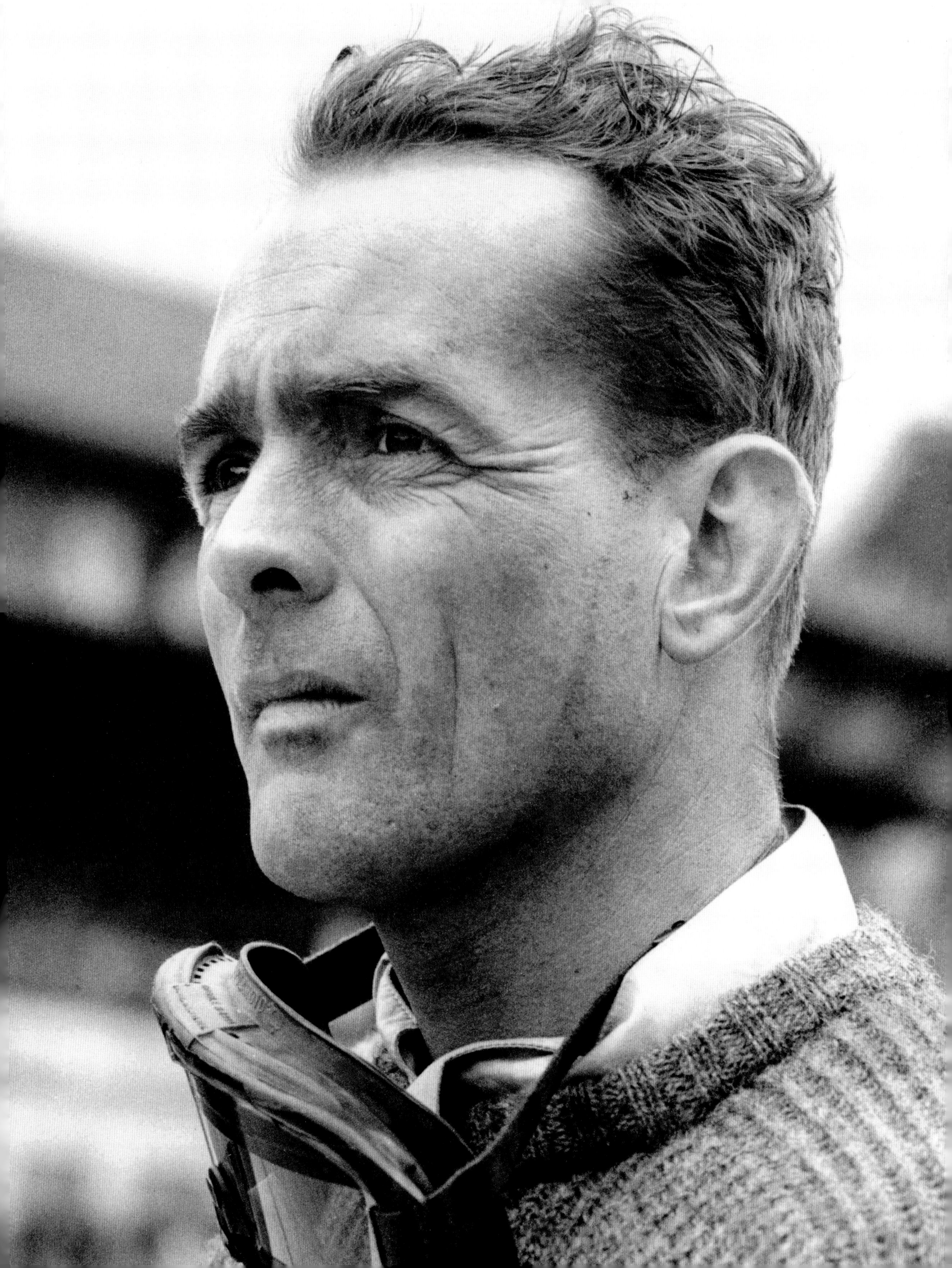

Alan Stacey

*1933 – †1960

▶ The 1960 Belgian Grand Prix was one of F1's most disastrous weekends, the other being that gruesome spring trauma at Imola, 34 years later. The parallels were frightening.

Practice had already been overshadowed by the huge accidents of Mike Taylor, practically ending his career, and Stirling Moss. Enormous skidmarks remaining on the last quarter of the notorious Burnenville right-hander told the story of the balding Londoner's near-fatal high-speed crash for a long time after. A wheel had broken away from the delicate suspension assembly of his Lotus, a risk the drivers of Colin Chapman's fragile creations famously had to live with.

Chris Bristow and Alan Stacey died on the Sunday within minutes of each other, not far from the scene of the Moss calamity – two very different men, singled out by the Grim Reaper in cold indifference from the small band of grand prix drivers of the time. Bristow, a potential star of the future, fell victim to his skirmish with the wild Belgian, Willy Mairesse. Stacey, as his team-mate Innes Ireland suggested, had been hit in the face by a bird before going off the track. The race continued.

He was no longer in his prime as an F1 driver, anyway. Some even thought that a grand prix car had become too fast for Alan Stacey. Many years later, British GP journalist David Tremayne described him as "a valiant soldier, plugging on gamely against mounting odds." Tremayne was referring to a physical handicap that not many people knew about: Stacey had an artificial limb below his right knee. To double-declutch, he had a motorcycle throttle fitted to the gear lever.

As his mechanic, Bill Bossom, had a missing arm, less sensitive characters in the paddock used to joke at the sight of the pair, that there were three legs and three arms under way. From 1958, though, Chapman had employed Stacey in his budding works squad.

So there must have been something to Alan Stacey, the grand prix racer.

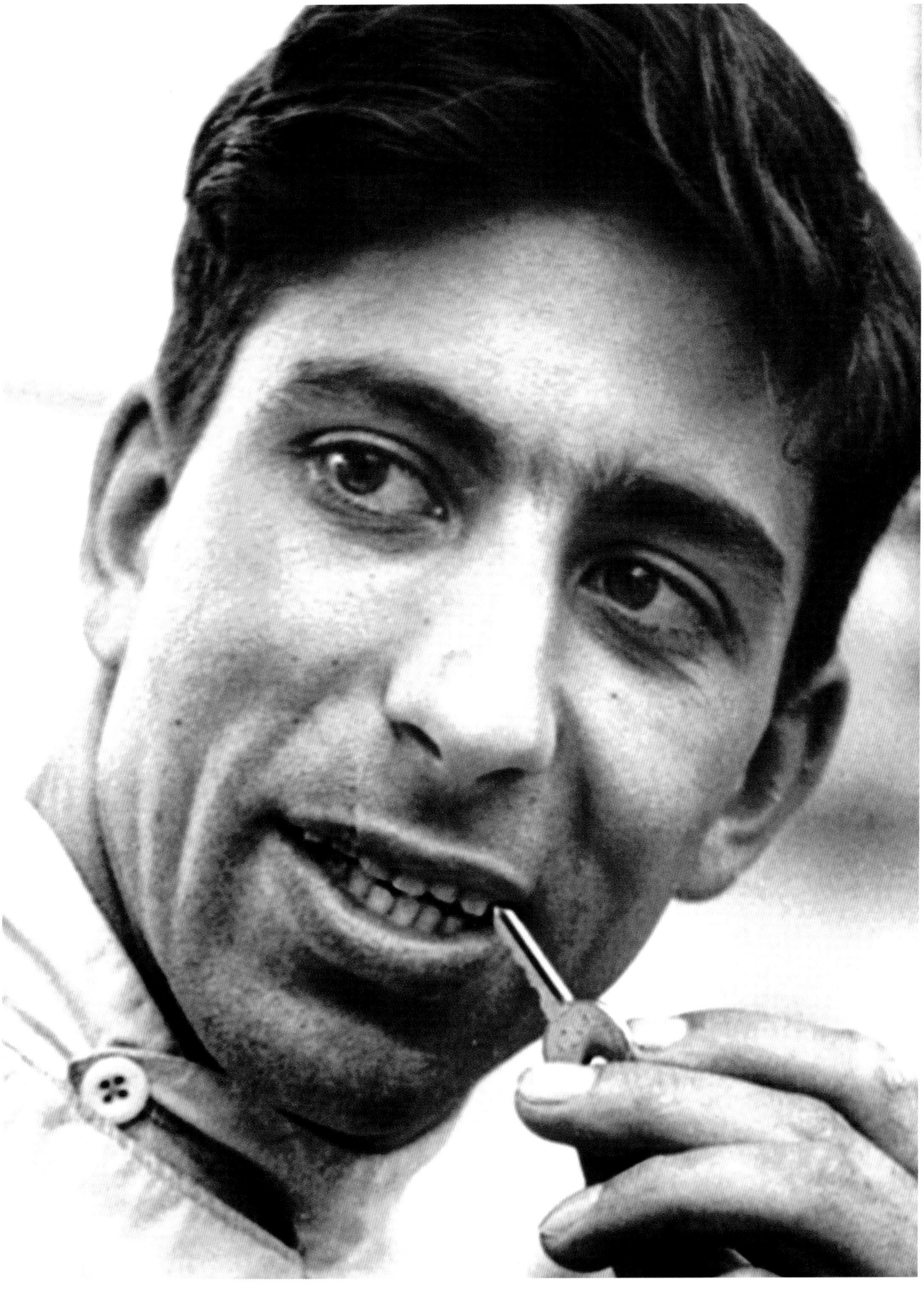

Bruce McLaren *1937 – †1970

▶ The US GP at Sebring on 12th December, 1959, and hence that year's F1 season finale, resulted in total triumph for tiny racing car manufacturer Cooper, from Surbiton, a suburban area southwest of London. Bruce McLaren won, Jack Brabham became world champion.

However, the paths that led them to that fabulous double couldn't have been more different. Brabham had to push his 500kg steed, whose tank was empty, for 400m up a slight gradient to the line, securing fourth place and providing the three points necessary for his first title. McLaren, by way of contrast, dashed fleet-footed past the chequered flag, having worked for some time to keep the back of the team's number one free from his pursuing rivals.

The augurs of the sport immediately smelled a future champion in the limping New Zealander – McLaren had suffered from hip trouble since the tenth year of his life. He would never attain that rank, but nonetheless left indelible traces on the history of his sport.

But first, he served others well. In 1962, for instance, and again for John Cooper, he smilingly ascended the steps to the royal box of the glamorous couple, Prince Rainier and his Gracia Patricia, as winner of the blue-riband Monaco Grand Prix. In 1966, together with fellow-Kiwi Chris Amon, he won the Le Mans 24 Hours aboard the mega Ford MkII. In Formula 1, McLaren entered his own products from that same year onwards, crowned by his Spa victory two years later. After 1967, together with compatriot Denny Hulme, he reflagged the CanAm series into the Bruce & Denny Show, with his mighty orange Group 7 cars. The future looked bright.

On 2nd June, 1970, however, Bruce was testing his latest weapon, ahead of the fourth year of his prestigious CanAm engagement at Goodwood. At 270km/h, its huge rear bodywork flipped open. The car morphed into a projectile, careering into an empty marshals' post, its brilliant driver subsequently ranking among the great racing dead of that terrible year.

He left behind his small family and his good name.

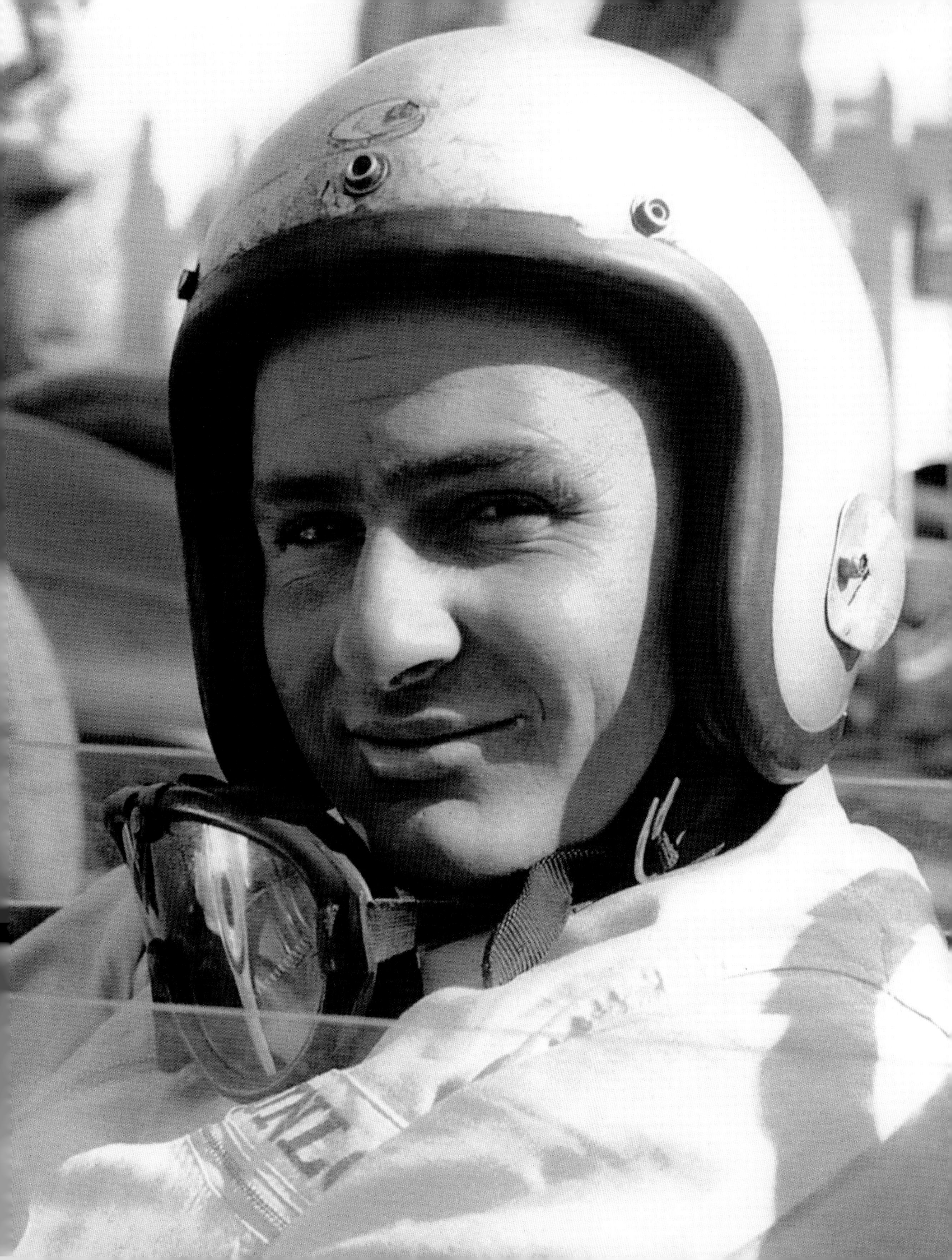

Lucien Bianchi   * 1934 – † 1969

▶ Evidently, the motor racing bug, highly infectious anyway, is often transported via the genes. Whole clans define themselves in terms of drift angles, braking points and clever slipstreaming tactics, such as the Andrettis, the Unsers and the Fittipaldis. In Formula 1, that has generated famous pairs of brothers, like the 'Schumis' and the two Belgians of Italian origin, Lucien and Mauro Bianchi, the Milan-born sons of an Alfa Romeo mechanic, who lived in Brussels from the fifties onwards.

But only Lucien, the elder, would occupy a special place in the history of the sport. The man with the precisely trimmed Menjou moustache busied himself in virtually every form of competition. He was said to have X-ray eyes, keeping a clear vision even by night, in drizzle, or dense fog, not least during his 13 Le Mans 24 Hours races.

Arguably, Bianchi's greatest year, 1968, showcased his versatility in a nutshell. After humble beginnings in the first half of the decade, his grand prix career seemed to gather pace as a member of the fading Cooper team, for instance with a third at Monaco, although four laps behind the winner, Graham Hill. In the same year, Lucien won at Le Mans, with Pedro Rodríguez, in John Wyer's Ford GT40.

Late in 1968, the Lucien Bianchi/Jean-Claude Ogier pairing, in a Citroën DS21, was in a commanding lead at the very first London-Sydney Marathon, until Ogier banged into the Mini of a non-competing motorist in the Australian town of Nowra, during the last 100 of the event's 10,000 miles.

A member of the Autodelta squad, Bianchi died during the Le Mans test weekend on 30th May, 1969, when his Alfa Romeo T33 hit a telegraph pole at the end of the Mulsanne straight. Australian Paul Hawkins was following in his wake, driving a Lola T70. The impact had been incredibly brutal, he told me six weeks later on the weekend of the Spa 1,000km, and actually should have been the reason for him to give up this sport forever.

But then the writing was on the wall for Paul himself, too.

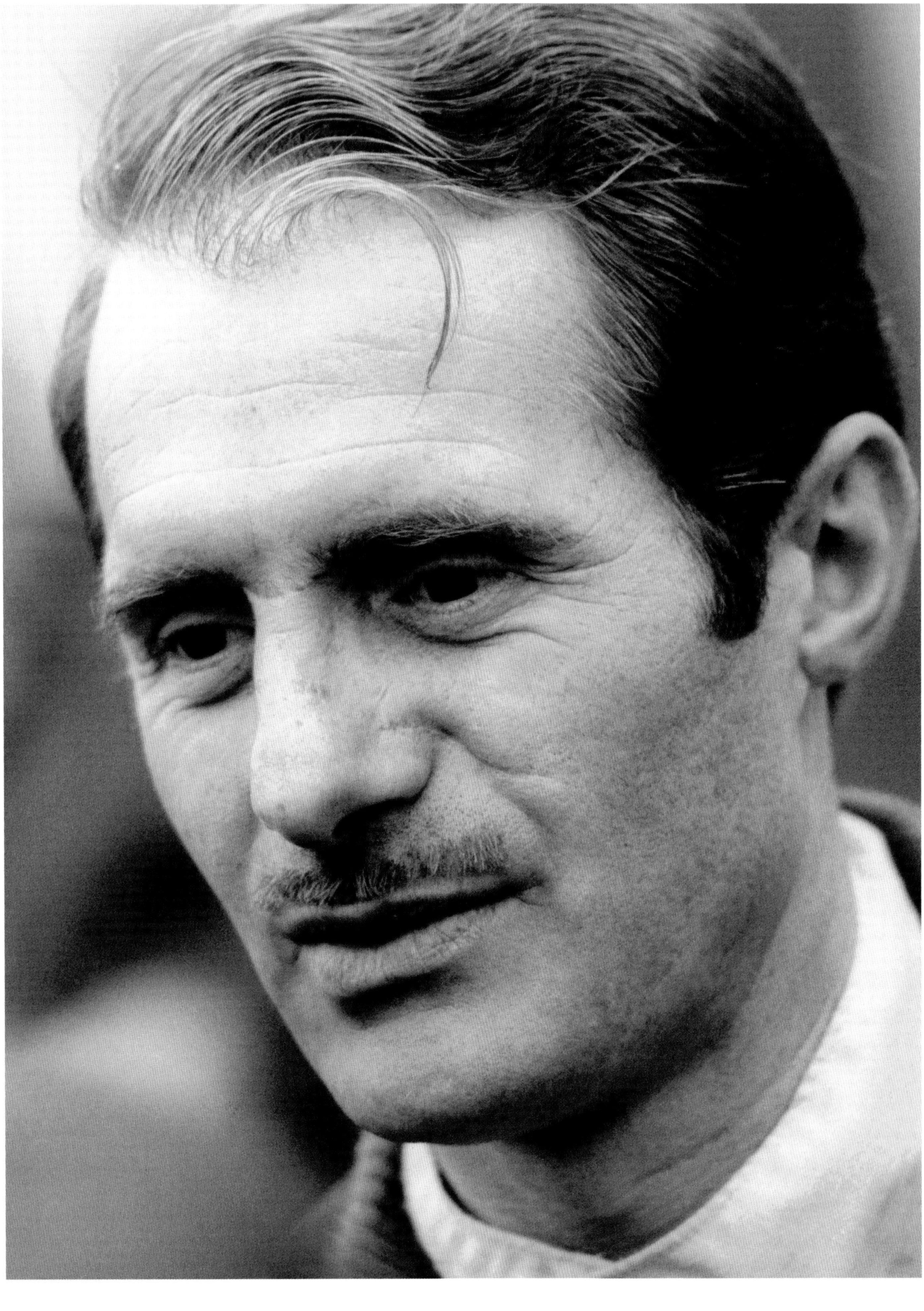

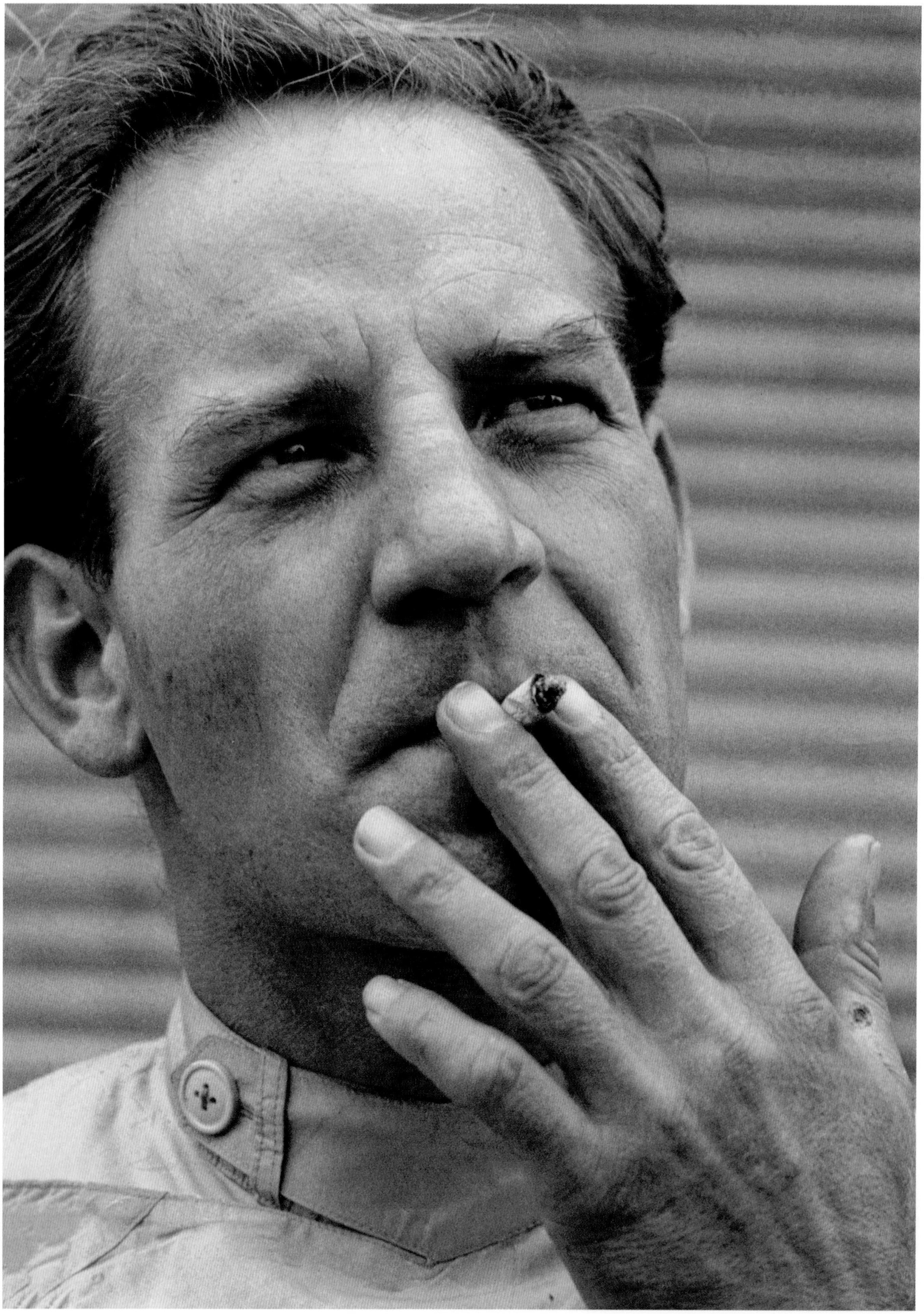

Innes Ireland * 1930 – † 1993

▶ "What a splendid character we had in Innes. One of the great flamboyant personalities enriching our sport for all of us lucky enough to be there with him." So read his obituary, from the pen of Jack Brabham, and basically there is little to add.

But it is worthwhile, indeed, to learn more about Innes Ireland. Fortunately, the pictures are still with us, along with his autobiography, *All Arms and Elbows*, once a big seller and titled after what spectators saw when a driver was at his limit, or in trouble. In it, Innes unfurled a wonderful panorama of big motor sport in the sixties. He recalled his races across the world, his triumphs and his defeats, the many tragedies in his working environment and also his own spectacular accidents.

Again and again, he praised the great camaraderie between the drivers of his era, though that didn't prevent them from playing hair-raising practical jokes on one another. Thus the occasion when Tony Brooks slipped beneath his blanket in the semi-darkness of some exotic abode, only to find a strange bedfellow in the shape of a huge, slippery, dead barracuda. Tony's revenge, Ireland related, was typical of him. Cunningly delayed, completely unexpected and terrible.

Innes also dismissed some familiar legends. One of them, made up by a major German tabloid following his 1961 Solitude victory in a Lotus, was that, roaring drunk, he had emptied a pistol into the ceiling of his hotel room, calling on the inhabitants of Stuttgart to surrender. Actually, journalist Bernard Cahier had only ignited some Swiss jumping jacks. But the episode fitted perfectly with Ireland's image, an ex-parachute regiment lieutenant who had fallen from the skies, professionally, in the fifties.

He also revealed the moving story of his early love, Jean Howarth. He lost her for 20 years, out of sight, but never out of mind. When the two met again, Innes asked her if she remembered the letter he had once written to her, while in a pensive mood. She had it in her handbag, faded, crinkled and a little frayed at the edges.

They remained together ever after, marrying shortly before his death from cancer – all those cigarettes.

Dan Gurney *1931 – †2018

▶ Sometimes, life hits a peak as it will never do again. You just don't appreciate it, or must sleep on it.

Daniel Sexton Gurney, with his triumphant Le Mans victory in the Ford GT40 MkIV a week before still prominent in the memory, experienced that magic moment on the afternoon of 18th June, 1967, smiling down at a sea of rapturous faces below him on the sloping finishing straight and pit lane of the Circuit National Belge, in his arms a huge floral arrangement.

There was something very special, in every respect, about Gurney's fourth and last victory in Formula 1. His blue car, sporting the ambitious Eagle name, and built at his Californian facility in Santa Ana, was his own product, unusually robust and one of the most beautifully-shaped racing vehicles ever. Impressive to look at and emitting a mesmerising *bel canto*. A bit too long and too heavy compared to the recently introduced Ford DFV power unit, the V12 behind Dan's back was manufactured in the modest premises of cylinder-head guru Harry Weslake at Rye, on the English south coast. On the iconic roller-coaster circuit through the Ardennes, Gurney had just driven the fastest ever grand prix until then, at a stunning 235km/h. The old record, established by Tony Brooks in 1959 in his Ferrari Dino 246 at the Berlin AVUS circuit and 5km/h slower, had indeed been ripe for beating.

Nobody envied Gurney his success. The tall American, son of a bass baritone at the New York Met and as versatile at the wheel as his compatriot, Mario Andretti, had no enemies. In suitable clothing, one might have imagined Gurney some 900 years before as a Viking leader, but also one who would help an old lady cross a busy street, and to whom you could entrust your briefcase.

After 1969, he was married, scandal-free, to Evi Butz, once personal assistant to Porsche's Huschke von Hanstein and as popular in the racing fraternity as Dan himself. The couple had five sons.

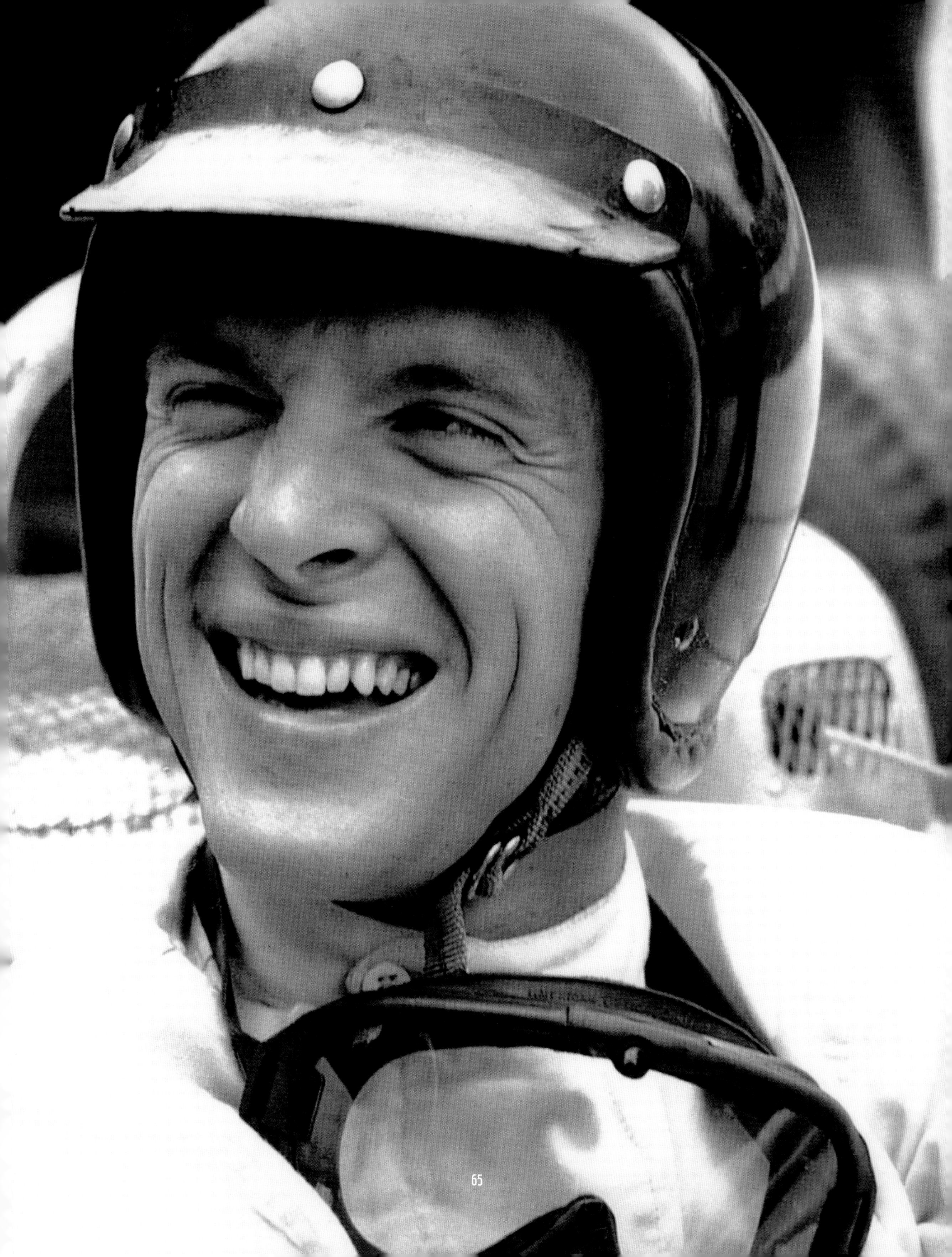

Chris Bristow *1937 – †1960

▶ The Grand Prix de Belgique, 19th June, 1960. At the beginning of lap 19, the two cars of Willy Mairesse and Chris Bristow hurtle down the descent towards Spa's notoriously dangerous Eau Rouge in close company. Trouble is brewing. Obviously, the two men are fighting it out, not unlike the famous final shootout in the cult western, *High Noon*, the stubbornly ambitious Belgian spurred on even more because this is his first GP, for Ferrari to boot, and in front of his home crowd.

Their careless game continues up the hill towards the Les Combes left-hander. But then Bristow enters the seemingly endless right-hand Burnenville corner into the valley on the wrong side, at full throttle. He never manages to get back on the ideal line. The Cooper's drift becomes a slide that carries the car off the track and into the fields, the driver decapitated by a wire fence. The tight-knit British racing community, Formula 1 and the racing sixties have lost a raw diamond of the calibre of Stefan Bellof or Gilles Villeneuve.

"Chris lacked patience in developing his undoubted talent with experience, and in its stead bravery was substituted, his death being something that shouldn't have happened," said Tony Brooks in his autobiography, *Poetry in Motion*. Close to the end of his own career, Brooks was Bristow's experienced team-mate that year in the Yeoman Credit Team, run by Ken Gregory, Stirling Moss's bustling manager, along with Stirling's father, Alfred.

Moss held his fellow Londoner in high regard. He had found himself behind Bristow in an F2 race at Clermont-Ferrand. When Gregory asked him what he thought about his driving style, he replied that it was neat and tidy. At the Monaco Grand Prix, in 1960, that became apparent to the F1 world when Bristow qualified for the first row on his debut visit to the Principality.

He had shown his potential everywhere in the minor categories. The rest remained speculation.

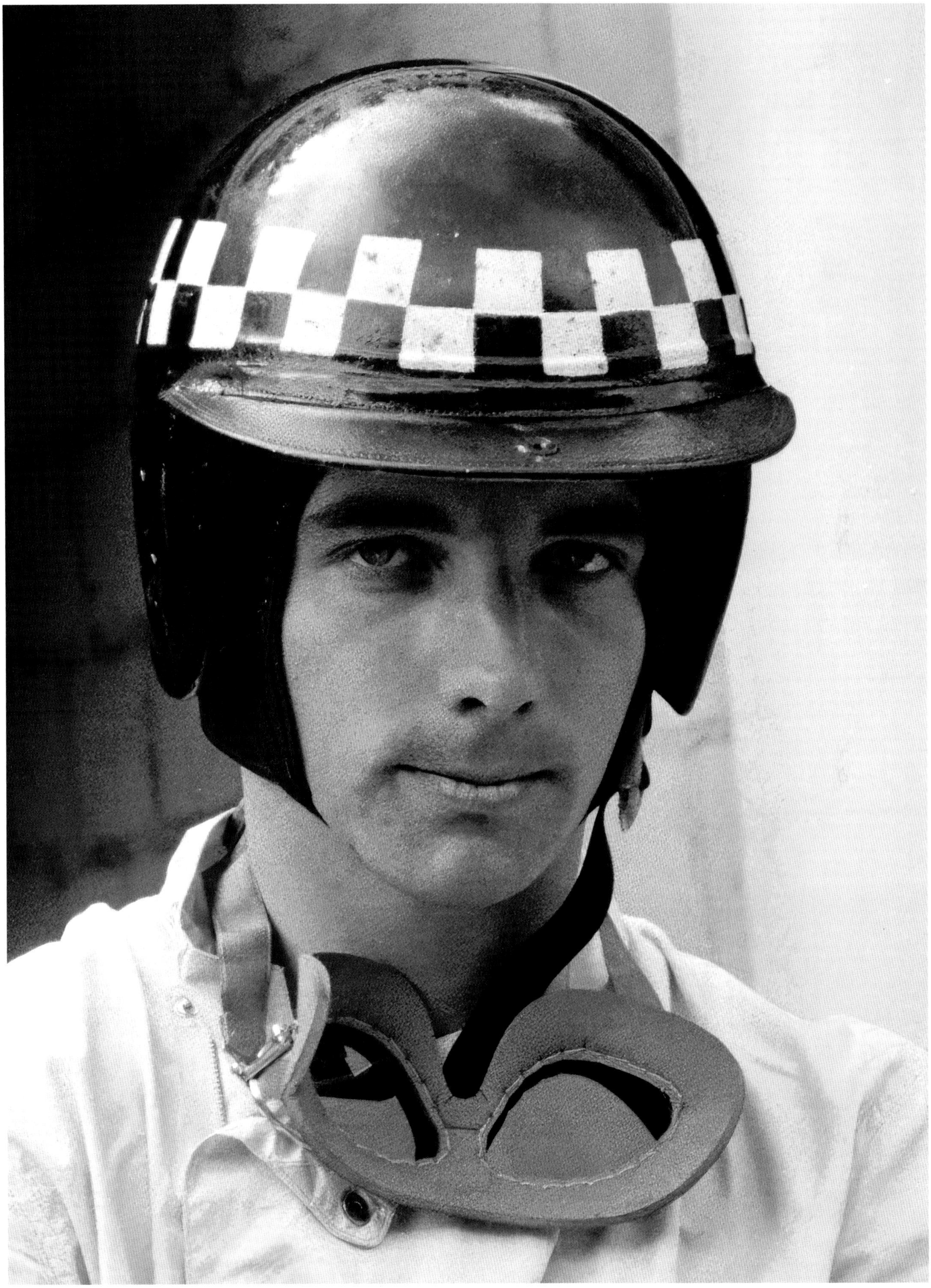

Richie Ginther

* 1930 – † 1989

▶ "Ginther", Enzo Ferrari said about him in *Piloti, che gente*, "was a curious little man whose lean face was all freckles and whose eyes were alternately sad and distracted and then smiling."

The Californian had been lucky. Ferrari's assessment of the chosen few who had the honour of driving for his Scuderia was seldom friendly. And Ginther had committed a cardinal sin: "He left us without any real reason and without saying a word." History has it that Ginther had been sacked, however.

Small, with red stubbly hair, Ginther hailed from Hollywood. His intimate knowledge of the insides of racing cars, coupled with his experience as a driver, enabled him to take a philosophical view of his job. "I'm not much of a charger", he said. "I just lie back and pace myself, picking off the front-runners as they falter."

On his day, however, beating him was not easy. For instance, at the Monaco Grand Prix in 1961, when Ginther, in his 'Sharknose' Ferrari 156, was the only driver to keep up with steering-wheel magician Stirling Moss, driving Rob Walker's Lotus 18. He would roar with laughter at such occasions. In the 1965 Mexican Grand Prix, he ran away from everybody else to score a triumphant victory in the final GP of the 1.5-litre era, a first for Honda, a one-off for himself.

It was the highlight of a Formula 1 career that had begun in 1960, when Ferrari had decided to employ his reliable services. He remained a paragon of stability – for BRM, when he finished all ten grands prix in 1964, and for Ford, providing valuable input in developing the GT40.

There was just one minor deficit: the charisma of the born winner was never quite his thing. Practising for the Indy 500 in 1967, he suddenly made up his mind that it was time to pull the plug on his racing career.

Four years later, he reconsidered his life altogether, continuing his quest for meaning in a mobile home – in the desert.

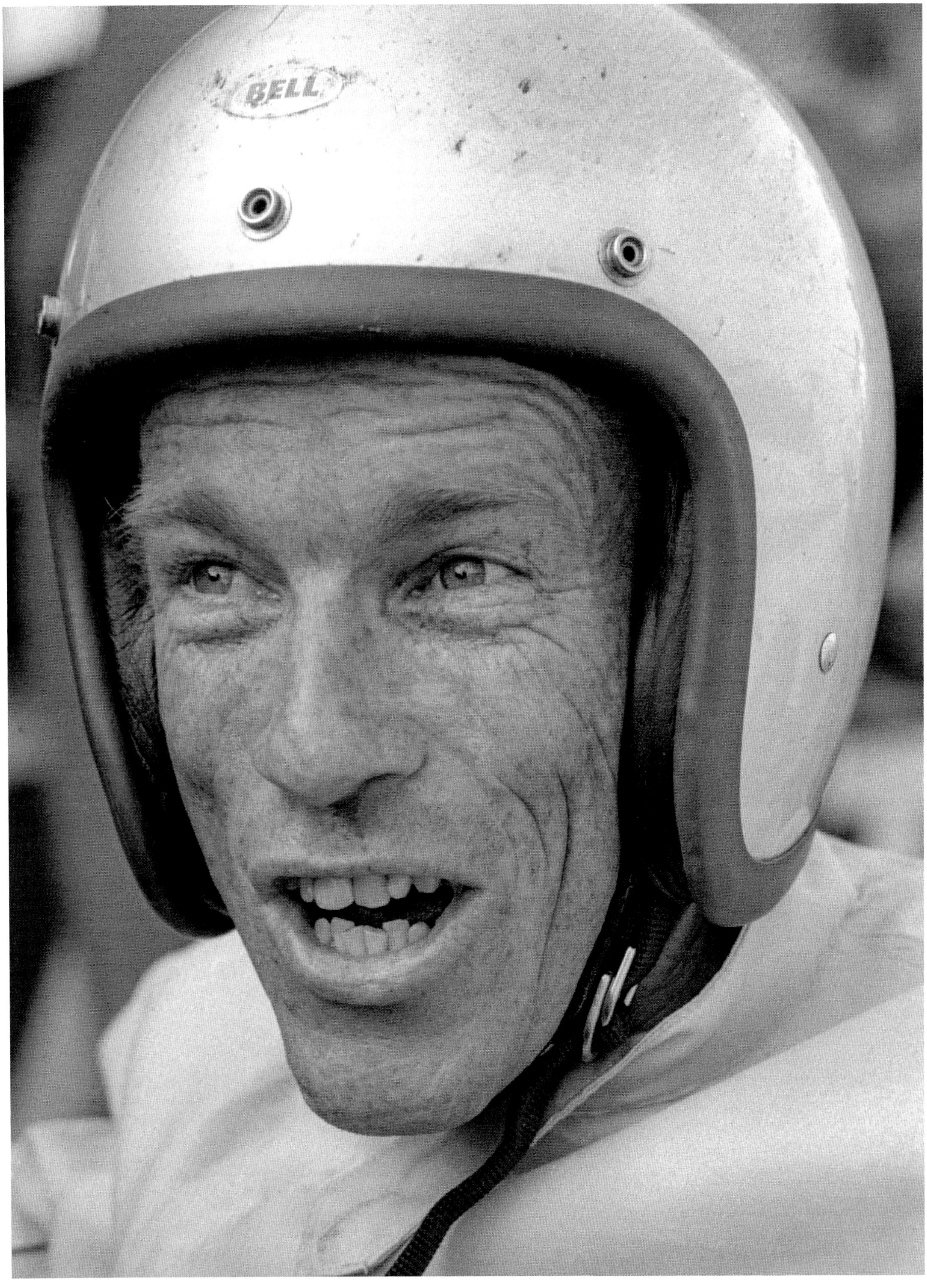
BELL

70

John Surtees *1934 – †2017

▶ The way John Surtees' championship came about seemed almost as though it had been dreamed up by a fanciful movie producer. For the 1964 finale at Mexico City, the usual actors, Jim Clark and Graham Hill, had arrived with three and two victories respectively. Surely, they would settle the matter between them. Surtees also had two wins behind him, but he was seen as having only an outside chance. But then the last minutes of the race, and of the season, confounded all speculation – the baffled Ferrari driver had grabbed the crown.

Nobody begrudged him his luck. Someone of Surtees' ilk, who had won four big events at the Nürburgring – the 1963 and '64 GPs, plus the two 1,000km races in 1963 and '65 – and all of them for the Prancing Horse, undoubtedly deserved the highest accolade.

And that's how the Ferrari connection became the most important one in 'Big John's' life. The honour was based on reciprocity. After all, the seven-times motorcycle champion had energetically pulled the Scuderia out of the doldrums after their downfall in 1962, but he had left them in anger by mid-season in 1966.

When he talked about that time, by the fireside at one of his beautiful properties near Edenbridge in Kent, fascinating details surfaced. For example, at the end of the 1963 German GP, he found himself sitting soaked in fuel after the Nordschleife had brutally twisted the chassis of his Tipo 156, holing the tank. One spark, he said, would have ignited an inferno. And that the real reason for his defection from Ferrari had been his continuous trouble with Michael Parkes, the other Brit in the SEFAC.

He compared Maranello to the castle of King Arthur, the mythological Romano-British leader, from whose Tintagel palace, the 'Knights of the Round Table' embarked upon their adventures. Sometimes, however, Ferrari would grumpily pull up the drawbridge, which made it even easier for his minions to whitewash the outside world for him.

The old man, angered by the Briton's stubbornness, certainly would not have liked that comparison.

72

Jim Clark * 1936 – † 1968

▶ In nine years of reporting on him, the media ran out of superlatives. Instead, ever newer literary arrows were drawn from their quivers to do justice to the Jim Clark phenomenon: "Superjim", exulted *L'Équipe*, "Clarkissimo", *Auto Italiano* rejoiced.

But soon, a noticeable cliché began to prevail: the simple shepherd from the Scottish Highlands who suddenly found himself in the glamorous world of the grands prix, a sort of 20th-century Parsifal.

Jimmy liked to play along, often with an elfish sense of humour, obediently sporting for the cameras the devotional objects of down-to-earth folklore, such as a kilt or bagpipes. But he had long since discovered the "glitter on the other side of the fence", as Innes Ireland, his team-mate at Lotus at the beginning of the sixties, used to put it.

Clark has been dubbed "The Shy Champion", but behind the boyish façade burned the fierce flame of his ambition. His rivalry with Graham Hill simmered continually, though rarely was voiced. While Hill crowned himself 'King of Monaco', with five victories, Clark never notched a single first in the urban canyons of the Principality. At Spa, however, the score was 4:0 to the Scot. They were both winners at Indy. Common wisdom had it that talent galore had been dropped into Clark's cradle and came naturally to him, whereas the moustachioed Londoner had to work for his achievements.

The bond between Clark and Lotus chief Colin Chapman went far beyond the usual relationship between boss and employee. Each of them made the other great, and both gave and took in equal measure.

At the end of all his days, Jim Clark was killed in a Lotus, during heat one of an insignificant Formula 2 race on 7th April, 1968, amid the slender trees that lined the idyllic first forest straight of the bland Hockenheim circuit. One can only guess how and why.

Alberto Ascari in 1955, Jim Clark 13 years later – sometimes champions die lonely.

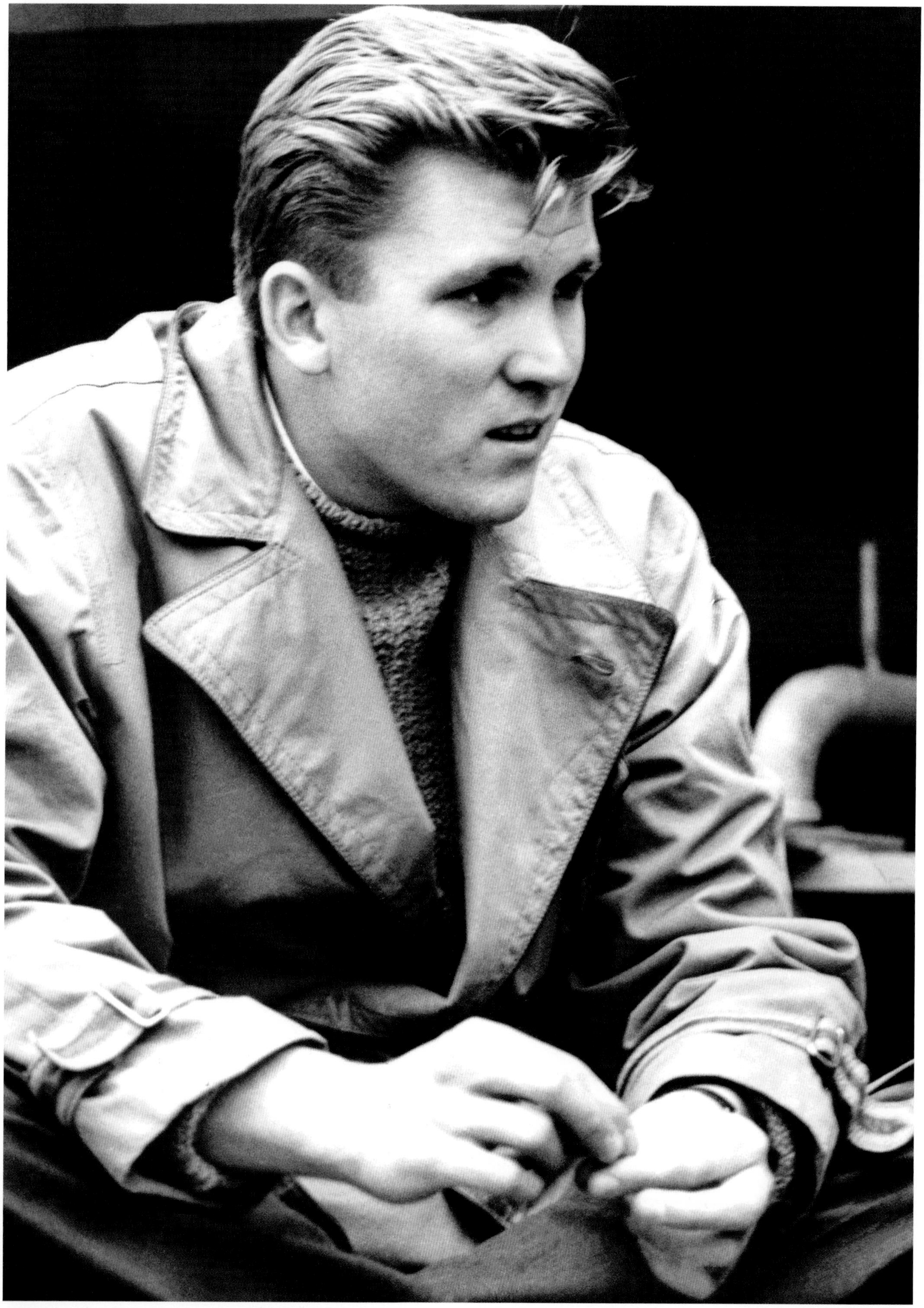

Lance Reventlow *1936 – †1972

▶ He had everything, in abundance, as a scion of the beautiful and immensely rich, though grief-laden and tragic, Woolworth heiress, Barbara Hutton, and a Danish nobleman. He was the stepson of Hollywood icon Cary Grant and friends with the film idols of his time, such as James Dean. A playboy, a jet-setter and a competent racing driver on the bustling North American scene.

Formula 1, however, turned out to be a step too far for Lance Reventlow, the more so because he entered it with the ambition of taking on the European elite, with his own vehicle, in the final year of the 2.5-litre formula. An 'anti-Ferrari', made in the USA, as it were.

He called it the Scarab, inspired by a beetle that is supposed by many to be a token of good luck. Work on the single-seater began in 1958 and led straight into a dead end, in spite of a sophisticated space frame, fuel injection and desmodromic valve operation, quite in keeping with the Mercedes-Benz racing cars of the mid-fifties.

The main deficit of the neat US machine, in an era of change, was its four-cylinder engine sitting in front of the driver, in time-honoured fashion.

Thus the appearance of Reventlow Automobiles Inc. in Formula 1 became a farce, as did Lance's spell in the highest echelon of motor sport. On his Monaco debut, at the end of May, 1960, he failed to qualify, 12 seconds behind Stirling Moss, who was fastest in practice. The trip to Zandvoort resulted in him failing to start because of a dispute with the organisers over start money. At Spa, the fragile powerplant in the never-ending bow of Reventlow's 2.4 Scarab 4 called it a day, at the very beginning of the GP.

Not even within the modest framework of the 1961 Intercontinental Formula could more fun, or positive results, be extracted from the US beetle, and Reventlow, disgruntled, pulled the plug on racing for good. An experienced aviator, he died in July, 1972, as a passenger in a plane crash in the Rocky Mountains.

Willy Mairesse

* 1928 – † 1969

▶ Not unlike Gilles Villeneuve's, the life of Willy Mairesse appeared to be an accident waiting to happen. But while the little French Canadian, darling of the gods and the masses, seemed like the nice boy next door, whose scooter had been taken and replaced by a far more dangerous toy, the little Belgian drove with gritted teeth and a frown on his face, a man possessed, and, as such, a crowd-puller as well.

Two scenes are ingrained in my mind, both from 1963. The first, in a recurrent pattern over the 36 laps of the Spa 500km on 12th May, where, near the exit of the sweeping Burnenville right-hander behind the two farmhouses, the cars' suspensions are compressed in a little dip for an instant, and the movement of Willy Mairesse, winner of the Ecurie Francorchamps in the Ferrari GTO, is faster than fast, like a mad apparition. The second, on lap two of the German GP on 4th August at the Nürburgring's Flugplatz: Mairesse crashes in his Ferrari, suffering severe injuries, as so often occurred. A Red Cross volunteer sitting next to the track has vanished, dead in the ditch, covered by a blanket until the end of the race.

Splendour and misery were bedfellows in the far too brief lifespan of Willy Mairesse, his path littered with a plethora of broken and blazing racing cars.

Splendour: whenever he won, as in the 1963 Nürburgring 1,000km, or the two Targa Florios of 1962 and '66, preferably against his laid-back compatriot, Olivier Gendebien, whom he couldn't bear, and vice versa.

Misery: as 'Kamikaze Willy', the notorious crash-pilot, at Spa in 1962 having it out with Trevor Taylor, then at Le Mans a year later, emerging from his burning Ferrari 250P like a human torch, and again at Le Mans in 1968, trying to shut the door of his Ford GT40 on the Mulsanne straight.

Willy Mairesse died far from the racing circuits, however, in a lonely suicide, having overdosed on sleeping pills, after he became unable to win anymore because of his wrecked body and tormented soul.

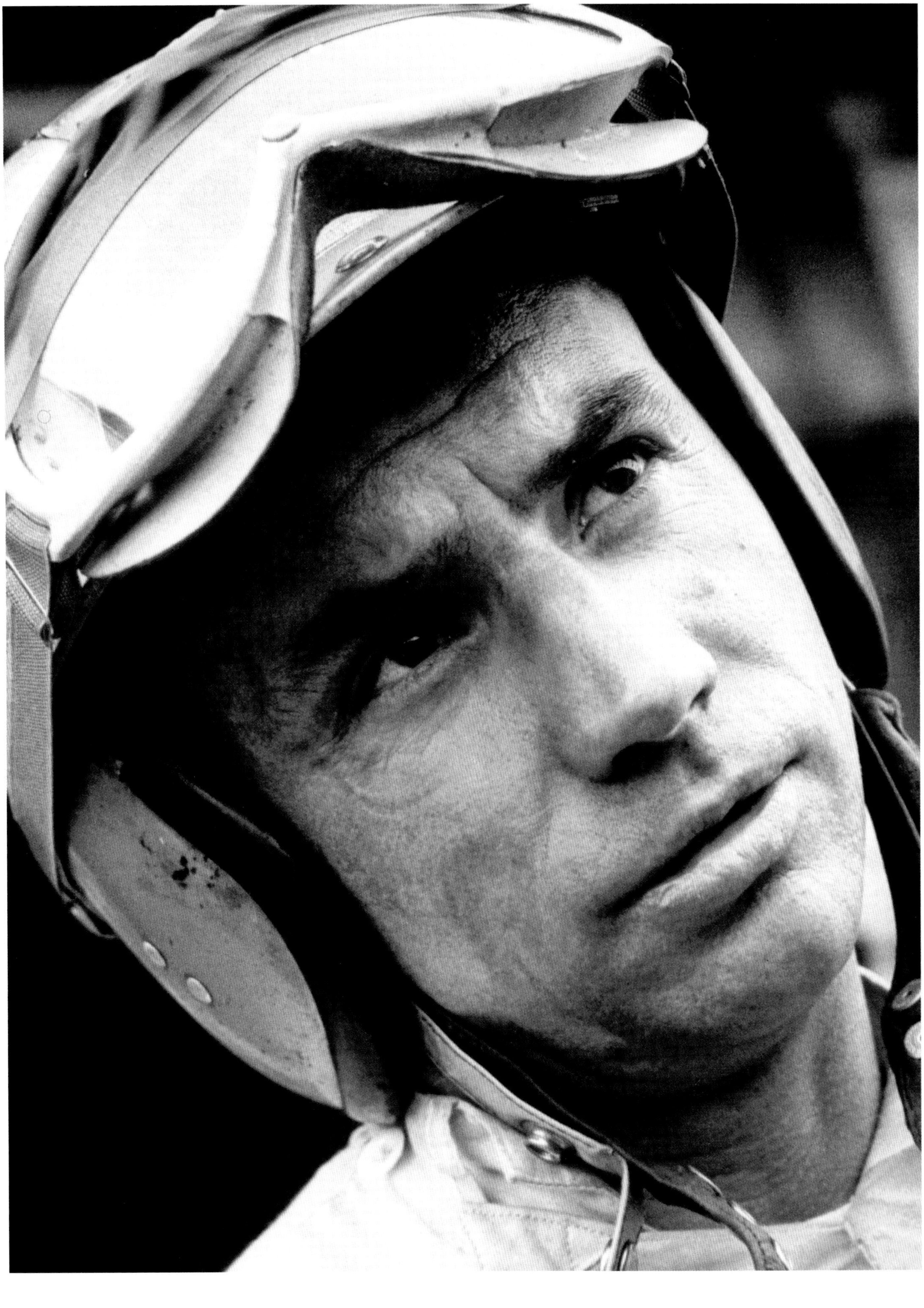

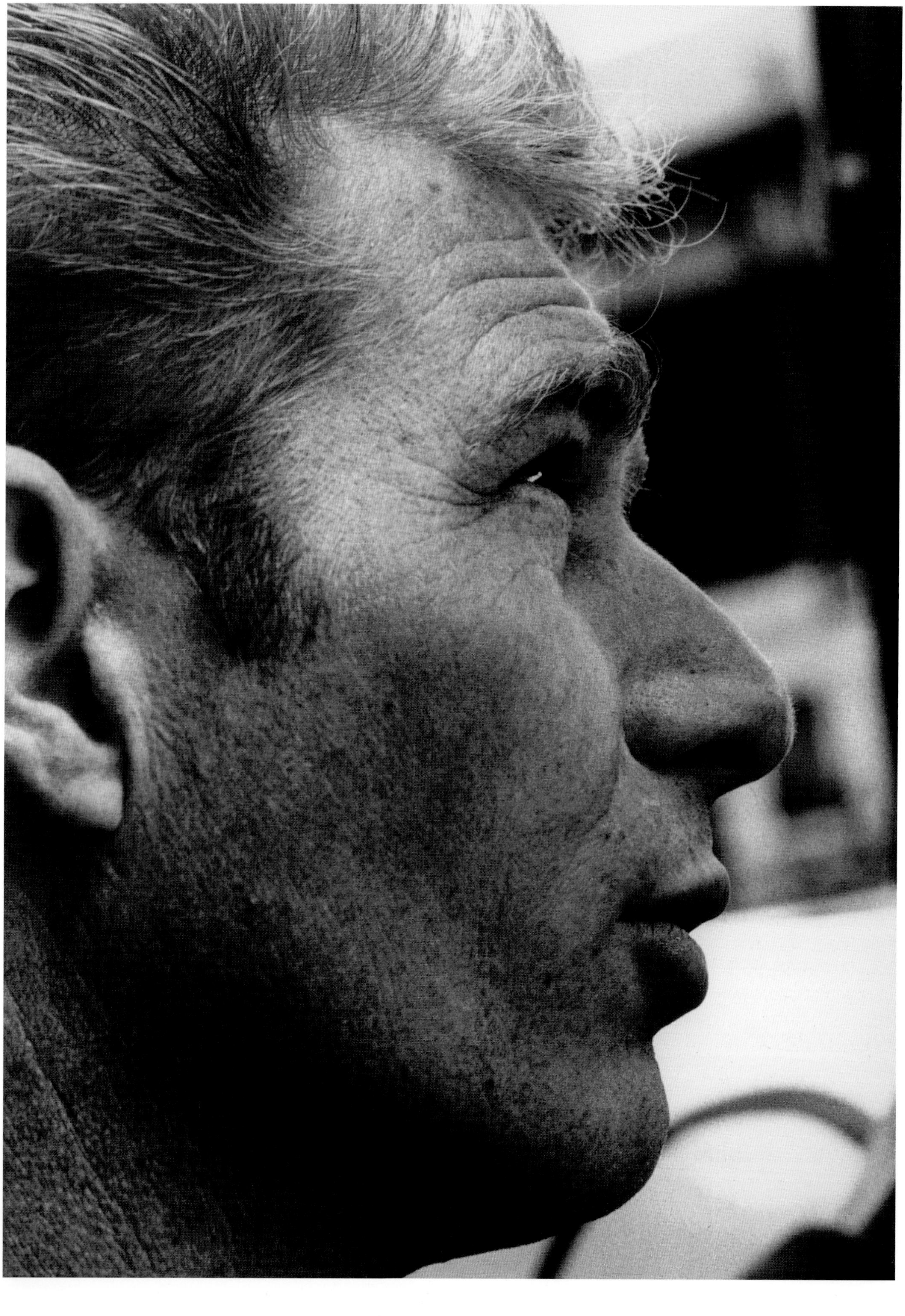

Jim Hall * 1935

▶ Jim Hall set out to conquer Formula 1: "Of course, I wanted to be world champion, like all of us". But then he had to make do with just three points from his 11 GPs between 1960 and 1963, with fifth at the 1963 German Grand Prix as his personal best – one lap behind winner John Surtees in a Ferrari. Having started out as a tiger, he ended up a bedside rug.

Hall wouldn't like that comparison, standing tall, with his customary cowboy hat on his head, a commanding presence, still, at 89. Perhaps inferior cars prevented him from achieving better results: the Lotus 18 customer car he had bought for himself, or the lime-green Lotus 24 with a BRM V8 in its rear, entered in 1963 by backbencher outfit British Racing Partnership, run by Stirling Moss's father, Alfred, and his manager, Ken Gregory. Or maybe it was due to repeatedly bad weather: it rained continuously during Hall's first European venture, he complained with hindsight.

His great years were still to come, however, as the creator of racing cars that were revolutionary. That began with their name. Chaparral was taken from a rather obscure species of the bird world, namely a cuckoo known as a roadrunner. Hall was the Texan equivalent of Britain's Colin Chapman, whom he admired. The moustachioed Briton, though, had been as closed to him as an oyster, he grumbled, unprepared to utter a revealing word.

Like Chapman, Hall gave plenty of headaches to the guardians of the rules, for example with the Chaparral 2D, aboard which Phil Hill and Jo Bonnier had won the 1966 Nürburgring 1,000km, pampered by the luxury of an automatic transmission. Or the 2F, a year later, with its enormous rear wing. Most of all, however, with his CanAm model 2J in 1970, as ugly as sin and sucked to the surface of the road by means of two ex-military tank-derived fans driven by a separate blaring two-stroke engine.

His competitors were livid, and rightfully so, until the FIA pulled the plug on the latest monstrosity from oil-rich Midland, Texas.

Trevor Taylor * 1936 – †2010

▶ Four British drivers named Taylor could be found on the F1 starting lists of the sixties: Henry, John, Mike and Trevor. A fifth, Dennis, was killed in the FJ race preceding the 1962 Monaco GP, together with Luigi Fagioli and Lorenzo Bandini, one of the surprisingly few victims of the iconic street circuit.

But only Trevor really made a splash, not only because he would climb into his race cars clad all in yellow, but also because he shrugged off the most enormous accidents, and made buffoons wonder whether he or his sister, Anita, was the prettier. At the beginning of the decade, he was a promising prospect in British motor racing, underlined by his successes in the speed classroom of Formula Junior. In 1961, he secured his country's title, which he had shared with Jim Clark the year before. Amazingly, the pair had collected the same number of victories, second and third places, and fastest laps – all for Lotus.

The careers of Clark, Taylor and Innes Ireland were closely entwined, with Lotus boss Colin Chapman as mastermind. When Chapman fired Ireland at the end of 1961, despite his first win for the marque at Watkins Glen, Taylor settled into the number two seat at Team Lotus, behind Clark, without grumbling. Two years later, Chapman insinuated that focusing on F2 for a year would do him good. Taylor didn't like the notion and spent 1964 with the largely uncompetitive BRP outfit, scoring just a single point.

Ironically, the number one driver was Ireland, still annoyed about his Lotus dismissal two years earlier. During an F1 event at Reims, things escalated. The rugged Scot, though, by his nature, preferred harmony, so over a couple of beers one night, they rapidly became friends and left the bar clasping each other in brotherly fashion around the neck on their way to their hotel.

But, after a chaotic final stint in his 1966 home GP at Brands Hatch, driving the F1 oddity Shannon Godiva, Trevor Taylor was lost to the highest realms of motor sport, but made a stirring comeback in the newly introduced F5000 formula in 1969.

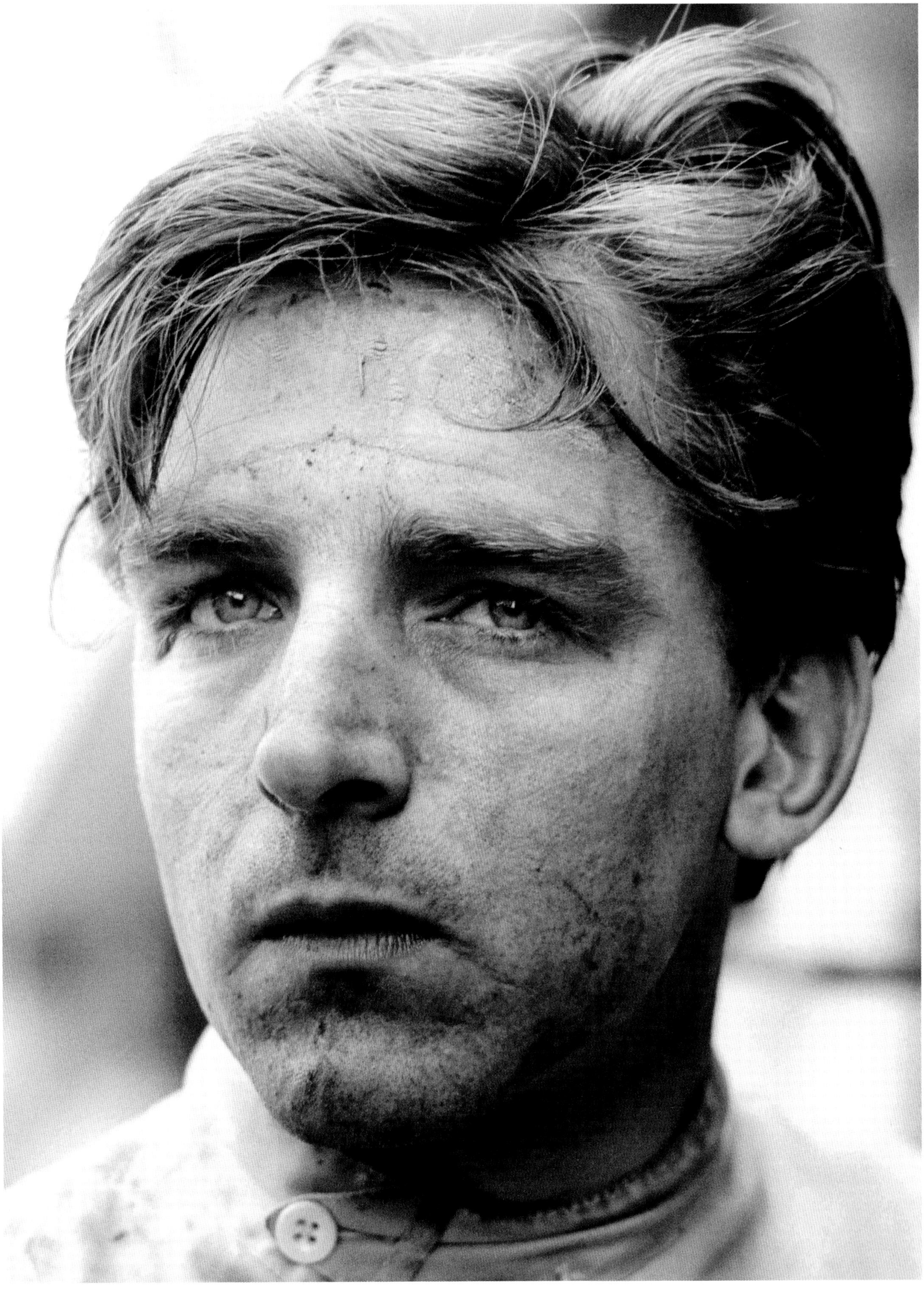

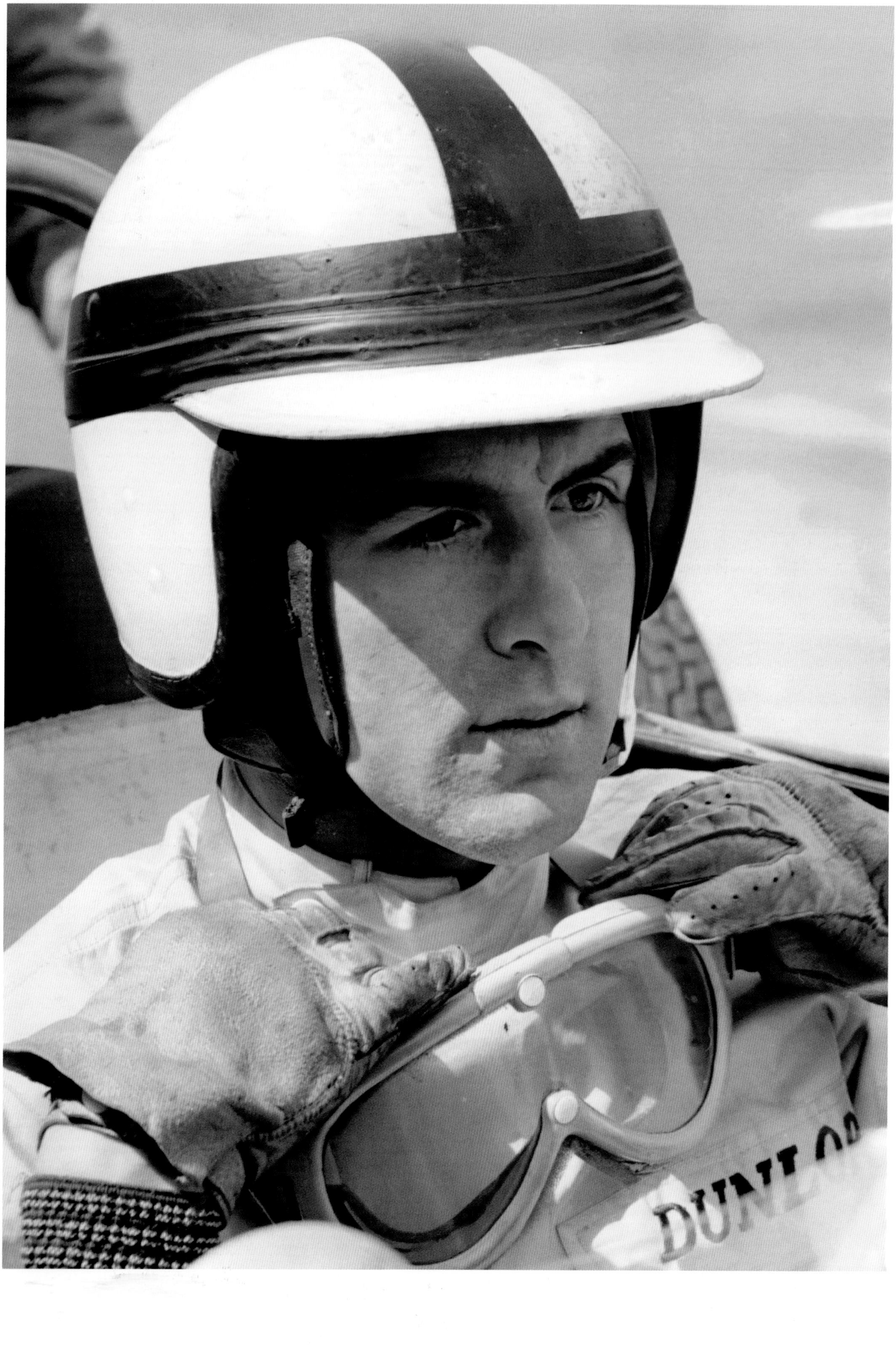

Jack Lewis * 1936

▶ Jack Lewis was truly a high-flyer who seemed to storm up the ladder towards the racing-driver Olympus two rungs at a time: Formula 3 in his first season in 1958, yielding three wins; moving up to Formula 2 in his second; then winning the Aurora F2 British Championship in 1960. Of course, motor racing is dangerous, and a photographer's lucky shot showed Jack 'Jackie' Lewis at Brands Hatch rolling his F3 Cooper-Norton. He appeared to be supporting himself and the car with his hands on the track. The nation was horrified, but young Jack remained undaunted.

With his ascent to Formula 1, Jack's trend curve levelled off considerably in 1961, not least as he belonged to the endangered species of private drivers. The purchase, maintenance and use of his Cooper T53-Climax were financed by his family business, H & L Motors, which kept its head above water by selling motorcycle parts. This was also the name of his team, run jointly by Lewis and his father, who approved of his son's escapades. Subsequently, it was rebranded as Ecurie Galloise in 1962.

Jack's talent stood out and paid off, with a fourth place at Monza in 1961 and a solid performance at the Nürburgring in the same year, the race in which Stirling Moss, driving 'Gentleman' Rob Walker's Lotus, outclassed the Ferrari 'Sharknose' strike force in changeable weather. In the end, Jack Lewis nestled into ninth position and at least kept the experienced, but already somewhat tired, Tony Brooks at bay.

However, he was always annoyed by the arbitrariness of the men who pulled the levers of Formula 1, for example, when he was denied entry to the 1962 Monaco GP because slower drivers in works cars were guaranteed access to the grid. And even more so when BRM sold him a barely competitive P48/57 at the beginning of 1962. The bad purchase was quickly cancelled.

By the end of that season, though, Lewis had had enough, and from then on devoted himself, like young Jim Clark, to breeding sheep, but also Arabian thoroughbreds, with the greatest of pleasure.

Nino Vaccarella * 1933 – † 2021

▶ In the night preceding the Targa Florio, the 'real' Targa Florio up until 1977, the Sicilian Madonie, south of Cefalù on the Tyrrhenian coast, changed from a haven of calm, vaulted by a star-studded sky, into a noisy fairground. In their hundreds of thousands, the Sunday visitors turned off the major coast road, flocked uphill in the direction of Collesano or Cerda, looked for a parking space in vain, and ended up next to or even halfway on the track, obscuring the ideal line.

Again and again, the drawn-out cry of "Niiino!" echoed from the mountain slopes, with "Forza Nino" having been painted everywhere on billboards and crumbling walls in crude letters. The object of these cult-like actions was Nino Vaccarella, headmaster of the Maria Montessori private school in Palermo, also lovingly dubbed *Il Preside Volante*, or 'The Flying Principal', because of his second profession as a *pilota*. All of these encouragements were completely unnecessary. Vaccarella always gave his very best, and that was a lot, and he also knew the 72km-long *circuito* almost as well as Targa founding father Vincenzo Florio or Baron Antonio Pucchi, another racing local. Nino, said his rival and friend, Vic Elford, was certainly familiar with every single square metre.

Vaccarella's impressive reward: three firsts, in 1965 in a Ferrari 275P2 (with Lorenzo Bandini), in '71 aboard an Alfa Romeo T33/3 (with Toine Hezemans), and in '75 at the wheel of an Alfa T33/TT12 (with Arturo Merzario). The racing pedagogue was not just a local matador, but world class in sports cars, with victories at Le Mans and the Nürburgring 1,000km in 1964, as well as the 1970 Sebring 12 Hours, to his credit.

Nino would pay only fleeting visits to Formula 1, however, not least due to the fact that in three of his four GPs, the ageing vehicles provided for him by Conte Giovanni Volpi's Scuderia Serenissima had already put fulfilling race-car lives behind them.

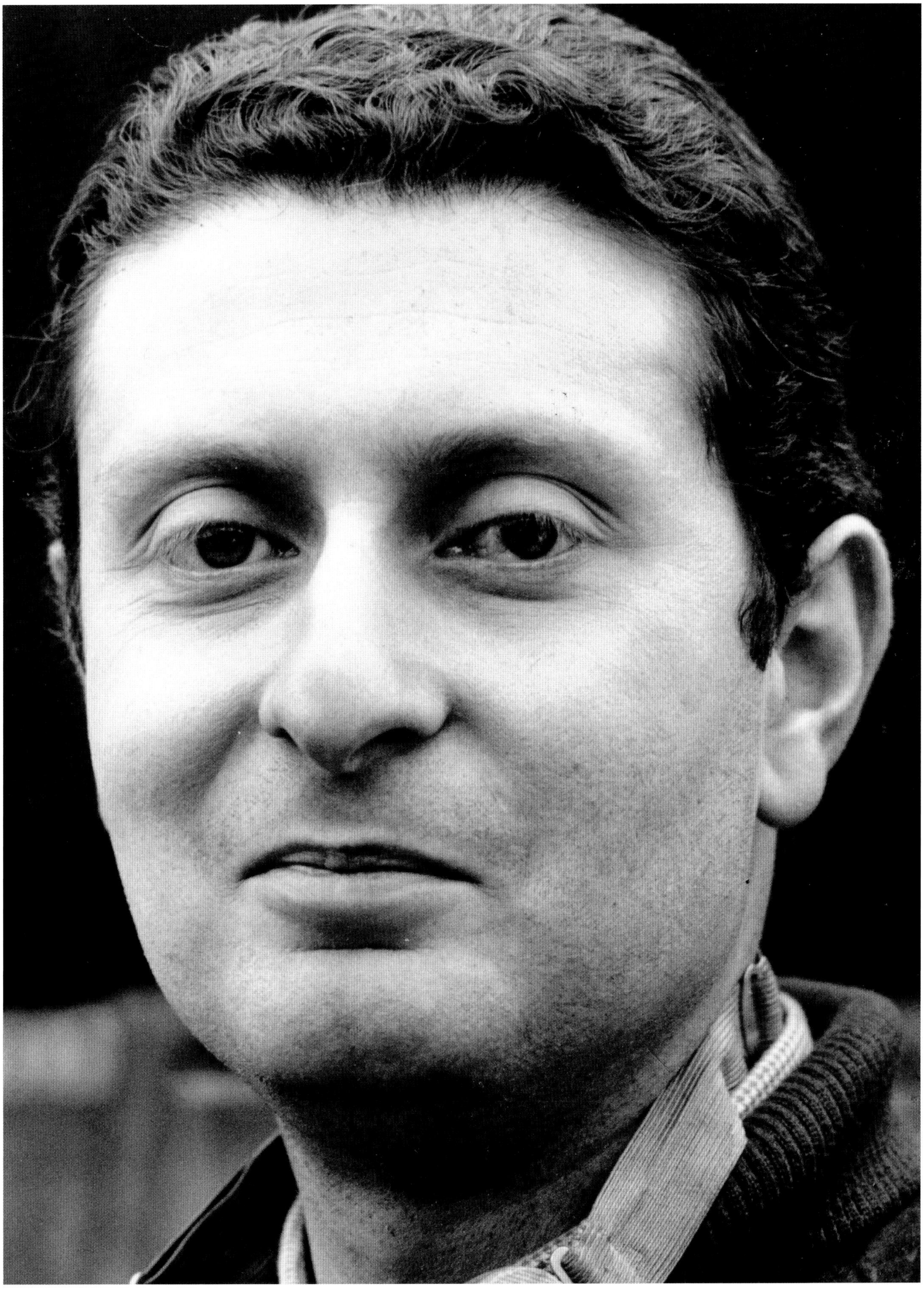

86

Lorenzo Bandini * 1935 – † 1967

▶ As usual, Enzo Ferrari watched the 1967 Monaco Grand Prix on TV, in the seclusion of his office at Maranello. On lap 82, a portentous black cloud of smoke rose above the harbour chicane. RAI TV commentator Piero Casucci was at a loss for words, but Ferrari instinctively knew that one of his cars was ablaze. He even sensed that the driver was Lorenzo Bandini.

Ferrari liked Bandini, born into a family of impoverished Italian immigrants in Libyan Barce, today el Merdj. Before Lorenzo became a member of his illustrious Scuderia, he had to make the hard slog, spurred on by a tremendous will, unlike, for instance, his compatriot and long-time rival, Ludovico Scarfiotti. When he stood on the podium after his first single-seater race in Syracuse in 1958, won at the wheel of a Volpini Formula Junior car, he rejoiced in dark presentiment: "A new world beckons to me – a terrible world."

For Ferrari, he rendered somewhat dubious merits when, during the 1964 season's finale in Mexico City, he elbowed title contender Graham Hill of BRM into the barriers. It was his 17th grand prix for SEFAC, and his infamous deed paved the way for the world championship of his team-mate, John Surtees.

It also endorsed his renown as a racing ruffian. But there was another side to him: when Surtees was about to leave Ferrari in anger after the 1966 Belgian GP, Bandini beseeched him, in tears, "John, please, don't go." Surtees confirmed this many years later, contradicting a persistent narrative that there had been much poison between them.

It might have been Bandini's year in 1967. He had already caused a splash, with sports car victories at Daytona and Monza in the mighty P4, and a second place at the Race of Champions at Brands Hatch. But then it all turned out differently. Three days after his fiery Monaco accident, the news of his passing made the rounds.

All Italy mourned.

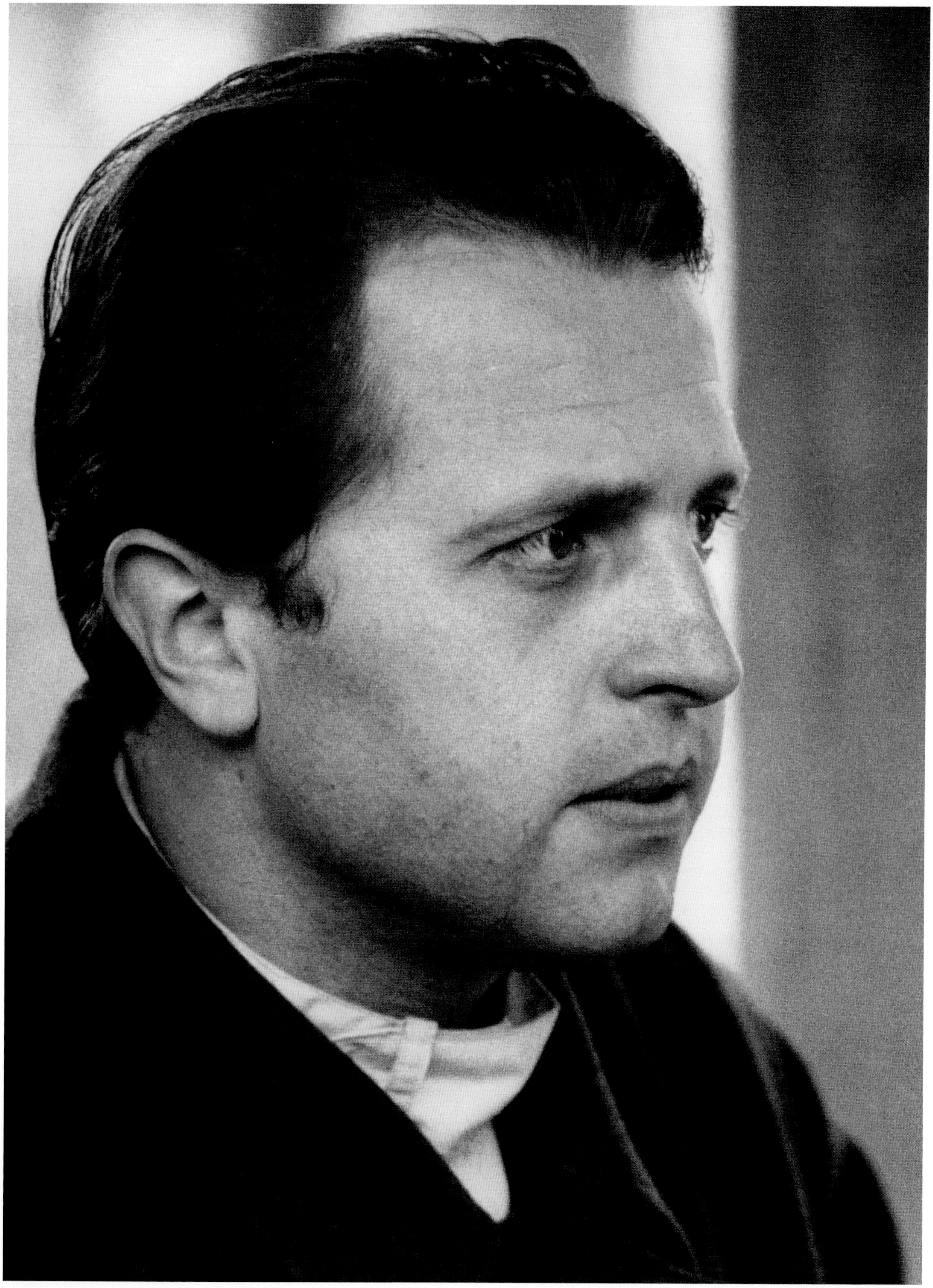

Giancarlo Baghetti

* 1934 – † 1995

▶ The opinions voiced in Enzo Ferrari's late work, *Piloti, che gente*, as collected by his close confidant, Franco Gozzi, are brief and often caustic, actually betraying much more about the old man himself than the people of whom he talks. The red cars from Maranello are untouchable icons, but their drivers come and go.

About Giancarlo Baghetti, he had this to say: "When I met him, he struck me as a cold-blooded, cautious and reserved young man. The press hailed him as another Varzi." As a matter of fact, the laid-back Milanese, scion of an affluent family of industrialists, enriched GP history with a statistical one-off, winning his first three Formula 1 races in 1961.

Only the third, however, was a 'real' grand prix, with Baghetti's vehicle being a rental car, a Dino 156 'Sharknose', loaned by FISA (Federazione Italiana Scuderie Automobilistiche), a coalition of Italian automobile clubs.

Not before the Grand Prix de France, on 2nd July, did Giancarlo face the GP field in full combat strength. The works cars had to retire, and Baghetti, in the FISA 156, led for seven of altogether 52 laps, emerging as winner from the uncomfortable slipstream bunching of the Reims straights like a shrewd and seasoned campaigner. Ferrari gave him a works contract for 1962. So far, so good.

Then, however, he was entered only four times, with poor results. The 1962 season was bad for the Scuderia anyway, left entirely in the doldrums after its 1961 glory. In the end, Ferrari went for Lorenzo Bandini. Baghetti sought refuge at ATS, an F1 team set up by Ferrari renegades Carlo Chiti, Giotto Bizzarrini and Romolo Tavoni. "His luck began to wane," said the *Commendatore*, unruffled.

On 7th May, 1967, and about to become a GP pensioner, Baghetti was confronted with the ugly face of his sport, as a witness at the Monaco harbour chicane where his old nemesis, Bandini, suffered lethal burns.

Baghetti died of cancer three years later, also far too early.

Tony Maggs * 1937 – † 2009

▶ In the sixties, the path to the higher ranks of motor sport inevitably led through Europe and, more accurately, via Britain, racing's self-appointed motherland.

That's why South African Tony Maggs, against the explicit will of his family, headed north for the far-flung Eldorado of the drift angle in 1960, a trailblazer for future like-minded compatriots, such as Jody Scheckter. Maggs turned out to be the most successful representative of his country in the racing community, however, with the exception of the curly-haired 1979 world champion from East London.

He was also lucky, quickly meeting the right people at the right moment. Ken Tyrrell, a powerful player in this sport, who had just given up his own ambitions as a driver, ran the Cooper team in Formula Junior from a shed of his timber business at East Horsley, and he took the youngster under his wings. Maggs leapt to prominence, gaining the European Championship in 1961, while his victorious little Cooper T56 was sold to up-and-coming Hollywood star Steve McQueen.

Another fortunate coincidence brought Maggs together with Louise Bryden-Brown, heiress at Parke Davis, then the world's biggest pharmaceutical concern. As a personal little toy, she indulged in her own F1 team. Maggs drove her dapper Lotus 18 in that year's British and German GPs, with poor results, though not least because of Ferrari's crushing superiority in the 1961 season.

Nevertheless, Charles and John Cooper employed him as number two in 1962, behind Bruce McLaren, in the F1 squad from Surbiton. The best placings Maggs delivered were two seconds, in the French GPs at Rouen, in 1962, and at Reims a year later, profiting from numerous retirements in both cases. In 1964, he had to step down to Scuderia Centro Sud, with an elderly BRM, when Phil Hill joined Cooper.

In June, 1965, he took refuge in retirement, deeply moved by the death of an eight-year-old boy whom his Brabham had killed, in a prohibited area, after going astray during an F2 race in Pietermaritzburg.

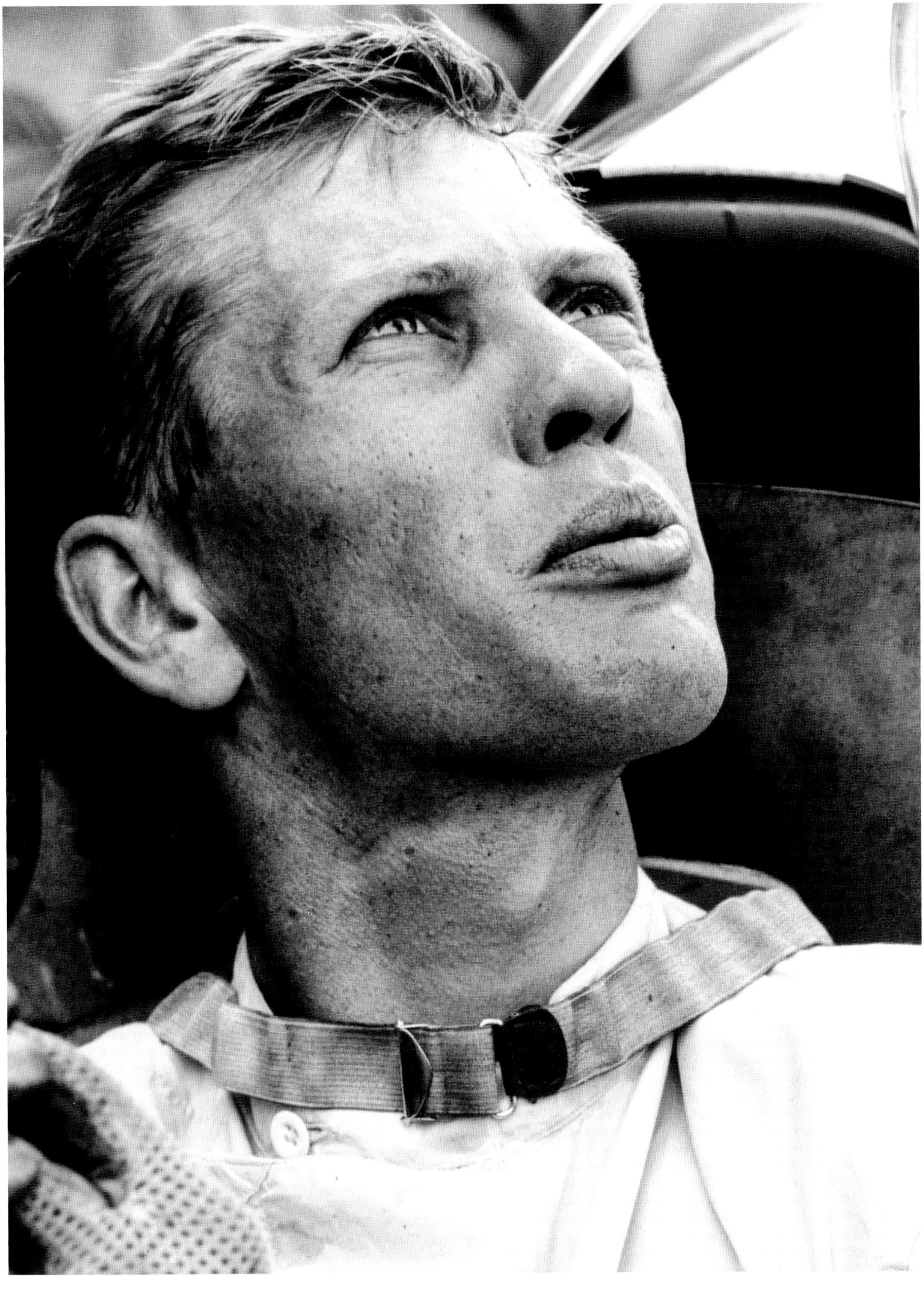

Ricardo Rodrìguez

* 1942 – † 1962

▶ As usual, the ADAC's seventh 1,000km, on 28th May, 1961, was good for a couple of surprises. For the second time in a row, the curious 'Birdcage' Maserati Tipo 61 crossed the finishing line as winner, sailing under the Stars & Stripes banner and stirring up a storm in a teacup.

However, a sensation was caused by the daring race of the vehicle in second position, Luigi Chinetti's Ferrari 250 Testa Rossa, whose nose had been modified in keeping with the 'Sharknose' design prevailing that year. At the steering wheel, the Rodriguez brothers, Ricardo and Pedro. The 270,000 spectators wondered how on earth those two managed to keep their screaming 12-cylinder mount between the hedges of the 'Green Hell'. Ricardo, the younger, crowned the spectacle when, with two laps to go and 15km from the pits, the Ferrari shed a wheel and he drove it back on three tyres and a brake disc.

The two Mexicans had shot into the racing-driver firmament like comets in 1960, with their schoolboy looks and a breath of exoticism. Smart, without fear of death, the devil, or the Nordschleife of the Nürburgring, and already in league with the illustrious Ferrari name. In their wake came their compatriot, Jo Ramirez, of later fame as F1 factotum and McLaren team co-ordinator. "They were like night and day," he remembered. "Ricardo had it all, didn't have to push the limits, a natural talent."

But Enzo Ferrari was worried. After the 1962 Dutch GP, he warned the younger Rodriguez that he must bridle his enthusiasm and refine his style, to behave like a pro. Ricardo, however, only smiled.

The wizard of Maranello was right, as 1962 was a rotten season for the Scuderia, quite in contrast to the preceding year. At the Mexican GP, a non-championship event, Ricardo wanted to show his mettle to his legion of fanatical supporters, driving Rob Walker's Lotus 24. Trying to beat an opponent's time, he veered off the track at the notorious Peraltada corner, of all places.

He was killed instantly, not even 21 years old.

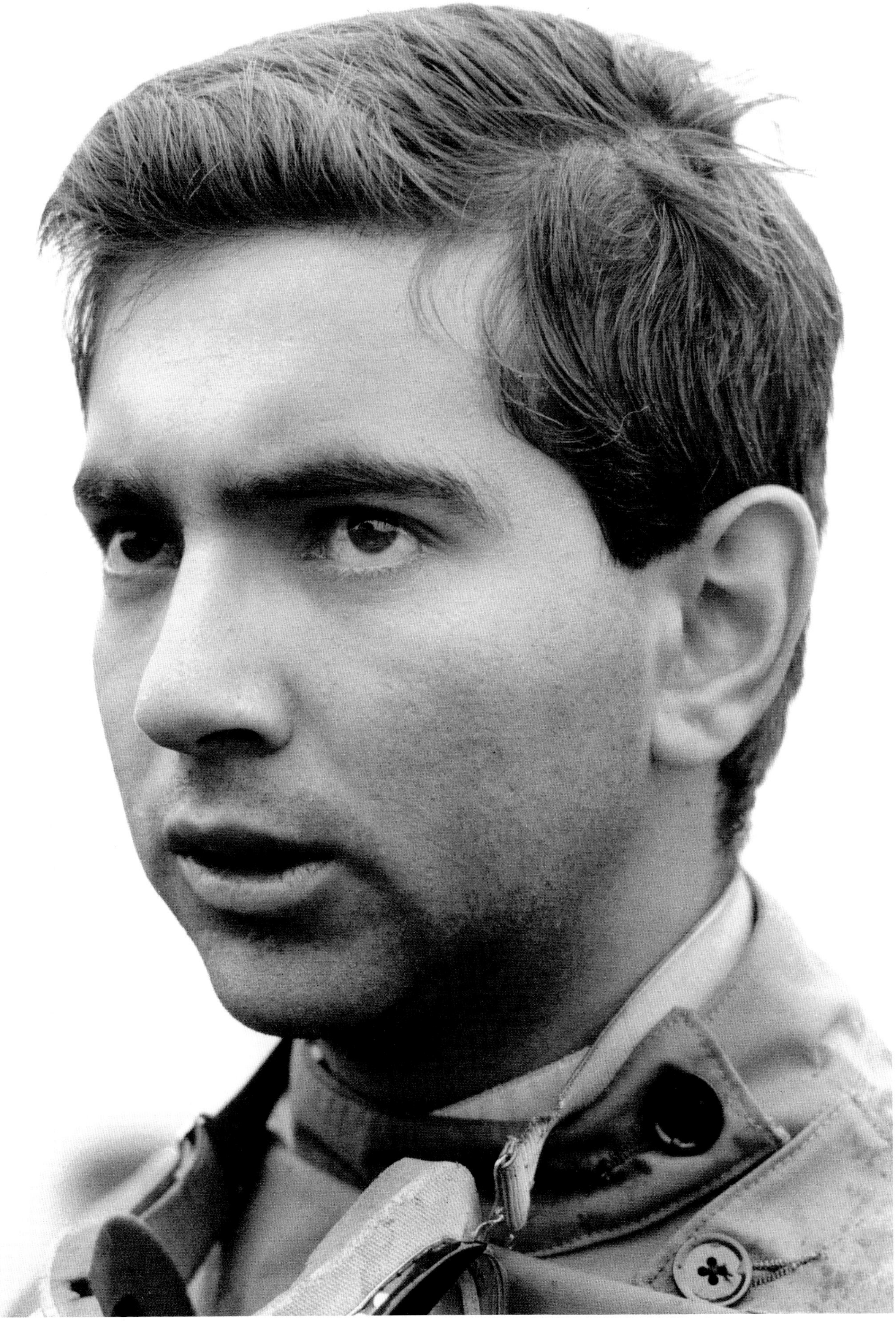

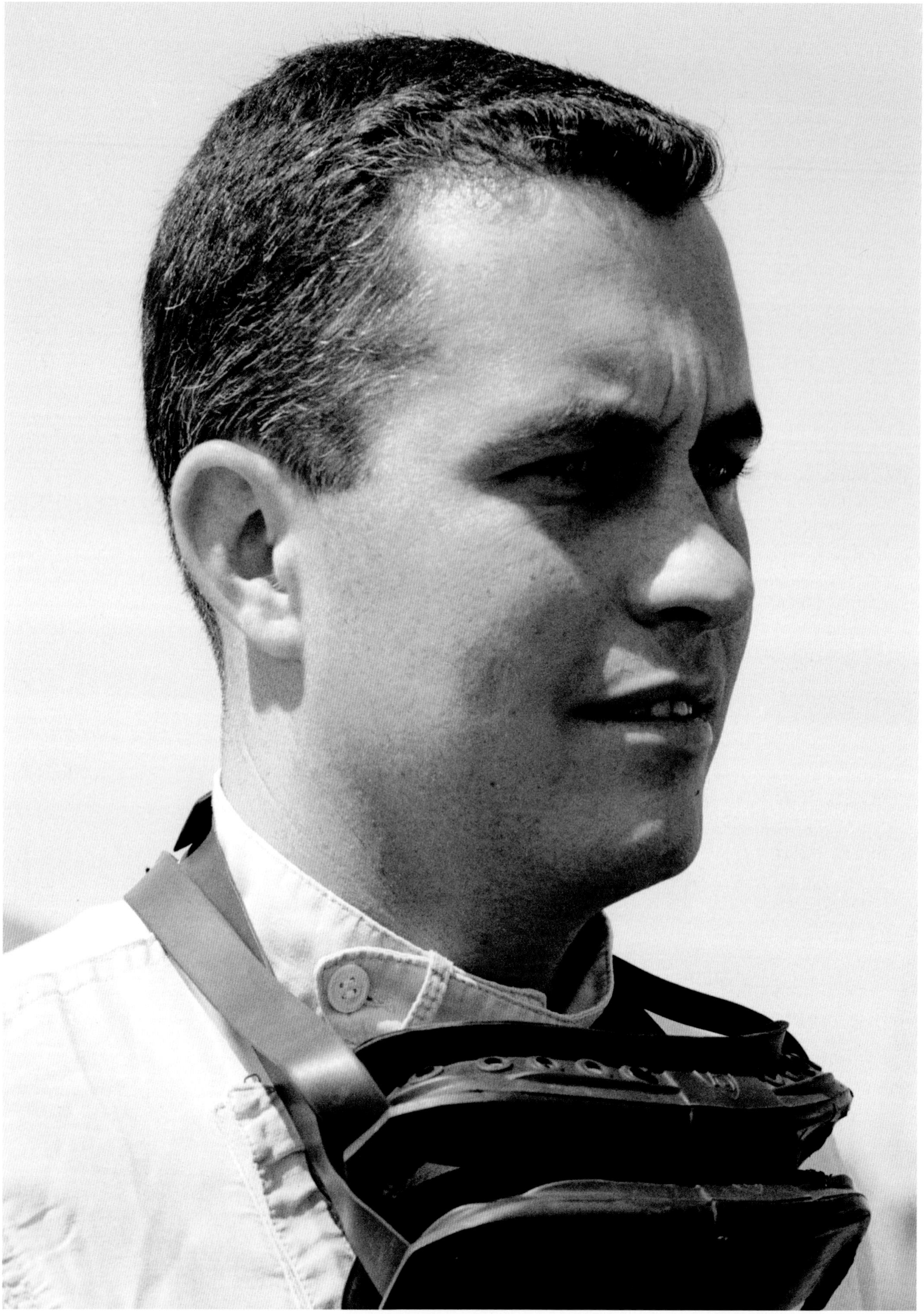

Roger Penske * 1937

▶ They call him 'The Captain', but, actually 'The Admiral' would be more accurate, as Roger Penske is not slowing down at the age of 87 and still reigns as the commander of an almost incalculable armada of often globally active companies. For example, owning the largest Porsche dealership in the United States, as well as being a globally positioned dealer for classic Ferrari parts and owner of the venerable British Ferrari dealership, Maranello Concessionaires. Recently, he added such treats as the IndyCar Series and the Indianapolis Motor Speedway to his opulent portfolio.

The core of this dazzling corporate hydra: a tough performance principle, tight hierarchies, meticulous cleanliness of the premises and assets, with strict adherence to the central star, Roger Penske. Perfection is not enough, as in the case of the Ferrari 512 S/M in the dark blue of the mineral oil giant Sunoco, which he sublimated from the rather crude basic product from Maranello and used successfully in 1971. How to keep such an empire in check? "Taking a few steps back and keeping an eye on the whole thing," Penske shrugged. Additionally, "Keep the fire burning."

In comparison to the abundance of his merits as a businessman and, above all, his value to American racing, with 20 first places by Penske drivers at Indy, and the two CanAm championships of George Follmer and Mark Donohue in 1972 and '73, Penske's excursions into Formula 1 dwindle to a footnote. A driver in 1961 and '62 in two appearances at home in Watkins Glen, then as the boss of his own racing team between 1974 and '77, competing in 40 grands prix and encompassing the entire spectrum from triumph to tragedy. The low point was the death of his driver and friend, Mark Donohue, at the Österreichring in 1975, while the highlight was the victory of John Watson in the Penske PC4, a year later at the same circuit.

Roger Penske says he's not interested in yesterday, but more in today and, above all, tomorrow. He has set in motion big plans for sports car racing, in league with Porsche, as he was 50 years ago, in the CanAm: dominance over the long distances, aiming for triumph number 20 for the Zuffenhausen-based company at Le Mans, with further victories in the US classics at Sebring and Daytona.

Tim Mayer *1938 – †1964

▶ Tim Mayer, the son of a stockbroker from Dalton, Pennsylvania, only drove one grand prix, on 7th October, 1962, at Watkins Glen, when the Cooper Car Company gave him a chance as third driver, behind Bruce McLaren and Tony Maggs. With an 11th place in practice and a solid performance in the rear third, before his retirement on lap 31 (out of 100) with an ignition problem, he did not set the GP world alight.

Nevertheless, an air of future greatness surrounded him as his maturity increased and, indeed, he had a works contract with Cooper for the 1964 season, as did his friend and mentor, McLaren. The fact that racing was no child's play was nothing new to him: on his debut in 1959, he had pushed his Austin-Healey 3000 into a pirouette in the middle of the straight, with a clumsy gear-change on a wet track; then, in 1960, his first test drive of a brand-new Lotus 18, in the Formula Junior version, ended upside down after ten minutes. Initially, Tim 'Timmy' Mayer was also in demand elsewhere, including at Yale University for his studies in English literature, then later in the course of his military service.

In 1963, Ken Tyrrell took on the talented youngster, but the BMC engines of his Cooper racers in Formula Junior were no match for the Ford engines of the competition, from Brabham, Lola and Lotus. In the winter of that year, Mayer was part of the British line-up for the Tasman Series, eight races, with four on each side of the Tasman Sea, which was always something of a welcome summer holiday, giving plenty of practice for the novice.

The finale in Australia took place on the hellishly dangerous street circuit at Longford. Mayer failed to return from the practice session on Friday evening, killed on impact with a tree at the side of the track. His teammates, Bruce McLaren, Tyler Alexander, Eoin Young and Tim's brother, Teddy, were all deeply shocked, but life goes on. Soon afterwards, they became the founding fathers of one of the most successful racing teams of all time.

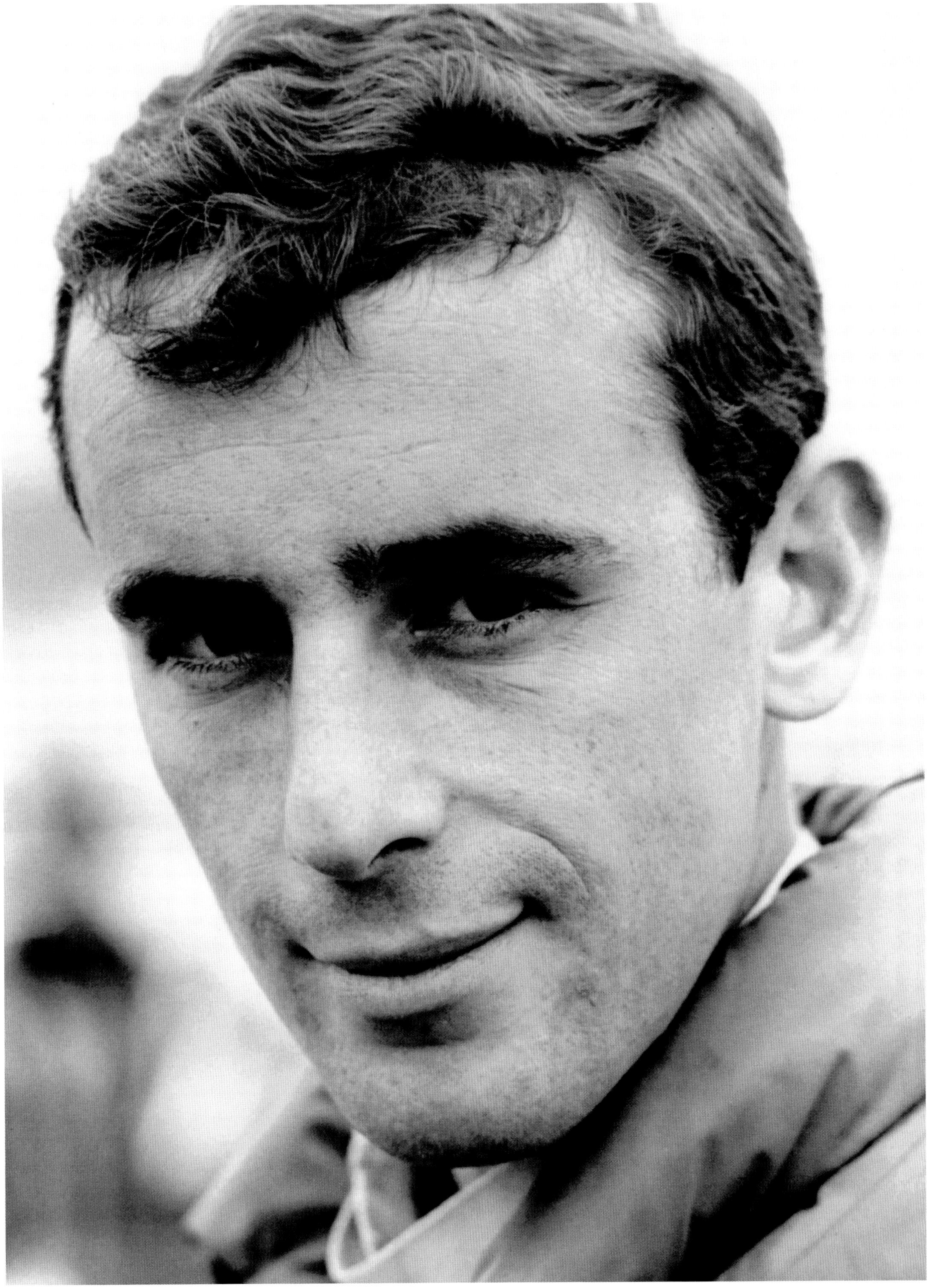

Neville Lederle *1938 – †2019

Never has the grand prix community been kept in greater suspense than in 1962, when the ninth GP of South Africa, the ninth and final round of the season, took place three days before the turn of the year on the Prince George Circuit in East London. The outcome of the world championship was still wide open – Jim Clark (Lotus) or Graham Hill (BRM)? That was the question that overshadowed all others.

The Scot had easily outpaced the field for the first 62 laps, but then he rolled to the kerb with an oil leak from his smoking Climax V8, allowing the moustachioed Londoner to drive the remaining 20 to victory and the title. A minor miracle was taking place four laps behind them, however, as sixth place, and with it a precious championship point, went to local Neville Lederle, in an immaculately prepared Lotus 21, leading the four-cylinder brigade in his very first grand prix. The newly retired Stirling Moss, who was present as a guest was effusive, saying that Lederle was a man to watch, and the renowned *Autosport* magazine agreed with him.

What seemed to be the beginning of something big, however, turned out to be the beginning of the end.

Certainly, the following year, the man with the German name won his country's prestigious South African Formula 1 Championship, which had been held since 1960, but then a serious accident during practice for the Kyalami 9 Hours, on 2nd November, 1963, thwarted all his ambitions, including his high-flying hope for the tenth South African Grand Prix among the illustrious circle of greats with whom he had felt completely at home. On the approach to the Leeukop bend, his right foot had become trapped between the pedals of his Lotus 23-Alfa Romeo and he slammed into the barriers without braking.

The healing process for the complicated double fracture of his left leg took forever. Once again, in 1965, his name appeared on the entry list for his home GP, but he was no longer able to qualify with the Lotus 21, now a tired secondhand car.

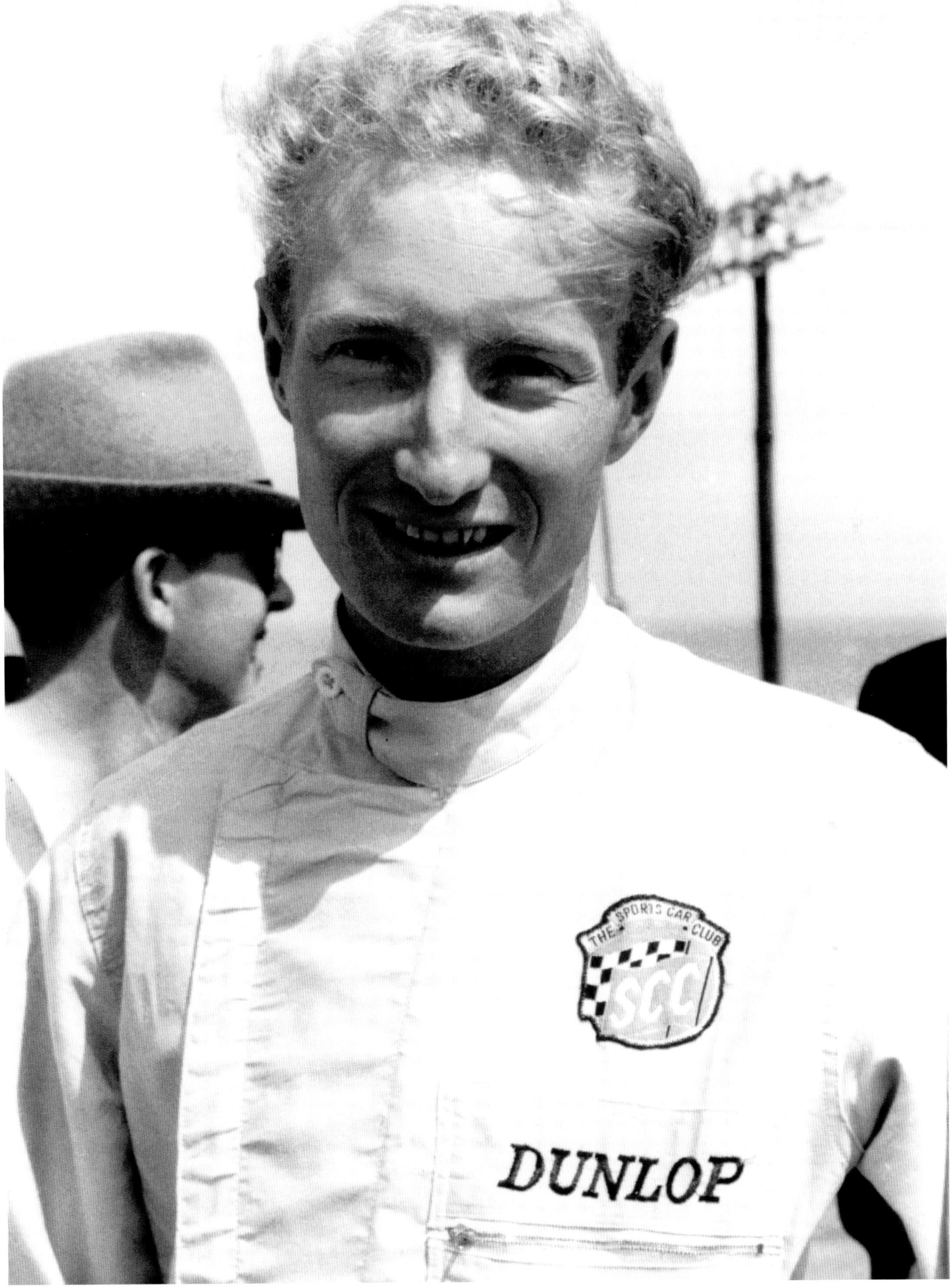
THE SPORTS CAR CLUB
SCC
DUNLOP

Jo Siffert * 1936 – † 1971

▶ It was 20th July, 1968, and a gloomy day at Brands Hatch. Rain threatened and there was a spell of drizzle. The Lotus works cars of Graham Hill and Jackie Oliver retired. Then Jo Siffert overwhelmed the luckless Ferrari driver, Chris Amon, and won the British Grand Prix, his first, as well as the ninth and last for racing stable owner Rob Walker, to whom Siffert's blue Lotus 49B belonged.

The car was brand new; only on the Thursday before the GP had Walker's dedicated crew tightened the last screws. After a devastating fire in March at Rob's famous Pippbrook Garage in Dorking, it had looked as though his small enterprise would never recover.

In his 96 grands prix after 1962, the moustachioed Swiss Siffert grabbed only two victories, the other one being in 1971 at the Österreichring, driving a Yardley-BRM. But Jo was a tough customer, the ideal choice for endurance racing. He won 14 long-distance events from 1968, all of them in Porsches, ten for the works and four for John Wyer, with two each at Zeltweg and the Nürburgring.

Then came 24th October, 1971, a brilliantly colourful autumn Sunday, with gossamer clouds drifting through the sky over Kent. The race had been included in the calendar to commemorate Jackie Stewart's second title, a non-championship F1 event that actually replaced the Mexican GP, which had been thrown out after the 1970 scandals.

On lap 15, however, the engines died down at Hawthorns in the back half of the circuit. Silence followed, except for the loudspeakers blaring trivia while a black cloud of smoke bore witness to a tragedy. After an eternity, the cars returned. Jo Siffert was missing, and the closed-circuit TV in the room of press officer Graham Macbeth showed in an endless loop how a valiant marshal had ventured again and again into the fiery inferno to pull Siffert out of the BRM.

After more than half a minute, there was that telltale gesture of resignation, body language that told it all – a horrific end to a race, to a season and to a charming man.

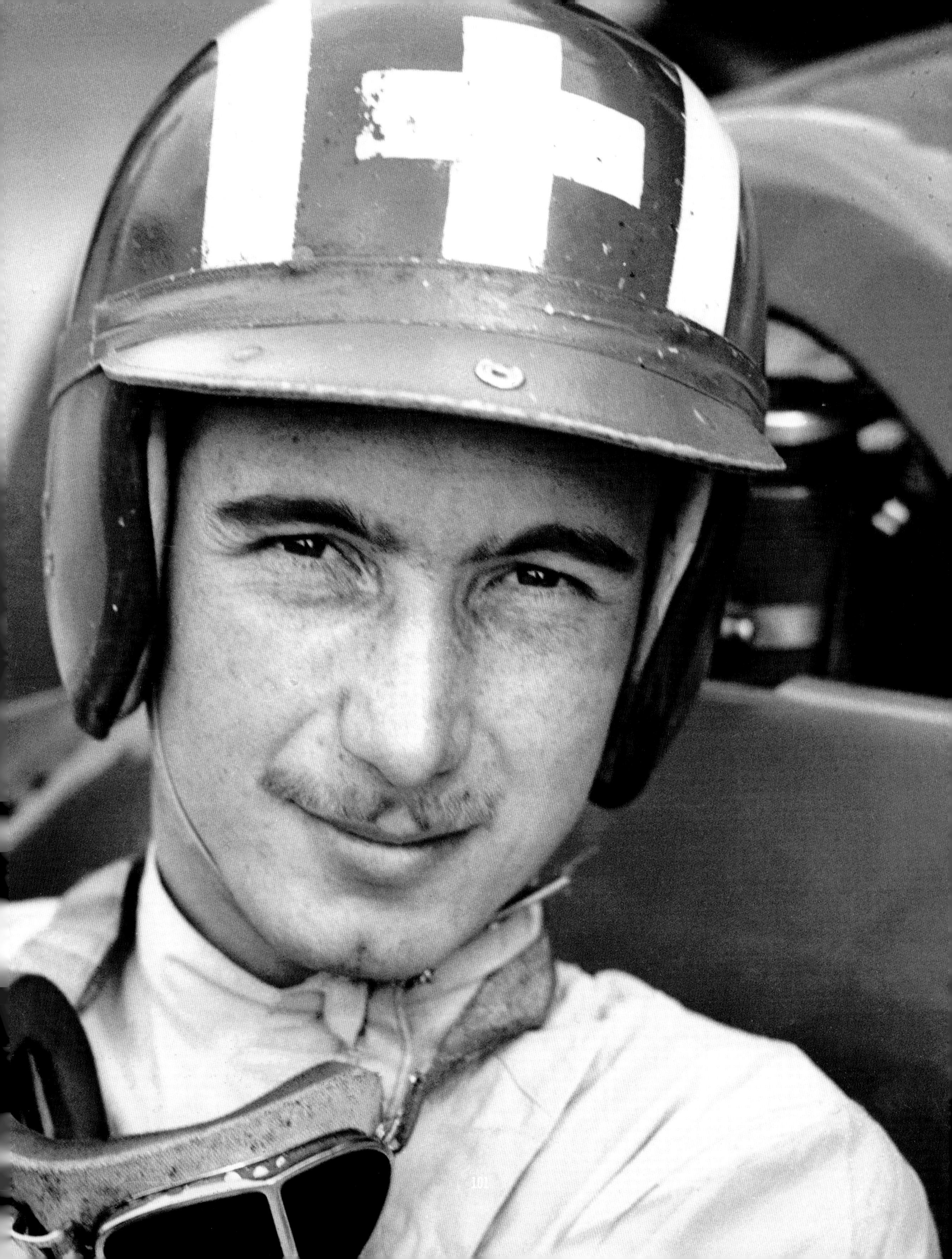

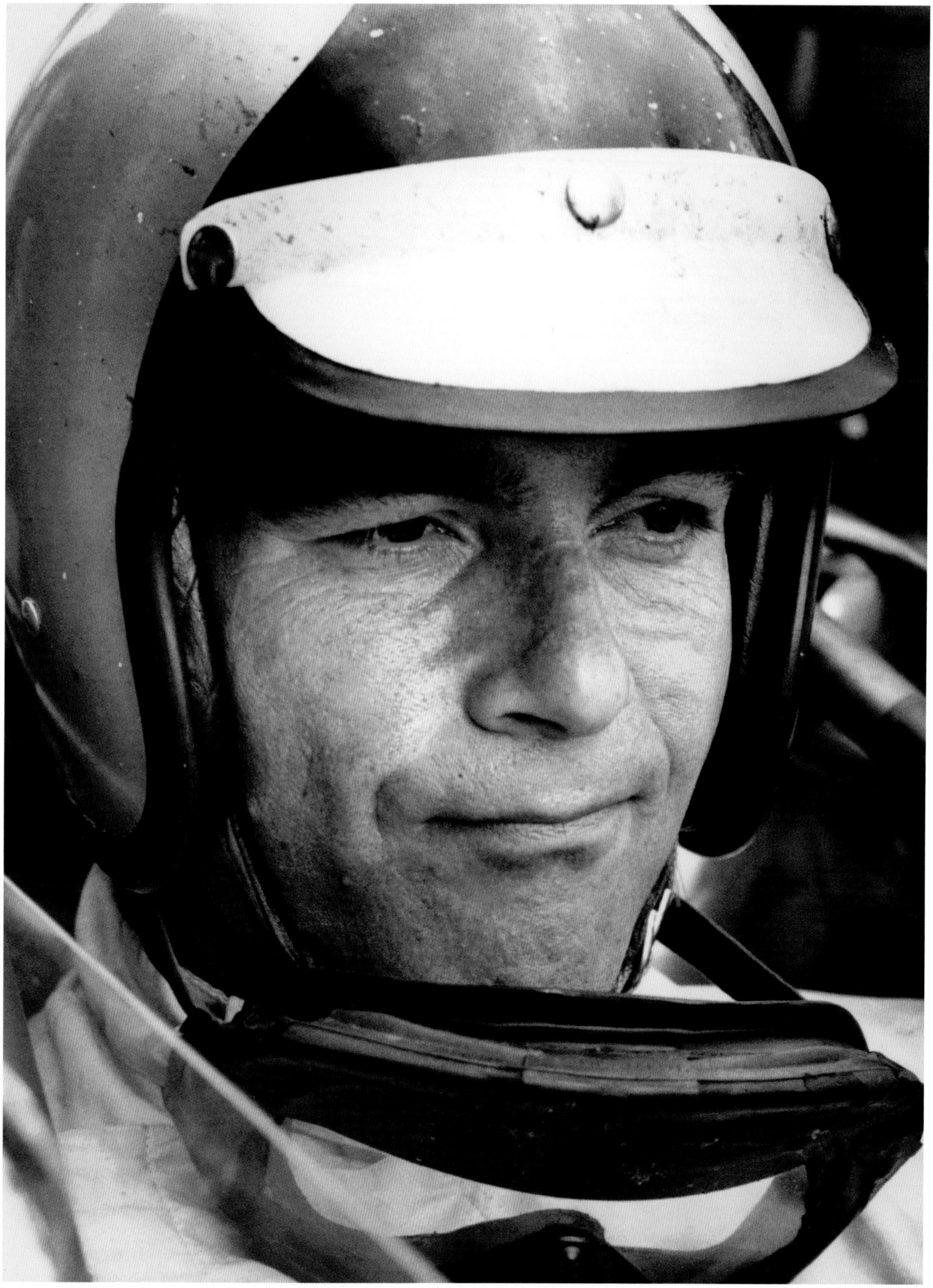

Tony Settember

*1926 – †2014

▶ In the gigantic hidden-object puzzle that is the world of grand prix racing, the man and his name have almost been lost, although Manila-born Californian Tony Settember did add a couple of colourful accents.

His moment of glory occurred in the first seconds of the 1962 Le Mans 24 Hours when he led the race until Dunlop Bridge, before being overwhelmed by the usual suspects. It was a gift, though, courtesy of the regulations: Tony's Corvette C2, pigeonholed as a GT car, happened to be the highest-displacement vehicle in the field, with its 5.4-litre V8. Thus it had been given the number '1' and a comfortable place at the front of the starting line-up. The roaring coupé was entered by US team Scirocco-Powell Racing Cars, called into being by Settember, and his youthful and immensely rich friend, Hugh Powell, and named after a scorching African desert wind.

A splash was also caused by the Formula 1 escapade staged by the two Americans in 1962 and '63 on their own, under the Emeryson and Scirocco labels, and run from London. They were rewarded with an utter lack of success in altogether six GP starts, apart from a second place that practically fell into Settember's lap, in a 1963 non-championship F1 race at the Hinterstoisser airfield in Zeltweg.

A key figure in this joint venture was British racing driver and constructor Paul Emery, boldly creative, but as poor as a church mouse, so the dollars were immensely welcome. The backyard of his tiny garage on Aspenlea Road, in the London district of Hammersmith, was crammed with curiosities, such as a Mini with two engines, one in the usual place and the other where normally the rear passengers were squeezed.

For 20 years, Tony Settember remained faithful to the sport he had first tackled in 1955 with an MG, through to commitments in CanAm and L&M F5000 – a textbook example of an amateur racer and true enthusiast.

Chris Amon *1943 – †2016

▶ Chris Amon was one of the best ever, in the assessment of Jackie Stewart, who numbered him among the competitors whom he respected most of all. Amon could fine-tune a racing car like nobody else, but unfortunately had no talent whatsoever for being in the right place at the right time. On the contrary, he would join teams that were on the verge of decline, while others blossomed as soon as he had left them. His grand prix results sheet can be read like a psychic profile, a record of how a good man can be worn down and crushed by life: 14 seasons, with ten teams over 96 races. One of these, in 1974 at the Spanish Jarama circuit, piloting his self-developed, but virtually un-driveable, Amon Ford. There were no wins, in spite of five pole positions and 19 starts from the first row, yielding only two second places and three fastest laps.

He had led the field for 850km during his GP races, however, and shining like a beacon in all that misery was his 1966 Le Mans victory, driving the mighty 7-litre Ford GT40 alongside fellow Kiwi Bruce McLaren.

Eventually, someone tagged him with the label, "The greatest driver never to win a grand prix", and worse still, a "notoriously unlucky wretch". Such verdicts stick like glue and tend to become self-fulfilling prophecies, which develop their own dynamics as time passes. Amon himself reacted irritably to those simplifications, but the statistics worked against him. He countered that he had actually been lucky, unlike his deceased former team-mates, Bandini, Scarfiotti, Siffert, Cevert and all the others.

So, at the tender age of 33, following four years in the dim glow of undeserved mediocrity that encompassed mishaps of all sorts, he called it a day and retreated to his native Bulls, on New Zealand's North Island. He lived there quietly and peacefully with his second wife, Tish Wotherspoon, and their three children, Georgie, and twins James and Alex, dabbling a bit in local racing, but never wasting a thought on the grim world of major motor sport, which had almost destroyed him.

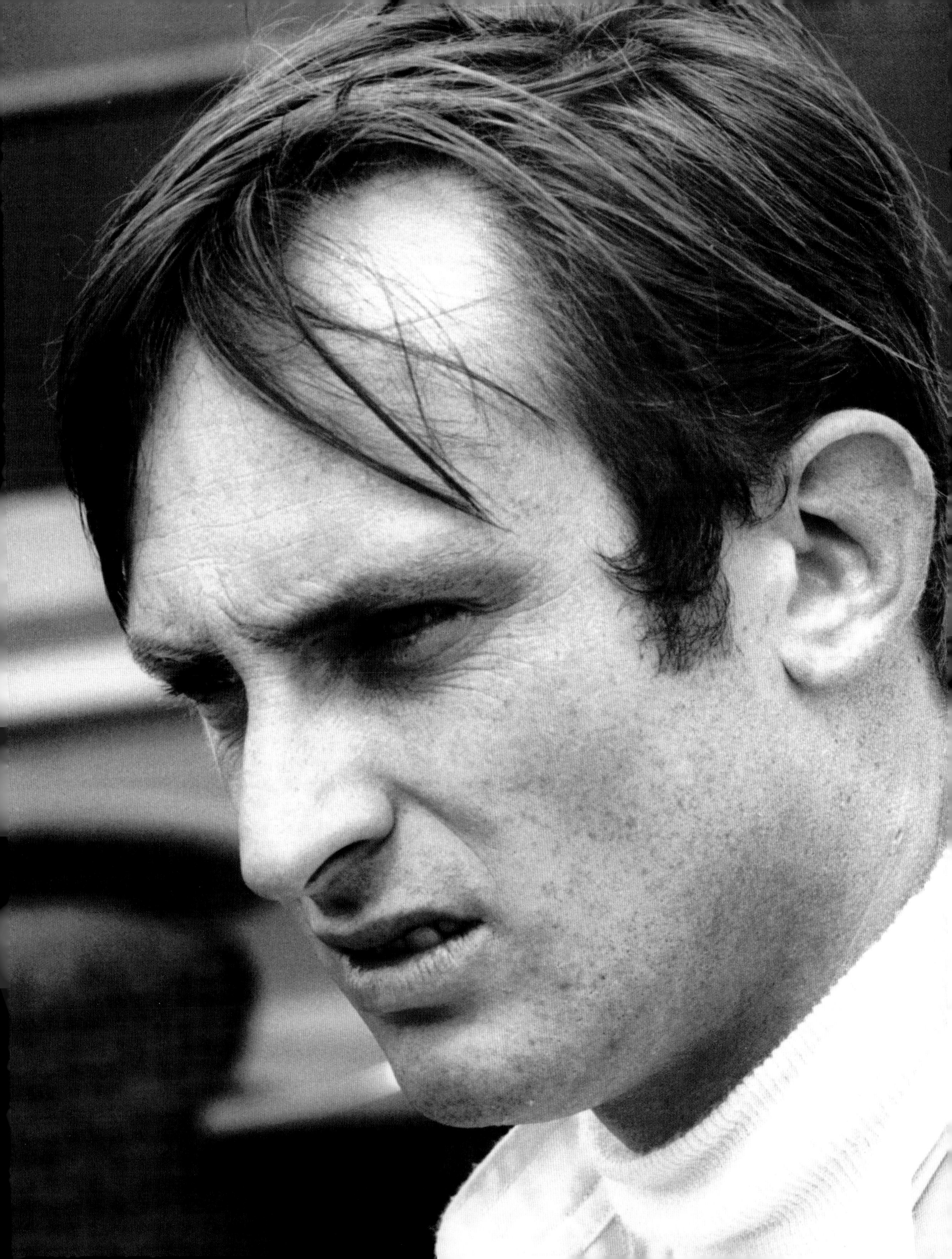

Ludovico Scarfiotti

*1933 – †1968

On 1st September, 1966, Ludovico Scarfiotti experienced all the happiness that can be bestowed upon an Italian racing driver: starting from the first row at his home Gran Premio d'Italia at Monza, then the fastest lap and finally victory, all in a Ferrari. The *tifosi* went berserk. He already knew the feeling, only less exciting and less turbulent, having won the Le Mans 24 Hours in 1963, and the 1964 and '65 Nürburgring 1,000km in the red prototypes of the SEFAC.

His triple triumph, however, was the swallow that doesn't make a summer. In *Piloti, che gente*, Enzo Ferrari contrasts his two Italian stars, Scarfiotti and Lorenzo Bandini, over several pages, team-mates in 1965 and '66 and united in seething rivalry. It is quite obvious where his sympathies lie: the talented have-not and son of a repatriated family, who took the uphill grind, versus the spoilt scion of the rich and influential Agnelli dynasty, who had it all laid on for him.

Exactly that, assumes Ferrari, had spurred Scarfiotti to distance himself from the Agnellis, to do something on his own, and seek glory and honour in other fields. He wonders, but also understands, why the driver risked everything in the process, although he approached racing as calmly as every other challenge in his life. However, "once he'd tried a Formula 1 car, he never wanted to quit." And that was a fundamental mistake: "Problem was, his style didn't match the refinement that it required." Of course, Ferrari admits, Scarfiotti would never see it that way, heading for new shores in Britain and Germany to seek the satisfaction he thought he deserved. His need to feel complete at the wheel of a racing car had got the better of him.

His quest to find himself ended tragically. On 8th June, 1968, Ludovico Scarfiotti, European champion in 1962 and '65 for Ferrari, lost his life during practice for the Rossfeld hillclimb – in a Porsche.

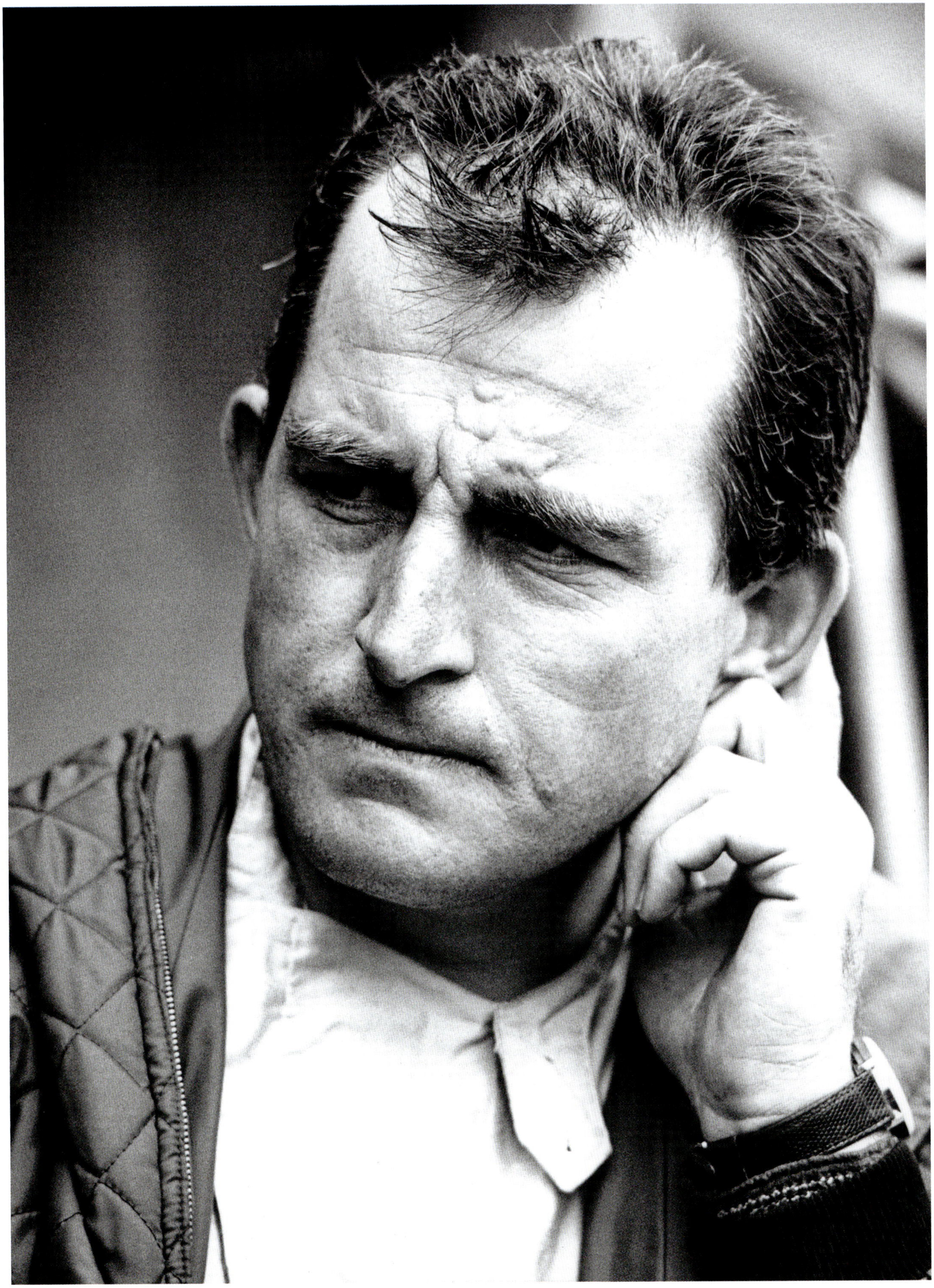

Gerhard Mitter *1935 – †1969

▶ During practice for the German GP on 1st August, 1969, the driver of start number '24', Gerhard Mitter, passed the timekeepers at 4:15pm in his BMW 269-4 seeking to improve his 11th-best time so far in the F2 category. He never returned from that lap.

At Schwedenkreuz, between Flugplatz and Aremberg, one of the fastest sections of the Nordschleife, the slender little BMW had suddenly veered from the track without apparent reason, arguably because of a steering failure. Gerhard Mitter was killed on the spot, his vehicle reduced to a mangled heap of junk. The few onlookers had just witnessed the sad end of a life dedicated to racing and the fervent ambition to be one of the chosen few in Formula 1.

Mitter was incredibly versatile, as a driver in sprint events for Porsche, with three European Hillclimb Championships between 1966 and '68 under his belt, as well as in long-distance racing, epitomised by his Targa Florio victory in 1969 aboard Porsche's 908/2, the spoils being shared with his friend, Udo Schütz.

He raced sports cars and saloons, F2 and Junior single-seaters, as well as being a technician who, for example, tuned blaring DKW three-cylinder two-stroke engines and installed them in his own Formula Junior car, then later into a Lotus chassis.

Mitter was extraordinarily tough, a stayer. While practising for the Spa 1,000km in 1966, the voluminous rear bodywork of his Porsche 906 abruptly flew open like a parachute. The car swerved into the Ardennes forest, but miraculously Mitter survived, continuing his season for a couple of weeks with his left foot in a plaster and plastic cast, which the Porsche mechanics had designed for him.

The Nürburgring was his destiny, his home GP, the playground in which on five occasions he faced the big names of the sport, such as Clark, Hill and Surtees. The first encounter, in 1963, turned out to be the most promising – fourth place in an old Porsche 718 F4, property of the Dutchman, Carel Godin de Beaufort.

Mitter had dreamed of so much more.

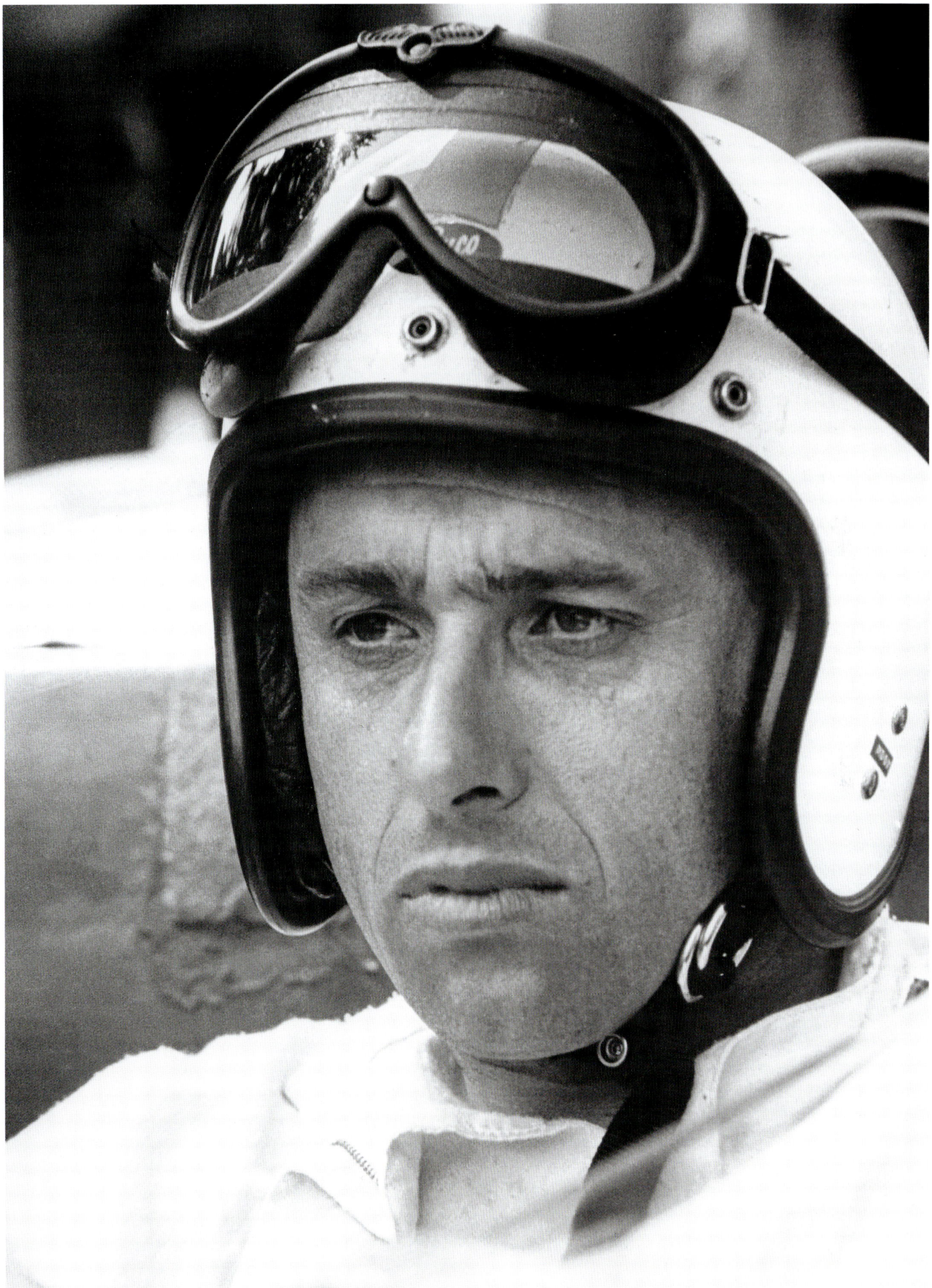

Bob Anderson *1931 – †1967

▶ Like John Surtees and Mike Hailwood, Bob Anderson came from motorcycle racing, but unlike his two fellow Brits, he never made it into the halls of fame of either sport.

Too much money, he complained, went to the top people. So he and his less-well-to-do peers would never be able to make ends meet.

Indeed, the Brabham BT11 Anderson could afford in 1964, by borrowing against his life insurance, had to last four long seasons, including the storm-and-stress phase of the 3-litre formula from 1966 onwards. Towards the end of 1.5-litre Formula 1 racing, he was not too badly positioned with the ubiquitous Coventry-Climax V8. But afterwards, his shoestring budget only permitted the acquisition of a secondhand FPF Climax 2.7-litre four-cylinder engine, which reduced him to the unattractive status of an also-ran.

Anderson had called his privateer équipe DW Racing Enterprises, an ambitious name, indeed. In addition to himself, DW Racing consisted of a lone mechanic, plus the odd volunteer. Behind, and often in front of the scenes, his wife, Marie-Edmée, a pretty former *au pair*, operated untiringly. When her parents had heard of her affair with a racing driver, they hurriedly fetched her back to France. But love was stronger.

Anderson's moment of glory during that time undoubtedly was his third place on the Hinterstoisser airfield near Zeltweg, picturesque venue of the 1964 Austrian Grand Prix, the very first GP in the Alpine republic. The delicate suspensions of most of his competitors had capitulated to the rough and bumpy concrete of the track.

On 14th August, 1967, Bob Anderson paid with his life for something that he had never been able to reach. When his faithful Brabham aquaplaned off the wet track during a testing session at Silverstone, a marshals' post stood in the way.

Irony of fate: BRM's Louis Stanley was considering a berth for him in the works team for 1968.

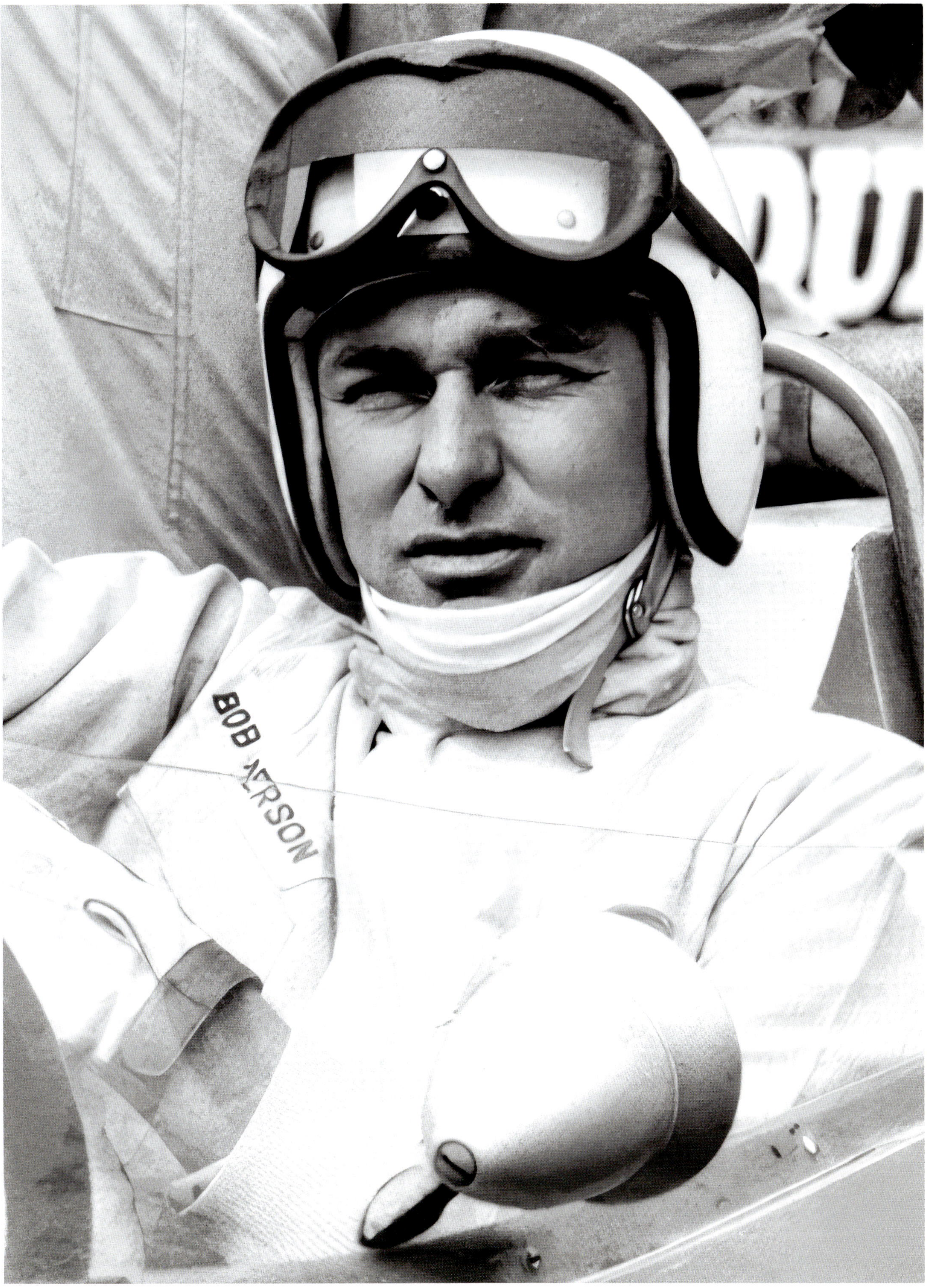
BOB
RSON

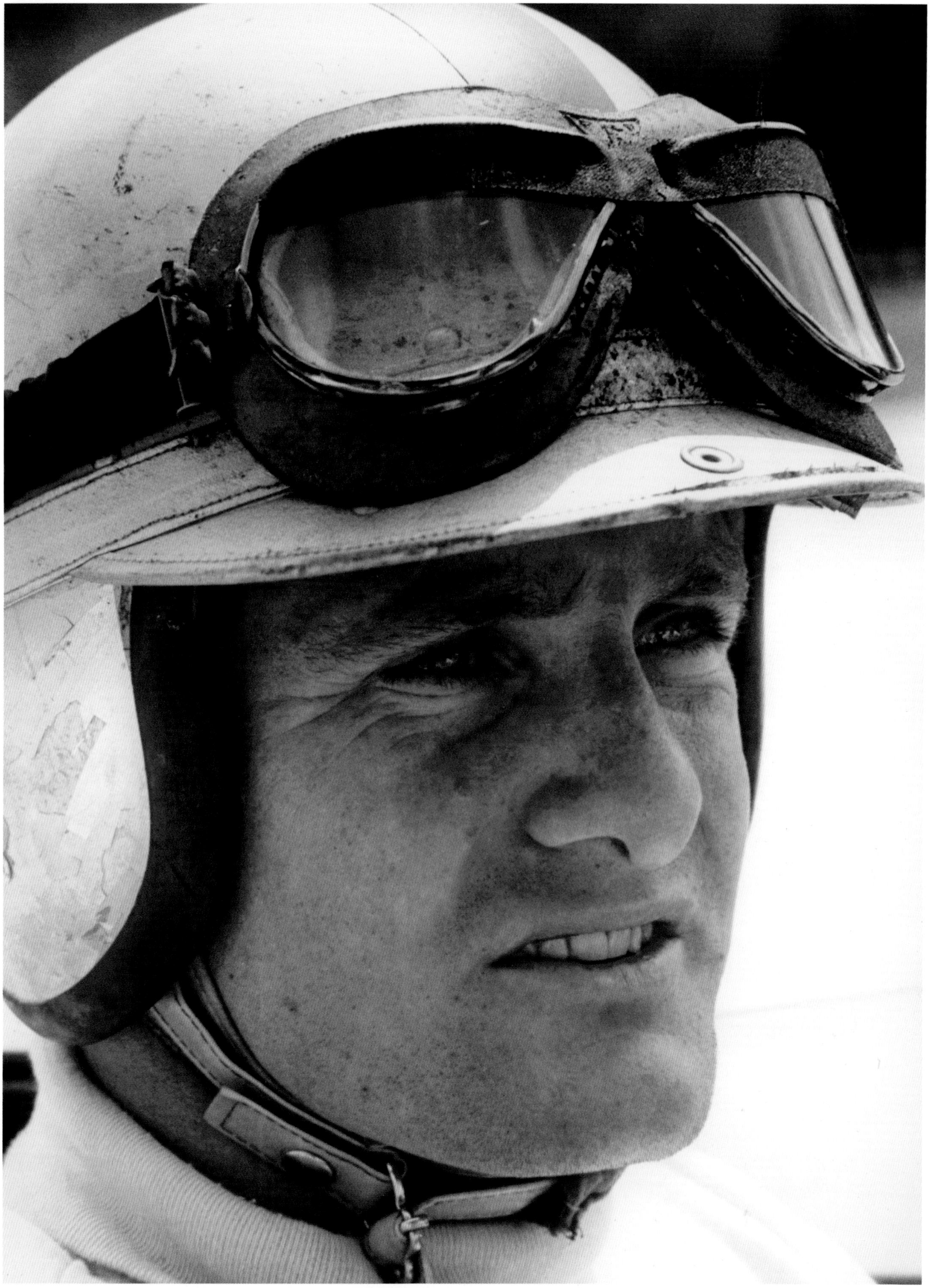

Mike Hailwood

* 1940 – † 1981

▶ Mike Hailwood was a Mozart of rapid movement, and not only on two wheels, which became an extension of his body, earning him the nickname 'Mike the Bike' and ten world titles, but also on four, regardless of whether it was F2, F5000, F1 or sports cars. Among the cars he raced were the Surtees TS10, the Lola T142, the McLaren M23 and John Wyer's Porsche 917.

There was no proper chronology, however, as in the career of John Surtees. In the aftermath of his big accident at the 1974 German GP, Hailwood retired to New Zealand, together with Denny Hulme and his former team boss, Phil Kerr, only to become bored stiff. Then he succumbed to courting calls and returned to Europe, winning the 1978 TT on a Ducati and the 1979 Senior TT on a Suzuki. That was the Hailwood rap, and his private life was fully in keeping with it.

To know Mike Hailwood was a blessing. He was sensitive, immensely musical and knew how to make people roar with laughter. He was also an indefatigable womaniser. The fairer sex made it easy for him, and as soon as he had moved into a hotel room, the telephone began to ring.

Three snapshots: a birthday party not far from the McLaren facility at Colnbrook. F1 fan Chris Barber and his jazz band were playing and at the microphone was trumpeter Pat Halcox, with Mike on vocals, singing 'Down by the Riverside'. Once the German photographer Jutta Fausel showed Hailwood a picture with his previous week's female escort. His response? "Who's she?" Serious, or joking? Nobody really knew. After his 1972 F2 victory (in the non-graded race) at the Österreichring, a stepping stone for his European title that year, the man with the champagne asked him, "May I pour you another?" "Yes, sir!" was the quick answer, and "Yes, sir!" again and again, until the bottle was empty. I loved assisting him.

Unforgettable: my nervousness, when he didn't return from his last lap of the 1974 German GP. And my grief, after the absurd death of Mike and his little daughter, Michelle, in a road accident on 23rd March, 1981.

It was somebody else's fault, but what did that change?

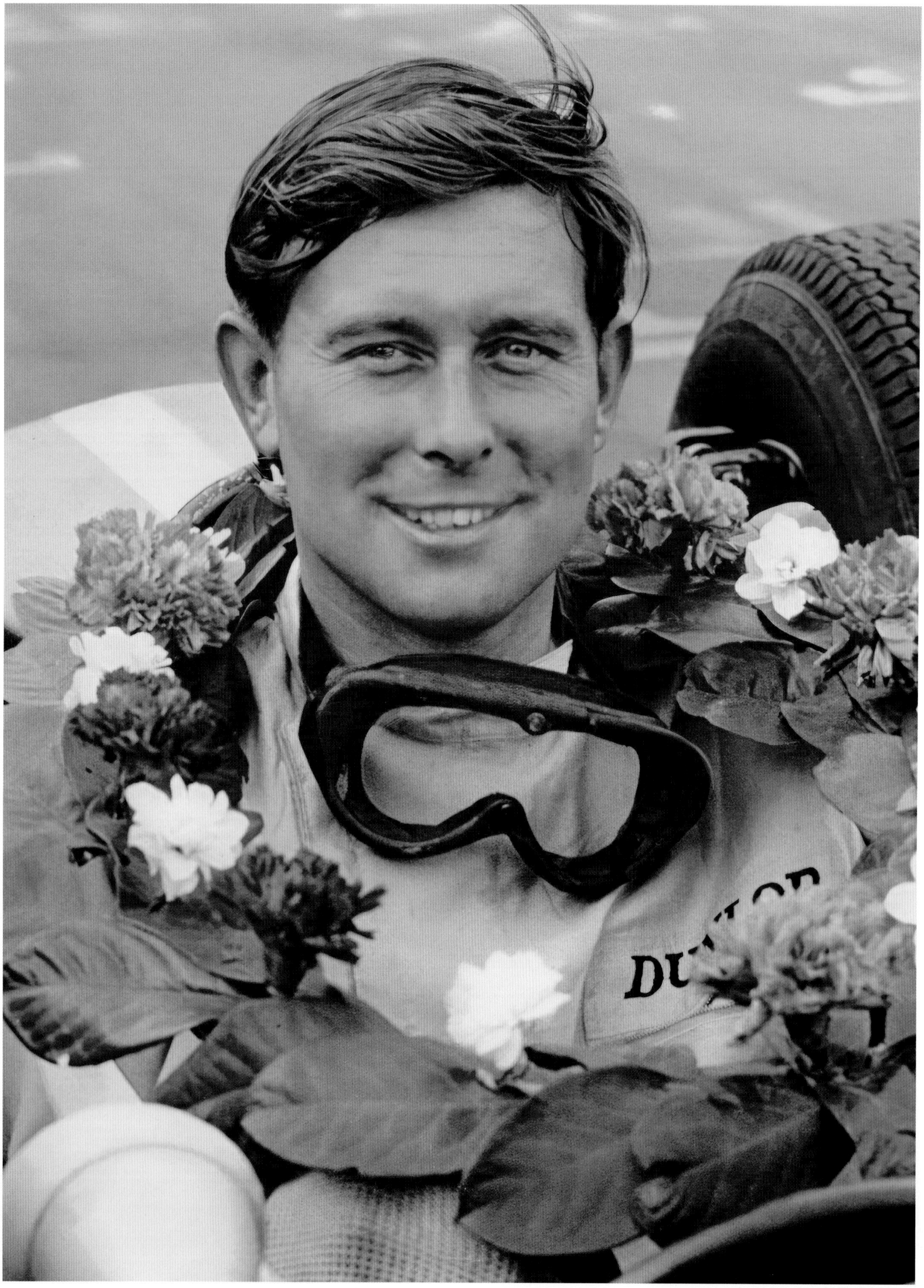

John Taylor *1933 – †1966

▶ On the first lap of the German GP at the Nürburgring on 7th August, 1966, a mushroom cloud of pitch-black smoke suddenly swirled up into the grey Eifel sky, above the dip before the short climb at the Flugplatz section of the circuit. While rubberneckers rushed downhill beside the track to the scene of the accident, the spectators at the crash site had already become eyewitnesses to a drama. The F2 Matra of Jacky Ickx and light-blue Brabham-BRM of Briton John Taylor had got in each other's way in the turmoil of the opening phase. Ickx escaped unscathed, but Taylor's Brabham slammed into a sign and was immediately engulfed in flames, along with the driver, who nevertheless managed to escape the inferno. There were different opinions about the chain of events that had led to the contact.

John Taylor was a nice guy with a penchant for unconventional behaviour. As a schoolboy, he would catch rabbits on his way to school and then hawk them to his classmates. During his military service in the Navy, he smuggled a motorbike aboard his aircraft carrier and roamed the spacious flight deck at night, until he was caught and disciplined.

After very promising beginnings in other categories, his F1 career turned out to be decidedly modest, apart from a few good placings in races that didn't count towards the championship. Primarily, this was probably due to his poor car material, the Cooper T45, an F2 car with which he made his debut in the 1964 British GP at Brands Hatch, finishing 14th, 24 laps behind winner Jim Clark. Also, the 2-litre Brabham BT11-BRM with which he had scored a precious world championship point in Reims in 1966.

Taylor was badly burnt in the Nürburgring crash, but had seemed to be on the mend when news of his death spread on 8th September of that year. "Thine Is The Victory" is carved on his gravestone in Newtown Linford. He would have liked to have made that his motto for life.

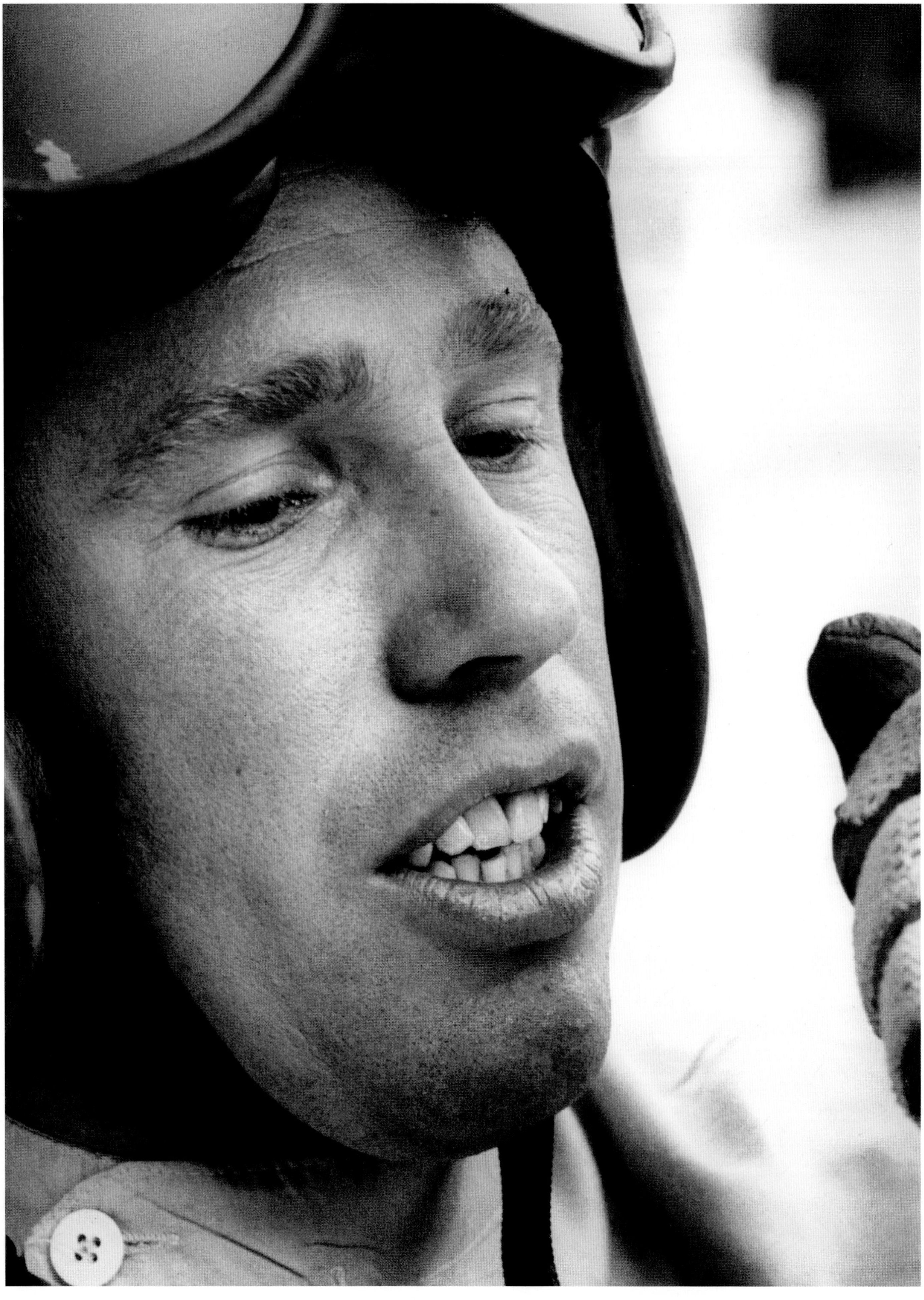

Mike Spence   * 1936 – † 1968

▶ Michael Henderson Spence was discovered on 2nd June, 1962, when the great Colin Chapman was watching the Formula Junior race from the balcony of his hotel room on the eve of the Grand Prix de Monaco. That man Spence, he kept thinking, looked like the stuff of which champions are made.

That's how this play in five acts began, but it ended with the death of the protagonist. Chapman remained a towering figure behind the wings, connected to the hero in a peculiar on/off relationship, while Spence himself was always rather in the shadow of the other Lotus hopefuls, Peter Arundell and Trevor Taylor. He wouldn't acknowledge any such hierarchy, but co-operated loyally with his undisputed hero, Jim Clark. Rumour had it that he had even considered pushing the Scot's stricken vehicle over the finishing line, and to his second title, with his own car at the 1964 season finale in Mexico.

The second act covered the formative years in Formulas Junior and 2, while in the third, during 1964 and '65, Spence drove F1 for Team Lotus, but always overshadowed by Clark. His best result was a fourth place in Mexico in 1964, but two victories in non-championship events really did his ego good: at the Brands Hatch Race of Champions, contested in two heats in 1965, and the South African GP in East London in 1966. In act four, he was searching for his own identity, grappling with the obstreperous BRM P83 H16, but winning the 1967 Brands Hatch BOAC 500 in the Chaparral 2F, with Phil Hill.

In April, 1968, when Chapman recruited the deserter Spence again – for his Indy efforts with the 4wd Lotus 56, a wedge sculpted with brute simplicity and propelled around the legendary Brickyard at record speeds by a whining turbine. During practice, Spence tested Greg Weld's similar car. Officially warned that he was taking a dangerous line through Turn One, he hit the wall and the right front wheel sheared off, smashing into his head.

Four hours later, poor Mike Spence succumbed to his terrible injuries.

Pedro Rodrìguez

* 1940 – † 1971

▶ Pedro Rodriguez was "as strong as an ox," said Jochen Rindt. His Austrian compatriot and top F1 journalist, Helmut Zwickl, detected "something sphinx-like" about him. Jackie Oliver put on record that, of all his team-mates at BRM and in John Wyer's Gulf squad, Rodriguez had been "the kindest, most considerate and gentlemanly".

However, Jo Ramirez, a constant companion of the Rodriguez brothers during their brief common spell in major racing, noticed that Pedro, the elder, "was getting faster each time he raced without the shadow of his younger brother." That view was shared by Enzo Ferrari, although he spared just a side note for him in *Piloti, che gente*. Only in 1970 did he begin to shine, a late bloomer. Pedro's brilliant victory at Spa that year certainly belongs to that phase, one of two in his 55 GPs and fought out in a bitter struggle with Chris Amon, who loomed in his rear-view mirrors.

In Rodriguez's slipstream, Amon drove a fastest lap of 3m 27.4s (244.744km/h). Eleven seconds fewer had been needed by Pedro himself three weeks earlier on the ultrafast Belgian circuit, during the 1,000km and driving JW Automotive's Porsche 917K. The mighty 917 was tailor-made for him, and Rodriguez in a sports car was one of the best ever, and not only because of his 14 wins in WSC rounds. He was supreme on wet tracks, his almost playful dominance during the permanent downpour of the 1970 BOAC 1,000km, at Brands Hatch, going down in the history of this sport as a unique feat.

The rivalry of the Wyer stars, Rodriguez and Jo Siffert, was palpable, almost physically. The famous picture of them on the notorious Eau Rouge corner at Spa in 1970, immediately after the start, speaks volumes. But the Mexican sphinx was a trifle quicker than the Swiss.

In 1971, both were killed on side stages within the space of three months, Rodriguez in Herbert Müller's Ferrari 512M, in a race of minor importance at Nürnberg. It had been a last-minute addition to his calendar. Chance or a quirk of fate? We'll never know.

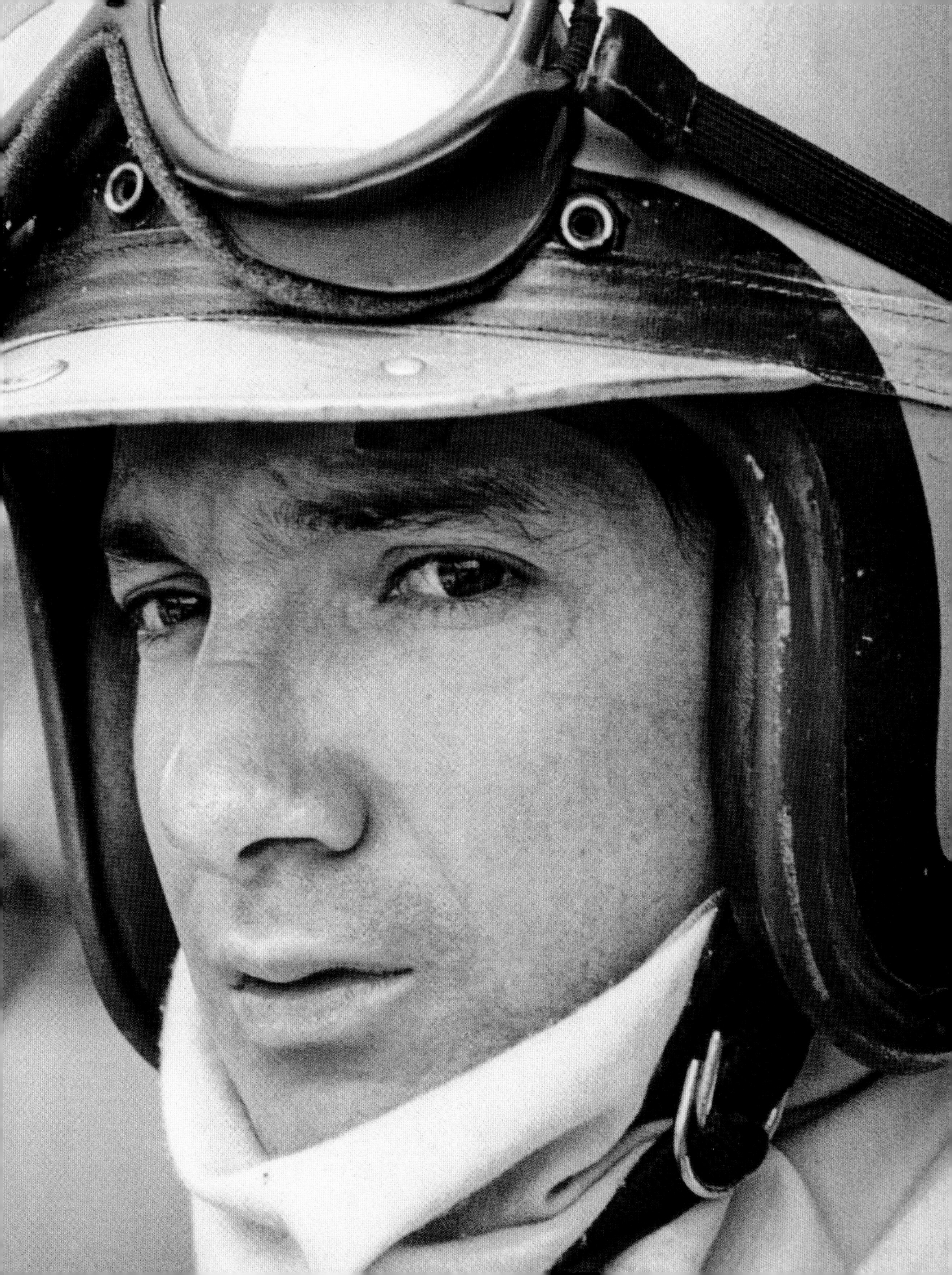

Moisés Solana * 1935 – † 1969

▶ Jai alai is one of the world's fastest games. Not unlike squash, it involves bouncing a ball around a walled space, where it reaches extremely high speeds. It requires lightning reflexes, keen eyes and nerves of steel.

Mexican Moisés Solana had all those qualities and made a fortune as a jai alai professional. But his bank balance melted away like the glaciers of the Popocatépetl because he invested in another, even more costly, sport: motor racing. Of course, his aforementioned qualities were helpful, as was the support of his father, José Antonio, a friend of Jean Bugatti.

Solana was a good racing driver, although he frittered away his energies and means over a wide range of categories. Towards the end of the fifties, the experts regarded him as being on par with the Rodriguez brothers. But, while his two dashing compatriots forced their way on to the big international stage at an early age, Moisés concentrated on Mexican competition, with only the odd excursion abroad, usually not too far across the Rio Grande. His flying visits into the world of grands prix, almost always spoilt by mechanical defects, were rare: eight races between 1963 and '68, six of which were on the Autódromo Magdalena Mixhuca in the thin air of the capital, and two at Watkins Glen in the neighbouring United States. His car material seemed to be promising, the more so as he managed six times to wrangle full-fledged Lotus works cars out of Colin Chapman.

Like wild little Divina Galica in the seventies, Solana had a foible for the start number '13'. On 13th July, 1969, however, what he had always supposed to be fun turned into bloody seriousness. Solana met his death in the Valle de Bravo-Bodencheve hillclimb. Even now, the mechanic who looked after his Cooper-Maserati in 1966, under the aegis of Roy Salvadori, has much to relate about Moisés Solana. He was Ron Dennis, then firmly on his way to becoming one of the biggest names in Formula 1.

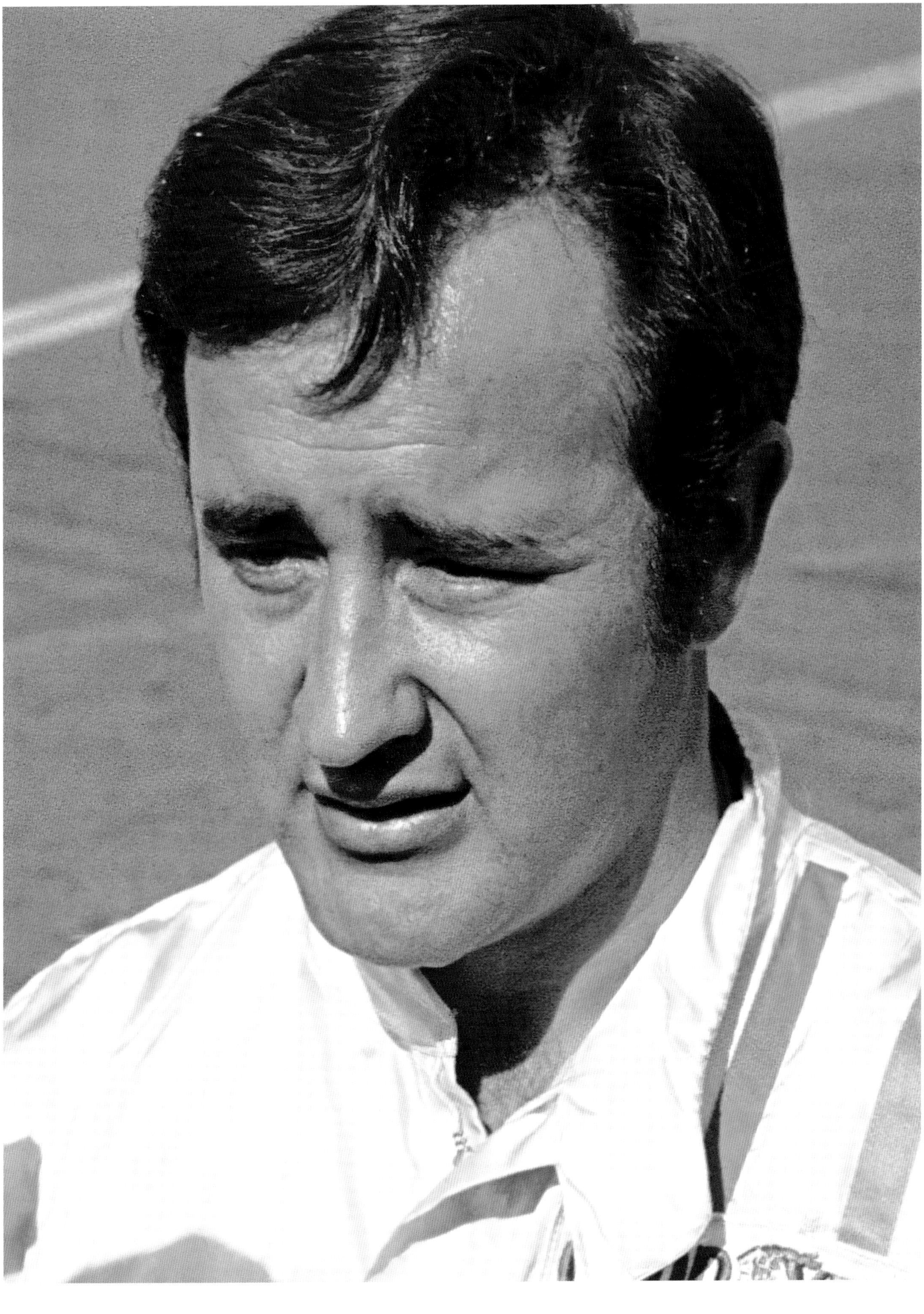

Peter Arundell *1933 – †2009

▶ In the final phase of the Grand Prix de Reims de la Formule 2, on 5th July, 1964, one of those ominous racing-car clusters had taken shape, which were so typical of ultra fast circuits like Monza, AVUS, and Reims.

With six laps to go until the end of that epic slipstreaming battle, Peter Arundell, driver of the Lotus 32 with race number 2, made a slight, but near-fatal mistake. In the Virage de la Garenne, a right-hander driven at full throttle, he looked into his rear-view mirror a trifle too long and drifted briefly off the track. When he had tarmac under his wheels again, he was hit by Richie Ginther's Lola. The Lotus was thrown sky-high, ejecting the driver, who was not wearing a seat belt. He crash-landed on his head and shoulders. For two weeks, Arundell remained in a coma, lovingly tended by his wife, Rikki.

It was 18 months before he sat in a racing car again, helplessly at the mercy of the Lotus 43 Colin Chapman had provided for him, a speeding work in progress owing to its heavy and complex BRM H16 engine.

Formula 1 had always been his goal with Lotus. But, from 1960 onwards, everything and everybody at Cheshunt was focused on new star Jim Clark. Strict team orders ensured that nobody and nothing would get in the way of the Scot, whom Arundell saw as being on equal footing. Chapman kept him waiting, though, until 1964, when he finally gave him an F1 seat, though as number two behind Clark.

Such treatment can sap a man's energy and self-confidence, even though it may appear to be chiselled in stone. After his Reims horror crash, he had lost some of his bite anyway, Peter Arundell, a promise whose fulfilment had been denied by fate. After the end of the 1966 season, he was ditched by Formula 1, the sport upon which he had pinned such great hope.

When Arundell's attempt at racing comeback fizzled out in Formula Vee in 1969, it went almost unnoticed. In motor sport, nothing ages faster than yesterday's glitz and glory.

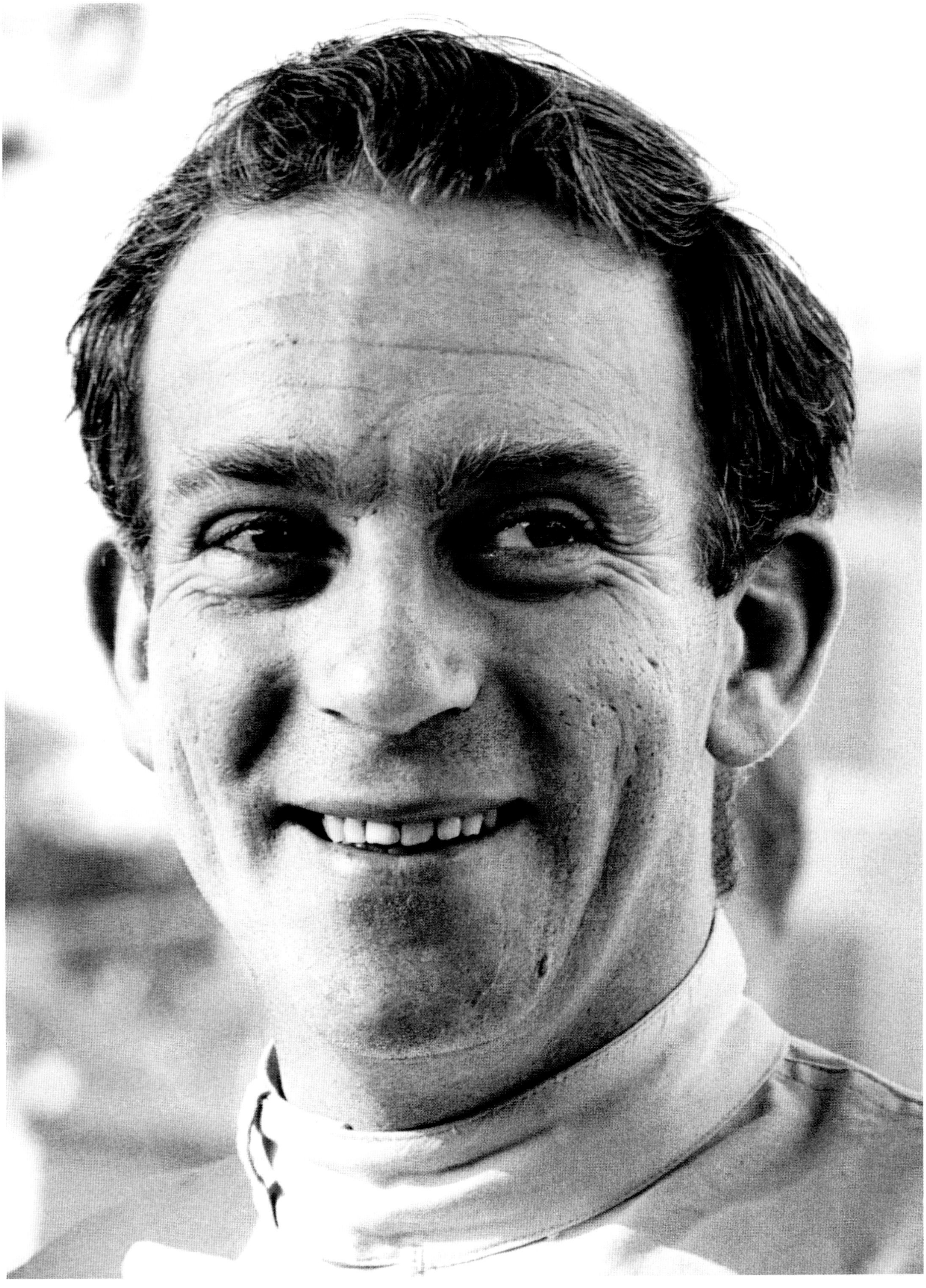

Richard Attwood * 1940

▶ "He (or she) doesn't suffer fools gladly," say the British when somebody shows no tolerance for idiots; actually it's a quotation from the letters to the Corinthians. In that regard, Richard Attwood sees eye to eye with St Paul, although that doesn't necessarily match his education at Harrow. One of the objects of his displeasure was BRM chairman Louis Stanley. 'Big Lou', bathing in the limelight of Formula 1, could be seen for many years majestically strutting up and down the pit lane, together with his wife, Jean, the sister of British Racing Motors proprietor Sir Alfred Owen.

A couple of days before the Grand Prix de Monaco, towards the end of May, 1968, the two men met at Nice airport. "What are you doing here?" Stanley asked in mock amazement. "I'll be driving for you," was Attwood's curt answer. He had only just been informed, over the phone by BRM chief engineer Tony Rudd, on the Tuesday before the encounter.

On race Sunday, Attwood launched a firework, writing a piece of motor sport history as well as a brilliant chapter of his own saga. On lap 17 of 80, he was already second in his elderly BRM P126 and, in the dying minutes of the GP, breathing down the neck of eventual winner, Graham Hill, with his Lotus 49. He also set the fastest time of the day.

Monaco suited him, tailor-made for his balanced and fluent driving style. In 1965, the Principality was the venue of his first GP, in a Lotus 25-BRM, then of his last in 1969, driving a Lotus 49, when his gear knob rolled about in the cockpit, leaving his right hand looking like a raw steak.

But the best was still to come, with Richard's 1970 Le Mans victory in a Porsche 917, together with old warhorse Hans Herrmann. From the end of the 1971 season, Attwood became absorbed by the family garage business, his young wife Veronica no longer prepared to postpone her wish to have children.

At the Goodwood Revival, however, Richard became a regular, driving as fast as he always could, which was very fast.

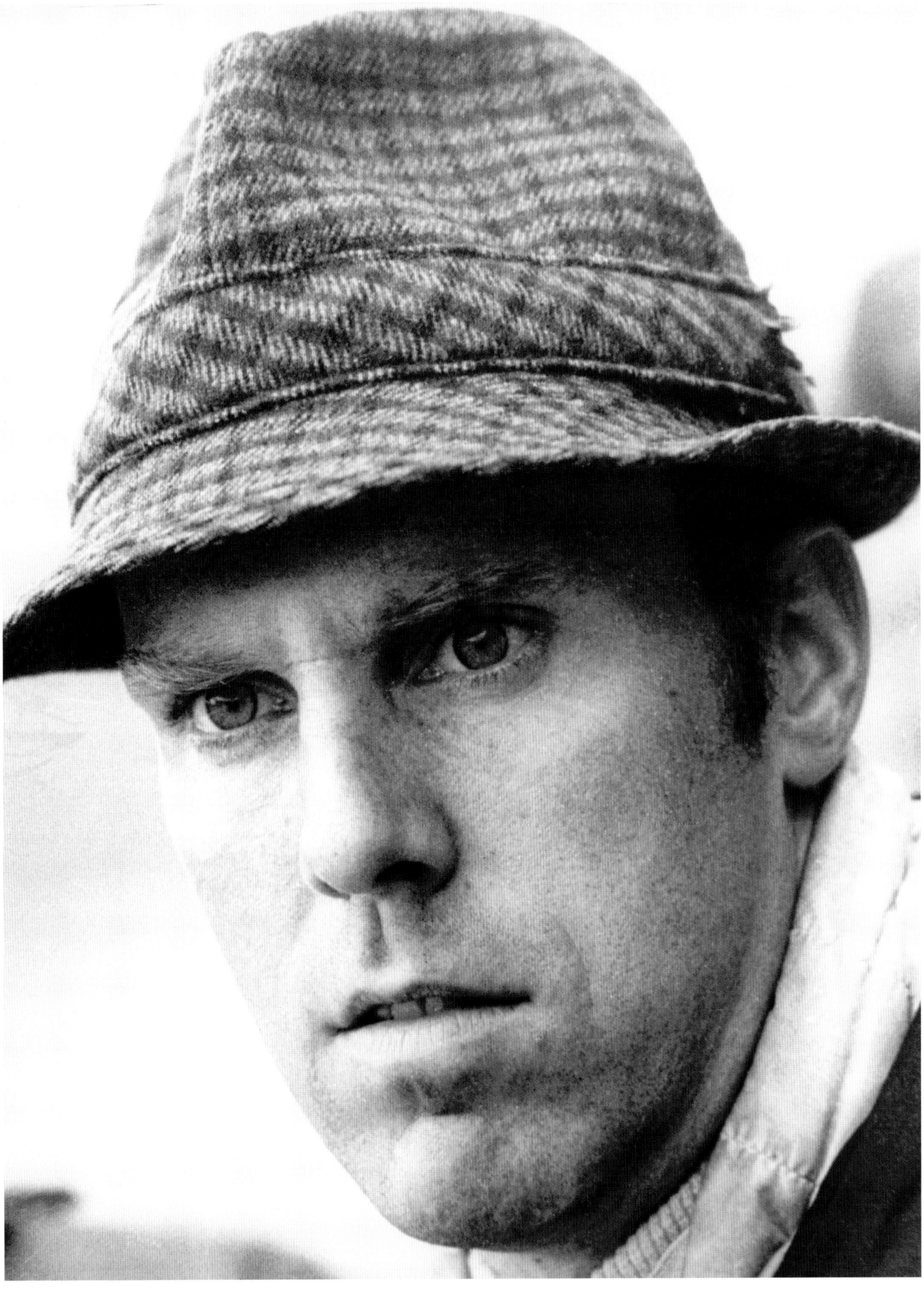

John Love * 1924 – † 2005

▶ During the second half of the South African Grand Prix on 2nd January, 1967, in Kyalami, a patriotic sensation was in the offing: John Love, as a citizen of neighbouring Rhodesia (Zimbabwe since 1980), was practically a native, and he led for 13 precious laps. Victory beckoned.

It would have been the triumph of David over Goliath. Love's car seemed to indicate this, being a four-year-old one-off, the Cooper T79, which the small factory from Surbiton had built for Bruce McLaren in the 1964 Tasman Series, but then sold on to Love. At the rear was the final development stage of the Coventry Climax four-cylinder FPF, with a capacity of 2.7 litres, basically a carp in the pike pond of the eight- and 12-cylinder engines.

Love had fitted the handy little racer with an additional tank so that it could get by without refuelling, but then one of the two Bendix fuel pumps failed, so he had to take on a few extra litres in the pits, allowing works driver Pedro Rodriguez to scurry past and win in his Cooper-Maserati.

He had already shown glimpses of brilliance during his flying visit to Europe in 1960, by then at the ripe old racing-driver age of 36. His podium finish in the Eifelrennen, driving the Formula Junior Lola, attracted the attention of timber merchant and master craftsman Ken Tyrrell. Under Tyrrell's energetic guidance, Love drove quite successfully in races across the Continent in the European Formula Junior Championship of 1961 and '62, together with South African Tony Maggs. Along the way, as it were, he also won the British Touring Car Championship, driving a Mini in 1962.

The reason, if not the cause, for his return home to Rhodesia was a serious Formula Junior accident in Albi during 1962, after which he was barely able to move his left arm. His nine GPs, in East London and later in Kyalami, were not particularly glorious. Instead, he shone elsewhere, on home soil for example, with six South African F1 Championships between 1964 and 1969. From 1970 onwards, his arch-rival and nemesis, Dave Charlton, didn't let himself down either by repeating this success.

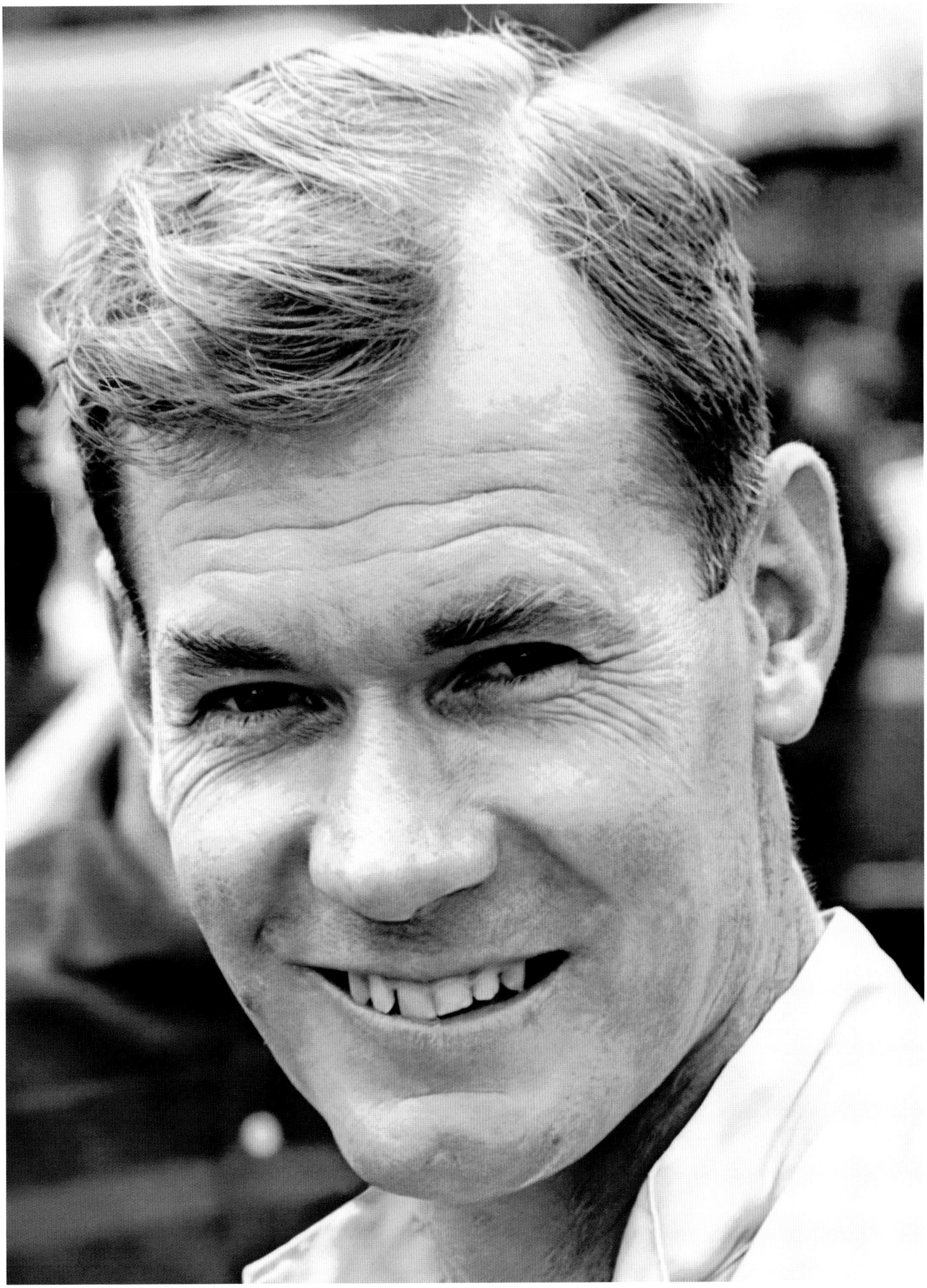

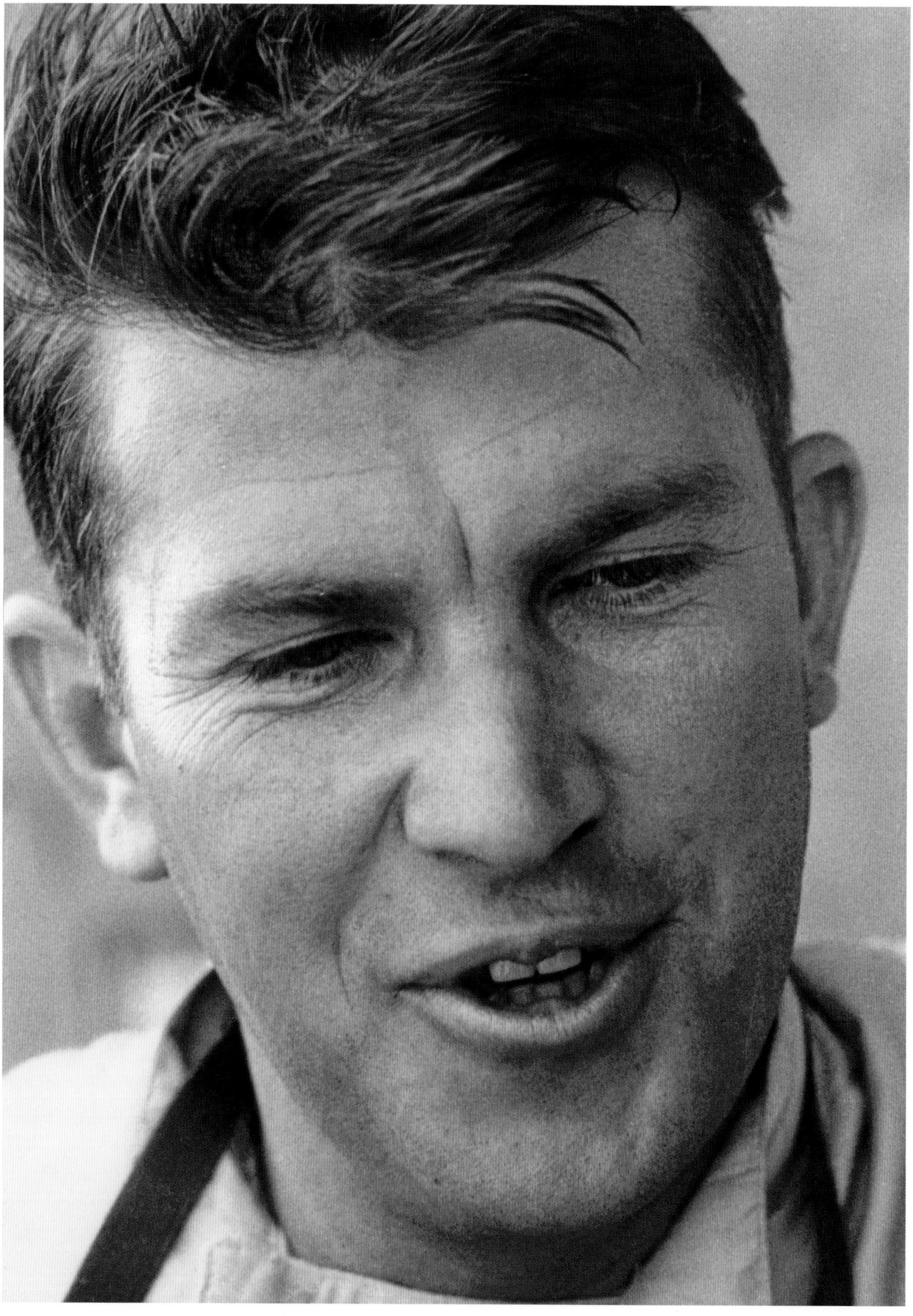

Ronnie Bucknum

*1936 – †1992

▶ The scene looked like an episode from the Second World War. Dozens of Japanese in identical outfits were combing a piece of forest in what seemed to be a mysterious military mission. Actually, it belonged to a different time. On the Saturday before the 1964 German GP, Honda mechanics roamed the dark Eifel woods seeking their charge, which had become lost somewhere in its depths, a stocky little white racing car with a transversely-mounted V12 in its rear. The mighty sounds it produced defied the tiny size of its cylinders. Eventually, the squad found what they were looking for at the Brünnchen passage, where the noisy novice Honda RA271 was silently parked beside the hedge.

Nothing made sense about that Far Eastern Nürburgring foray. To choose the 'Green Hell', the most demanding circuit of them all, as the venue of the small single-seater's baptism of fire seemed absurd. It was also the debut of its driver, Ronnie Bucknum, in three ways. The Californian was going to drive his first race in a formula car, and in his first grand prix to boot, the Ring also being a complete novelty for him, apart from a couple of laps in a Chrysler loaner.

On lap 11 of the race, the steering failed. Bucknum hit the banking at a frightening 100mph. He played down his shock and his injuries. Well, four stitches and a banged knee, that was all. However, it seemed an ominous debut.

But somehow, everything curiously went according to plan. His new employers had picked him out of obscurity at random, a nobody with some races on the US West Coast to his credit. If the car underperformed, Bucknum was the perfect scapegoat. If it was an instant hit, success would have many Japanese fathers.

The short career of the early Honda GP car was crowned by Richie Ginther's victory in Mexico City, in November, 1965. Bucknum was fifth, outshone by Ginther's arrival in the team for that year's Mexican Grand Prix. But he had some good seasons ahead of him back in the USA.

Walt Hansgen

* 1919 – † 1966

▶ To put it simply, Walter Edwin Hansgen was an exponent of the sports car. For more than 15 years following his debut in Bridgehampton, in 1951, he was usually to be found near the front, albeit without any major successes, apart perhaps from the four SCCA championships in his native USA, between 1956 and 1959. He took part in the Sebring 12 Hours on 15 occasions, and raced five times at Le Mans.

Initially, during the fifties, Walt Hansgen paid to race out of his own pocket, mainly driving Jaguars. However, after good performances in the D-Type, the dependable racer soon joined Briggs Cunningham's famous racing team. Then, following Cunningham's rettirement at the end of 1963, he moved to the Mecom Racing Team, whose fast-paced fleet of cars ranged from the Ferrari GTO and 250LM to the Lotus 19, a Scarab Chevrolet and various Corvettes, plus the Lola T70.

Formula 1 was by no means the otherwise customary top priority in Hansgen's CV. There were two US GPs at Watkins Glen in 1961 (he was 41!) and 1964, as well as the completely chaotic Mexican Grand Prix of 1962, with which that country wanted to recommend itself for inclusion in the official GP calendar, but that was it. Hansgen was entered for the first in the Cooper T53 of Cunningham's partner, Alfred Momo, but he retired after 14 laps due to a crash when Olivier Gendebien spun in front of him on an oil patch and there was no escape route. In his second US GP, Colin Chapman gave him a seat in the third works Lotus, alongside Jim Clark and Trevor Taylor. Hansgen returned this favour with a fifth place and two points. On the Magdalena Mixhuca circuit, Hansgen started from 13th place in a Lotus 18/21 and retired after 45 (of 60) laps with ignition problems.

At the beginning of 1966, it looked like being a good year for Walt Hansgen: third at Daytona and second at Sebring with the Ford GT40 MkII, on both occasions with his young protégé, Mark Donohue.

On 7th April, however, he passed away in a US military hospital in Orléans, three days after a serious and completely senseless accident during testing at Le Mans.

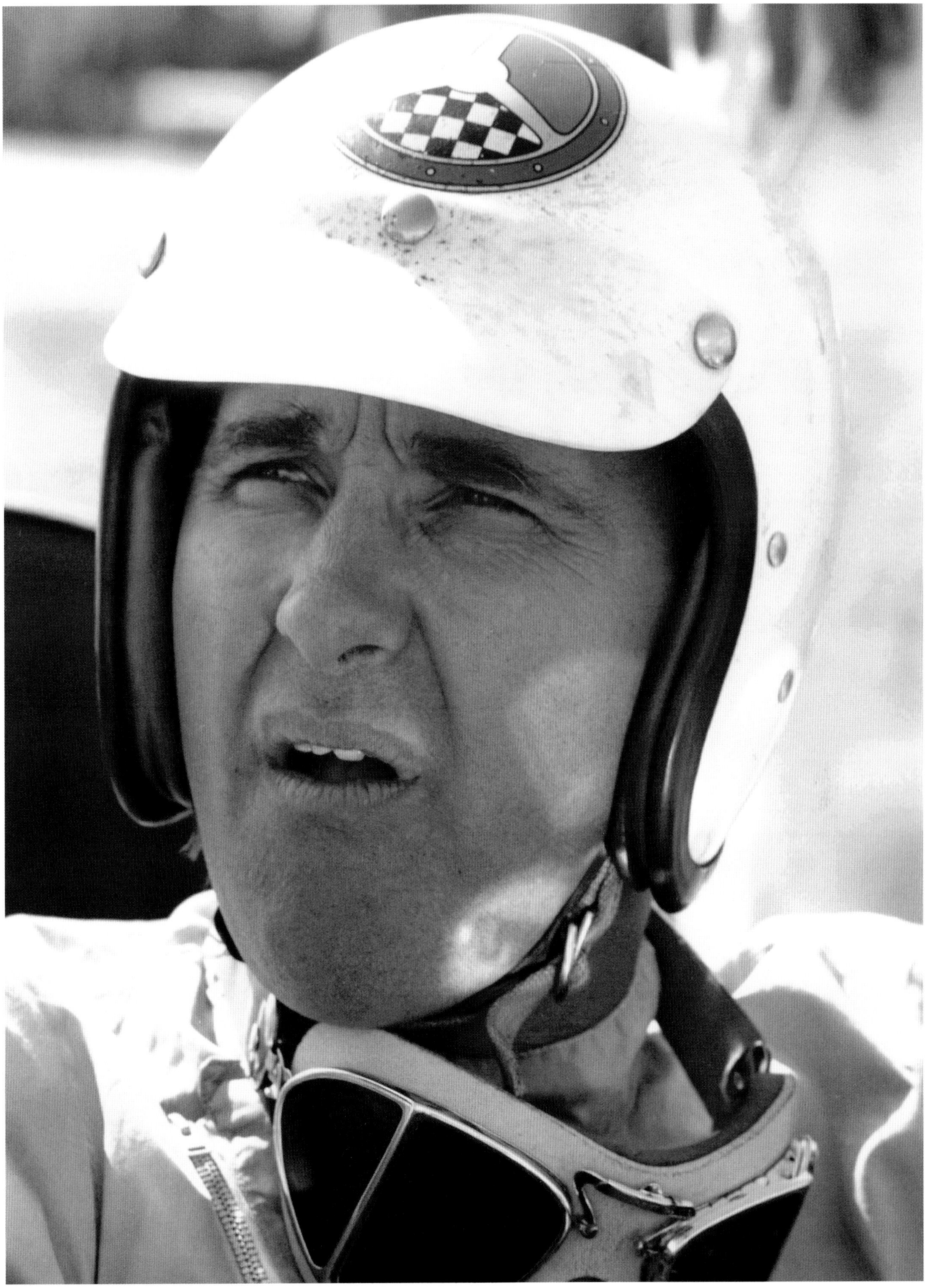

Jochen Rindt   * 1942 – † 1970

▶ Jochen Rindt certainly came close to the cliché of the racing driver as a pirate of the racetracks, with only the eye-patch missing, which would have grossly impeded him while exercising his fast craft. Otherwise, Karl-Jochen Rindt evaded all stereotypes, or even defied them, sometimes bordering on the paradoxical.

Obviously, that began with the gloomy phenomenon of becoming world champion only after his death unlike, for instance, Mike Hawthorn, who at least enjoyed his success for a few months before he was killed, on 22nd January, 1959, in a little road tussle with team owner Rob Walker on the Guildford Bypass.

His biographer, Dr Erich Glavitza, also saw that in the ongoing bickering regarding his nationality. He had been born in Mainz and grew up in Graz, and he insisted that he was Austrian, being celebrated by his compatriots as a national hero. But Glavitza also advanced convincing arguments that Jochen Rindt was the first German F1 champion, rather than 'Schumi'.

Rindt could show up in a long fur coat, looking like a member of the thriving Vienna *demimonde* of his time gone astray, without causing sneers from racing purists and other self-righteous individuals. His GP career took five years and 49 races before it really got going, with victory at Watkins Glen in 1969. But by then, he had already been dubbed 'King of Formula 2', with a Le Mans win under his belt in 1965, aboard the NART Ferrari 275LM.

In 1970, he caused a sensation at Monaco, where he hounded Jack Brabham into a rookie mistake and won the race. The young pretender had prevailed over the hard-boiled old hand.

Austrian motor sport in the late sixties, Formula Vee in particular, was a place of hilarity and youthful abandon. Drivers met, tussled with one another in the limitless freedom of the airfields and somehow seemed immortal.

But then came 1970, and the deaths of Bruce McLaren, Piers Courage and Jochen Rindt, a triple whammy of horror.

Afterwards, nothing was the same again.

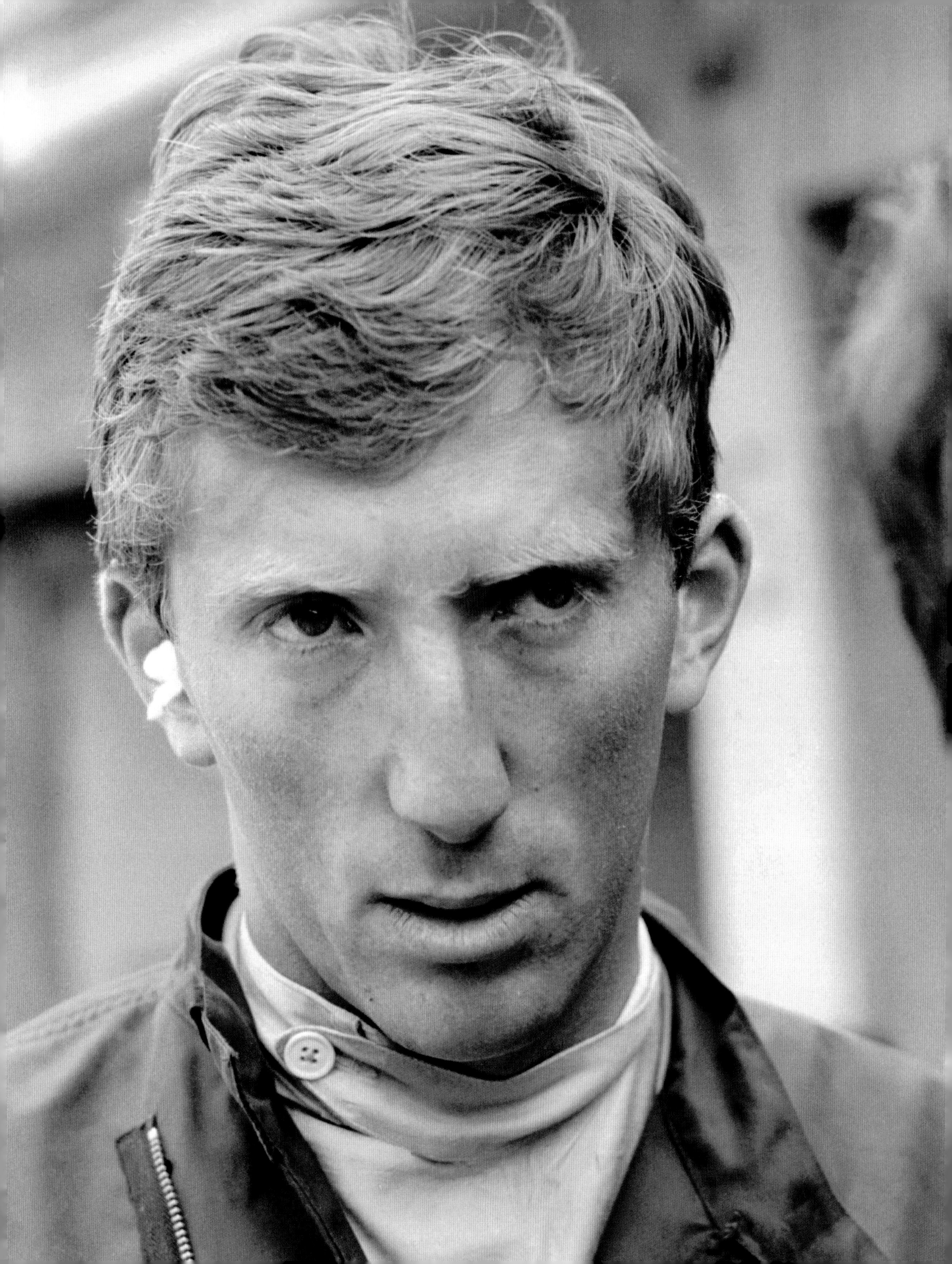

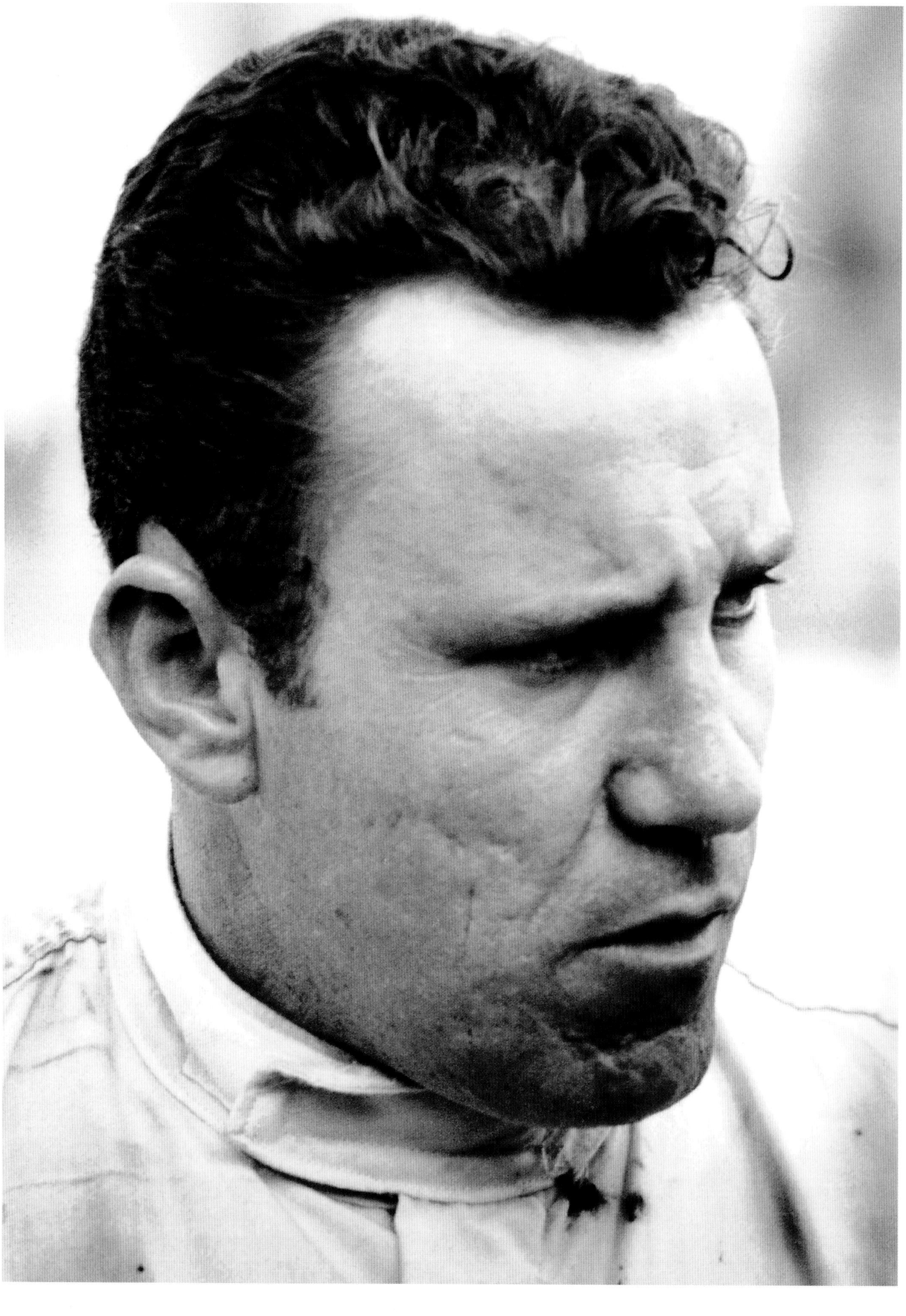

Paul Hawkins * 1937 – † 1969

▶ Lap 89 of the 1965 Monaco Grand Prix, the Lotus 33 with start number '10' and its driver, Paul Hawkins, exited the harbour chicane, spun, hurtled through the straw bales and dived backwards into the water. It was a strange *déjà-vu*. Ten years before, exactly the same fate had befallen Alberto Ascari in his Lancia D50.

Coolly aware of the damaging potential of his overheating Coventry-Climax V8 meeting the Mediterranean, Paul hit the 'kill' switch during his short flight, remaining calm while the car was sinking to the bottom, some 10m below. Then he bailed out of the cockpit, grabbed the mouthpiece from the frogman who had swum to his help, took several deep breaths and surfaced seconds later.

In his own words: "The car suddenly turned out to sea," and "That's one way to cool one's ardour." Of course, the scene grabbed the headlines and later achieved cinematic immortality when John Frankenheimer recreated it for the film *Grand Prix*, wrapped in even more drama, a year later.

For the rugged Australian, who had travelled to Britain in the early sixties with high-flying dreams, but no money, Formula 1 was only a footnote to his career. An untiring traveller in matters of motor racing, Hawkins was hailed sports car world champion in an unofficial ranking by *Autosport* magazine in 1967, with 32 events under his belt, from Snetterton in March to South African Pietermaritzburg on Boxing Day.

In that year, he even managed to be employed as a works driver by the competing outfits of Ferrari, Ford and Porsche, for whom he won the prestigious Targa Florio, with Rolf Stommelen.

He could swear like a trooper, being an expert at dishing out 'the Great Australian Adjective' and not sparing the weaker sex, who were quite fond of him, though.

He was liked by everybody. For the sport, his death at Oulton Park in May, 1969, was a heavy blow. For his friends, Paul Hawkins was irreplaceable.

Jackie Stewart   * 1939

▶ If Jackie Stewart pocketed only one euro for every selfie, that somewhat high-tech variant of the classic autograph, he would be a rich man.

But don't worry, the popular Scot will never struggle to make ends meet. Long before it was common practice, he cleverly capitalised on the value of his good name, assisted by his charismatic presence, plus a gift of the gab that could lure a ravenous terrier away from a sirloin steak, or so said Innes Ireland.

He still promenades affably through the paddocks of the world, clad in the trappings of Scottish tradition, such as tartan cap and trousers, a monument to himself and times past, and has long since arrived in the third phase of a life bursting with activity. The first: Stewart the racer, full of bulletproof intrepidity and fiercely competitive. The second: Stewart the superstar, radiating the ambiance of a pop icon and nicknamed 'Jack the Hair' for his shoulder-length mane. But already, he was becoming thoughtful.

Again and again, the breathless road movie that is his life took him to the Nürburgring as the measure of all things racing. Going by Stewart's guest appearances in the 'Green Hell', you can trace his evolution perfectly, between his iconic triumph over swirling Eifel mist and pouring rain at the German GP in 1968, and his last victory, again at the Grosser Preis von Deutschland, five years and two titles later. But by then, his brilliant team-mate, François Cevert, was breathing down his neck, and after that race, Jackie told his boss, Ken Tyrrell, that on that day, the handsome Frenchman could have beaten him. Stewart and Tyrrell – that was a man's alliance, not unlike that between Clark and Chapman, their common success had seemingly been pre-programmed.

After his austere farewell event in autumn, 1973, at London's Carlton Towers Hotel, deeply shaken by the death of his heir apparent and friend, Cevert, JYS never returned to the cockpit in anger. That decision, though, had been taken much earlier.

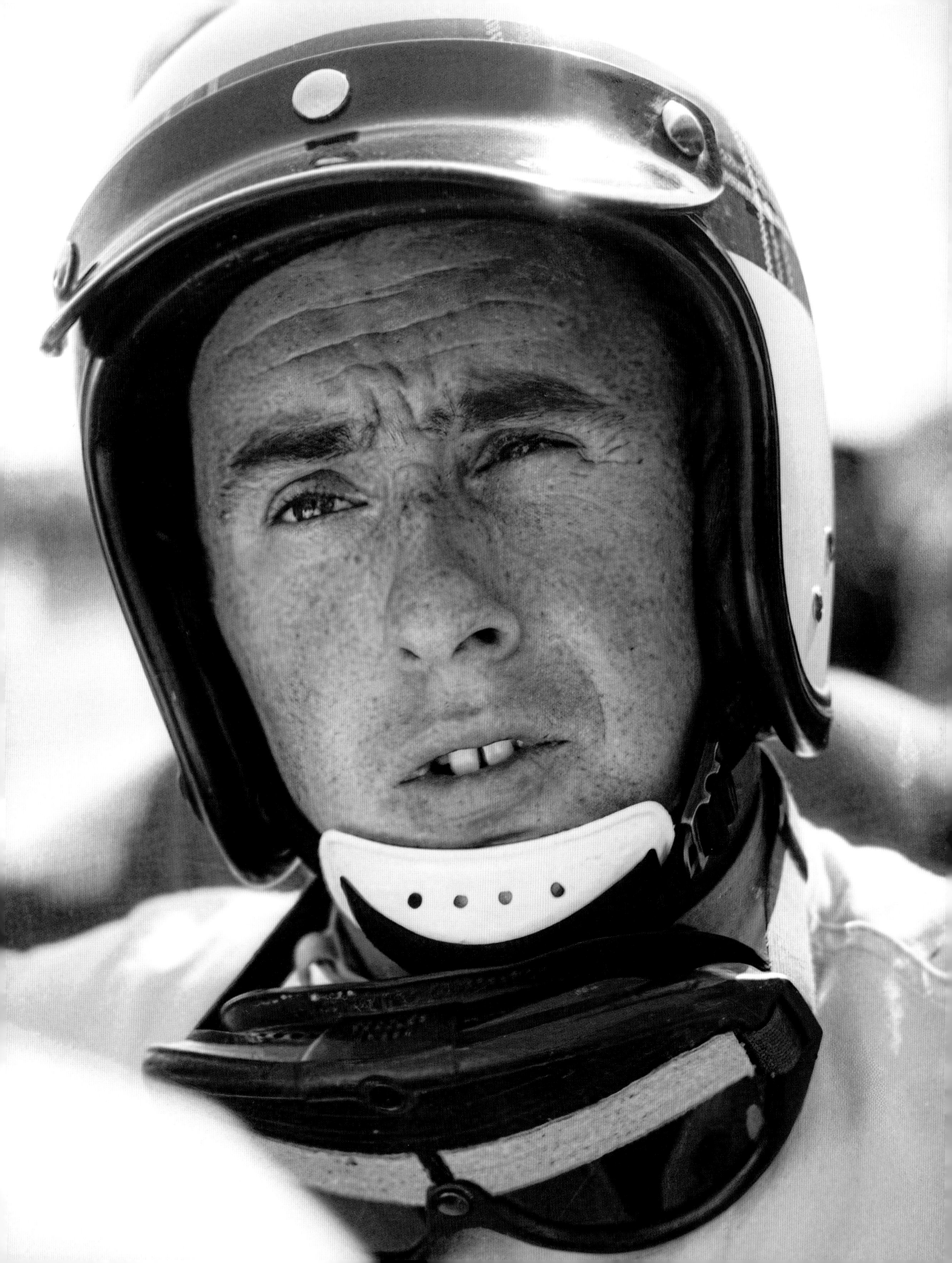

Denis Hulme   * 1936 – † 1992

▶ Watkins Glen, October, 1972. Young prodigy Jody Scheckter is about to burst upon the grand prix scene. On the eve of the race, the 22-year-old, curly-haired South African is seen with an older man talking at length, paternally, with him to alleviate his stage fright. That man is Denny Hulme, number-one at McLaren, F1 world champion in 1967, winner of the CanAm Challenge Cup in 1968 and '70.

That was not surprising, since possibly no other GP driver in those years would have been capable of imparting similarly calming encouragement than the even-tempered and patient New Zealander, called 'The Bear' by his American fans. He was never a daredevil. His Formula 1 figures tell it all, adding up to a sort of psychographic analysis: just one pole position, but eight grand prix victories, two in his championship year. In his 112 GPs, he could be found 61 times among the first six. All that spoke against any raging bravado – he hated any hoopla and public appearances, anyway.

He also showed unusual consistency in the choice of his teams. Between 1965 and '67, he drove for Brabham, until the tension between himself and 'Black Jack' became unbearable, so between 1968 and '74, he was a McLaren man.

Within his own four walls, Hulme valued calm and solidity as well. Together with his wife, Greeta, and their two children, Martin and Adele, 'The Bear' lived in a bungalow of futuristic appearance in Surrey. He used to say, though, that putting on a show was not his thing, but that everything should remind him of his home on the South Island, just a house with a parcel of land around it.

In 1975, he returned to the 'Land of the Kiwis', in the illustrious company of McLaren early retiree Mike Hailwood and his team boss, Phil Kerr. He continued to take part in the odd motor race, failing to completely kick the habit, as it were. But then, during the Bathurst 1,000km in October, 1992, his BMW M3 suddenly swiped the Armco barrier and veered across the track before coming to a standstill, as if parked.

At the wheel sat a dead man. Diagnosis: a heart attack.

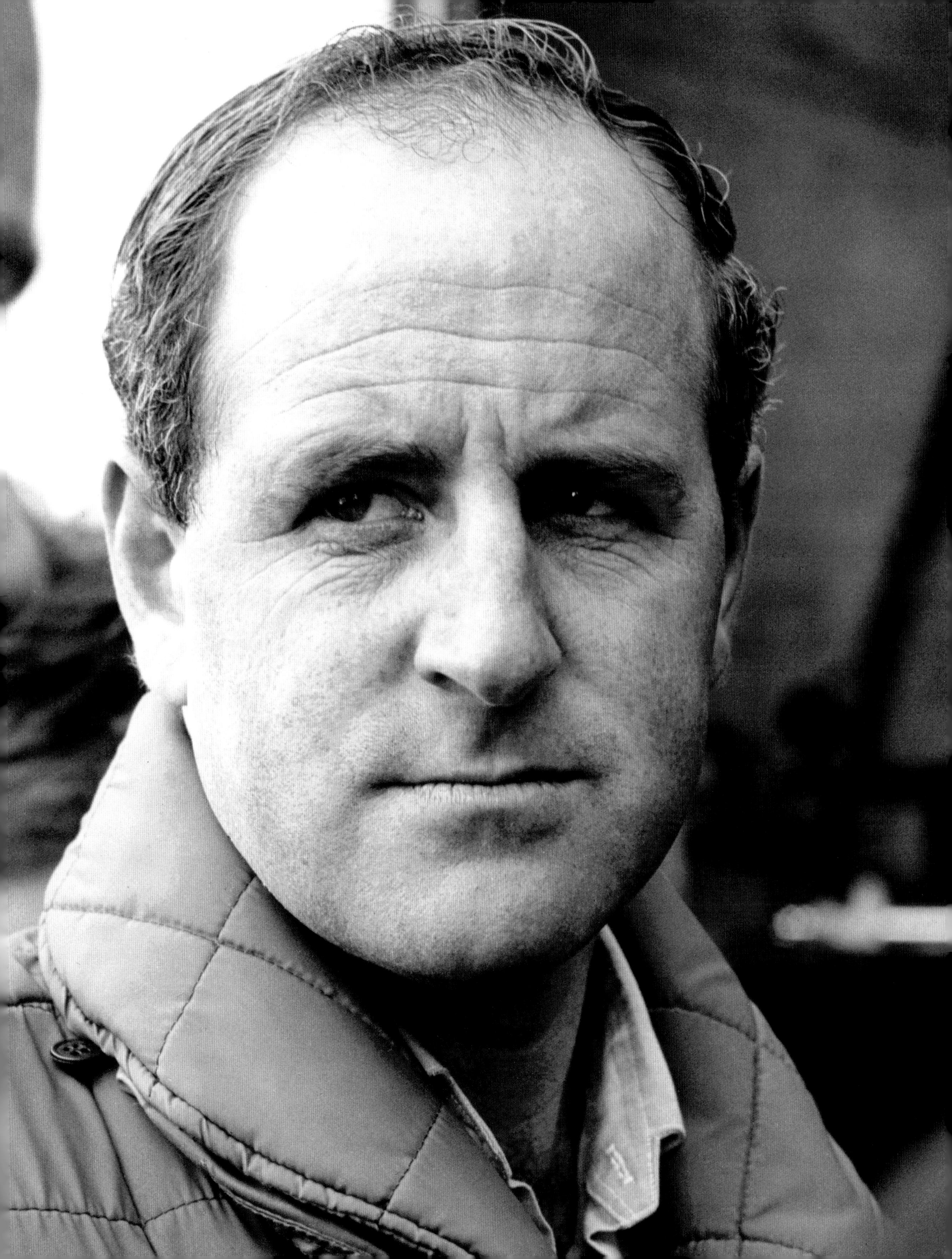

Bob Bondurant * 1933 – †2021

▶ Bob Bondurant – the mere name evokes dynamic situations: the Nürburgring 1,000km in May, 1965, the Flugplatz section. It's still the nasty old Ring, without Armco barriers and kerbs to protect the mortals hastening along the narrow stretch of tarmac between the hedges. Somehow faster than fast, the thundering blue Shelby Daytona Coupé, with start number '54', throws up a little cloud of dust at the same spot on every one of its 43 laps, a tough comrade for tough guys like Bob Bondurant and Jochen Neerpasch.

Their hellish ride in the recalcitrant beast bore fruit: first of the Division 3 GTs, seventh overall. Bob's name is inseparably interwoven with the 1965 FIA GT world title for Cobra creator Carroll Shelby.

Nevertheless, he also knew how to handle more delicate racing machinery. His win in the Coppa dell'Autodromo di Monza for F3 cars, in the supporting programme of that year's Italian GP, earned him an audience with Enzo Ferrari. John Surtees acted as an interpreter, but Bob did know some basic Italian: '*Formula Uno?*" he asked pertly. "*Possibile,*" the Maranello autocrat tortured him, "maybe". Obviously, he was talking sports cars rather than F1.

All the same, the man from Illinois sat in the red Tipo 158 in the following US GP at Watkins Glen, working his way up from 14th on the grid to sixth. Then came the rain. The elastic of his goggles had stretched, so he had to hold them in place, sticking a knee against the steering-wheel to change gear with his right hand. He ended up ninth, the chance of his lifetime gone.

In 1966, John Frankenheimer employed Bondurant's services for his racing melodrama *Grand Prix*, as both an adviser and instructor. The German track commentator, Rainer Günzler, even called him by his real name, unlike the film's semi-fictitious protagonists, Jean-Pierre Sarti (aka John Surtees), Scott Stoddard (Jackie Stewart), Pete Aron (James Garner, sporting Chris Amon's helmet design) and Nino Barlini (Lorenzo Bandini), conferring Bob with a bit of cinematic immortality.

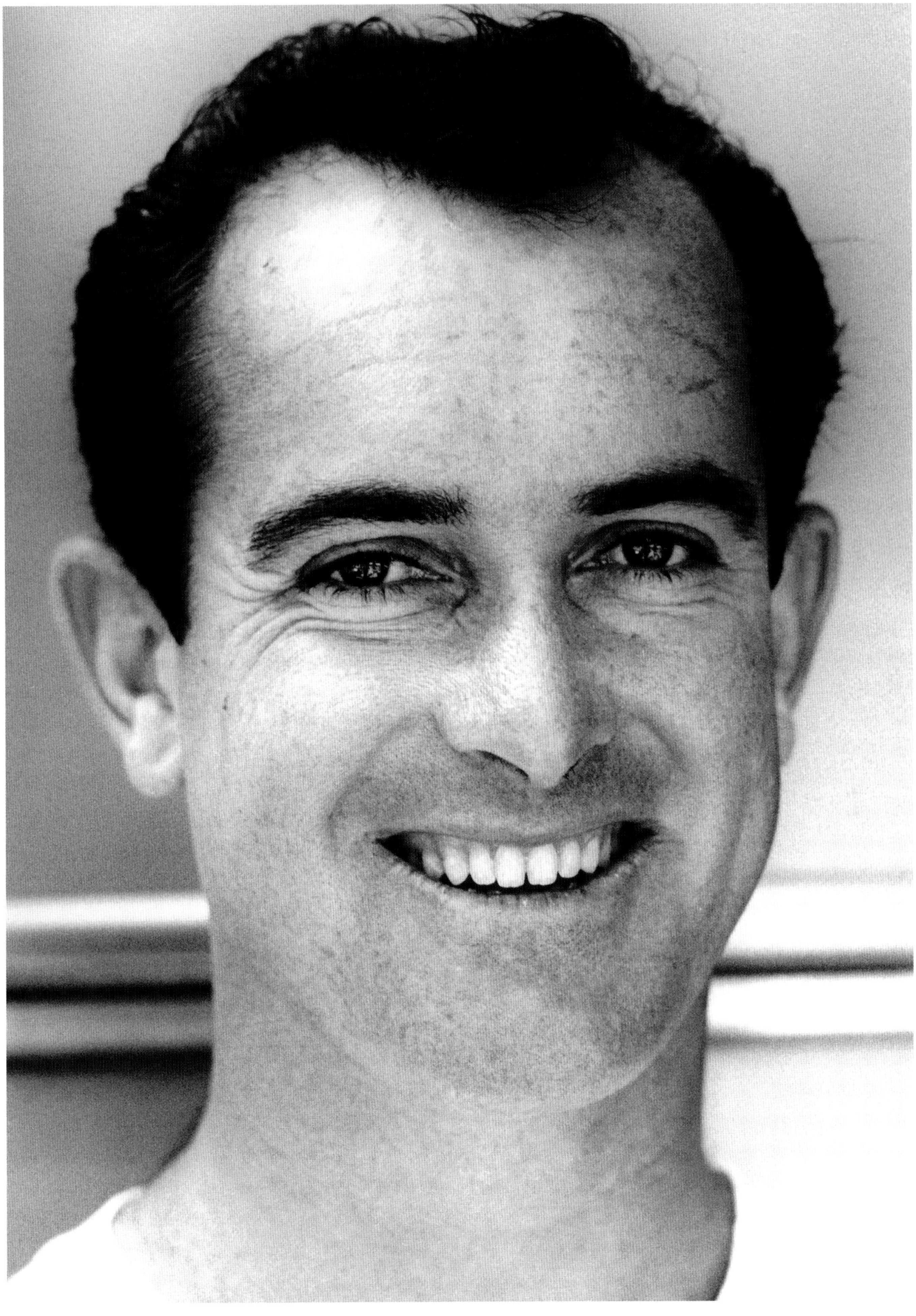

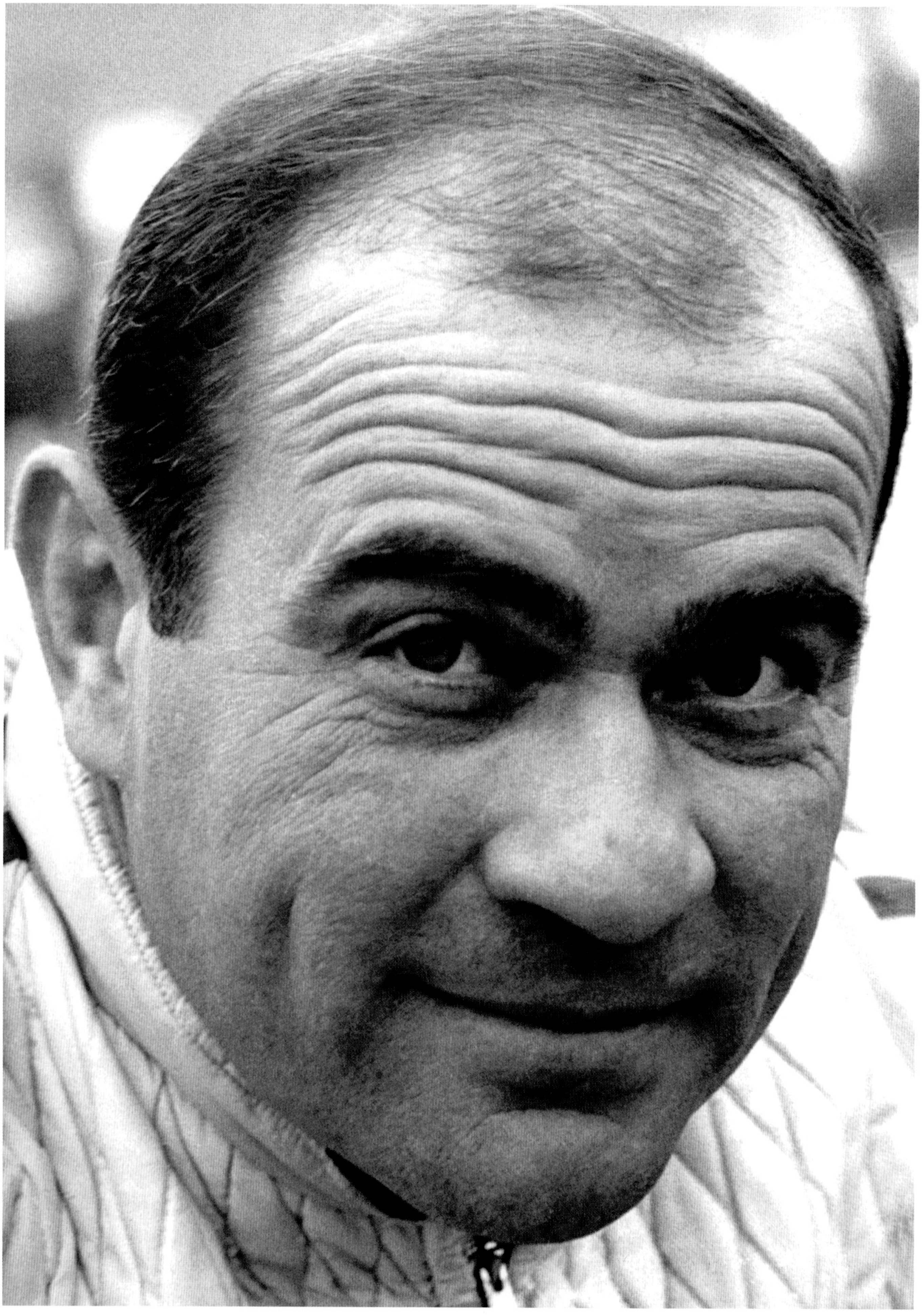

Guy Ligier * 1930 – ✝ 2015

▶ No doubt, given Guy Ligier's vibrant life story, one could cram in several curricula vitae into these lines. Nature had fittingly endowed the farmer's son and early orphan with a beefy physique and a fervent ambition. He was utterly irascible, and his temper tantrums were feared.

As a businessman, Ligier embraced the whole gamut, from a butcher, to a fertilizer producer, and then a building contractor who served his nation, constructing motorways, dams and bridges while also masterminding the Magny-Cours racing circuit. Really, a jack-of-all-trades.

He had a knack for wrapping people around his finger and managed to secure the friendship of French Socialist President François Mitterand. As a constructor and manufacturer, the chain-smoking Ligier enriched road traffic, mainly in France, with automobile oddities, like the JS4 microcar, which resembled a tiny telephone booth on wheels.

Ligier was an excellent oarsman, a member of his country's national rugby team, and a rally and racing competitor in a plethora of disciplines, not least on motorbikes.

At the ripe 'old age' of 36, he set his sights on Formula 1, acquiring first a Cooper T81-Maserati and later the Brabham BT20-Repco with which Denny Hulme had won the 1967 Monaco GP. This phase was rounded off with sixth place and a lonely championship point aboard the Brabham at the Nürburgring. The year before, he had hit his low point at the same event. After a practice crash into the woods at Hatzenbach, his right foot hung from the stretcher in the wrong direction. Only his furious protests prevented his smashed leg from being amputated.

In 1969, Ligier turned his attention to building his own vehicles, in the shape of the sports prototype JS1. With the JS acronym, he paid homage to his close friend, Jo Schlesser, who had been killed during the 1968 French GP at Rouen in a fiery accident, achieving posthumous fame through Ligier's Formula 1 cars. In 326 grands prix, between 1976 and '96, they scored nine victories – to the glory of France.

Chris Irwin * 1942

▶ During his second flying lap, practising for the Nürburgring 1,000km on Friday 17th May, 1968, the Ford F3L P18 of Briton Chris Irwin became airborne in the notorious Flugplatz section, somersaulted several times, then ended up in a ditch. Its Ford DFV engine was still running, but its driver was seriously injured, the edge of the windscreen having penetrated his skull. Irwin's team-mate, Frank Gardner, and others were sure that a fat Eifel hare had caused the accident.

The Ford prototype of the Alan Mann outfit was a most attractive racing car, but also difficult to drive at the Nürburgring, being something of a high-speed work in progress. "Leave it, Chris," John Surtees, originally scheduled to be his second driver, had warned in the run-up to the race. "The car is not fit to start at the Ring." But Irwin had a fiery ambition, and the prospect of getting a foot into Ford's door and a welcome salary of £500 was too tempting.

There was no doubt that, among the wild young men from Britain, he was one of the most promising, as was also Piers Courage. The two had been born within a month of one another, and their careers were intertwined, making them simultaneously friends and rivals. A month before the ADAC 1,000km, Irwin had stood out by winning an F2 race in the Eifel, driving John Surtees' Lola, though at the Südschleife.

Until then, his 15 months in Formula 1 had been less spectacular, with a fifth in 1967 at Le Mans, driving for the BRM 'B' team of Reg Parnell Motor Racing and finishing four laps behind the winner, Jack Brabham. His other best results, gleaned from a total of ten GPs, were four seventh places. In the last of those, at the 1967 German Grand Prix, to his frustration, he had to cope with the complex and troublesome BRM H16 engine, but nobody doubted his potential.

After the Ring crash, however, Chris Irwin the racing driver was history. He simply vanished. He is still with us, but for some time, not even his wife, Loti, knew whether he had not long since passed away.

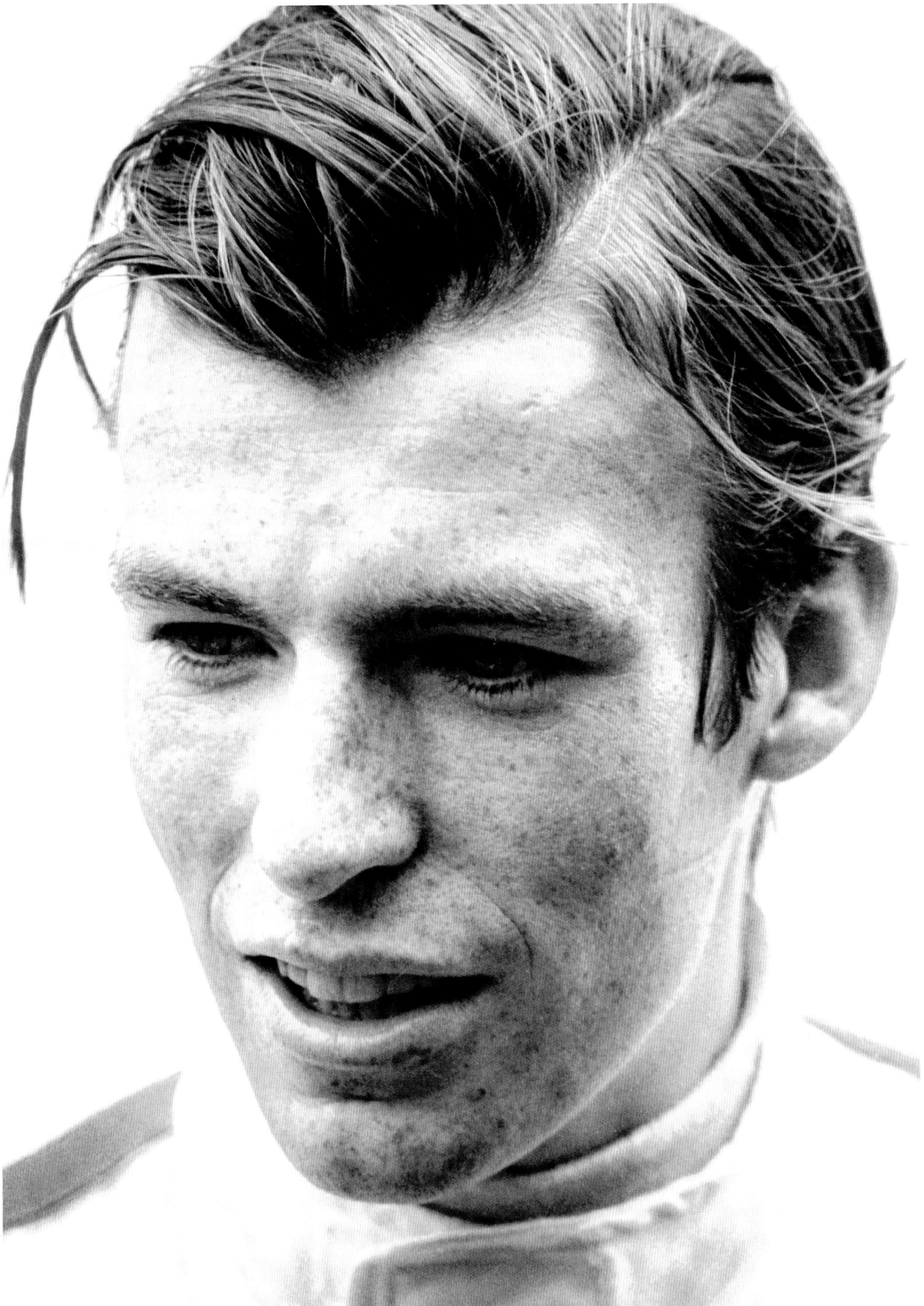

Michael Parkes   * 1931 – † 1977

▶ Michael Parkes was a Ferrari man at the same time as John Surtees and with similar functions. Namely, as team driver and technician, but he continued with the Reds for quite a while after the former motorbike superstar and 1964 F1 world champion had angrily departed the *Scuderia* following the 1966 Belgian GP. As a matter of fact, Parkes had been one of the reasons for 'Big John's' unusual departure in the middle of the season.

The frosty relationship between these two very different Brits sparkled with ice crystals. Even much later, Surtees breathed fire and brimstone whenever the talk turned to his tall compatriot. They certainly shared a commitment to the Ferrari cause, but while John Surtees was a commuter, travelling to Maranello as more of a visitor and leaving no doubt that Edenbridge, in the beautiful county of Kent, was his home, Parkes made the Emilia Romagna the very centre of his life. In *Piloti, che gente*, Enzo Ferrari pointed out that he had "refined his iron English will" with "fine Modenese lifestyle" and spoke Italian like a local. Surtees, he thundered by way of contrast, had exhibited "unbearable arrogance."

Parkes' contributions to the higher glory of the marque with the *cavallino rampante* as its emblem are usually underrated, considering his input as an engineer, his five splendid long-distance victories between 1964 and '66 and two second places at Le Mans in 1961 and '67. John Surtees' grim farewell seemed to open the door to a successful career in Formula 1, endorsed by two runner-up positions at Reims and Monza in 1966, plus victory in the 1967 International Trophy at Silverstone. But then a horrific accident at Spa's notorious Blanchimont corner in June 1967 put an end to such dreams.

Parkes was killed near the end of August, ten years later, when his Lancia hit the rear of a heavy goods vehicle at night in the pouring rain, near Turin. "The poor man," Enzo Ferrari lamented, in one of his rare displays of compassion.

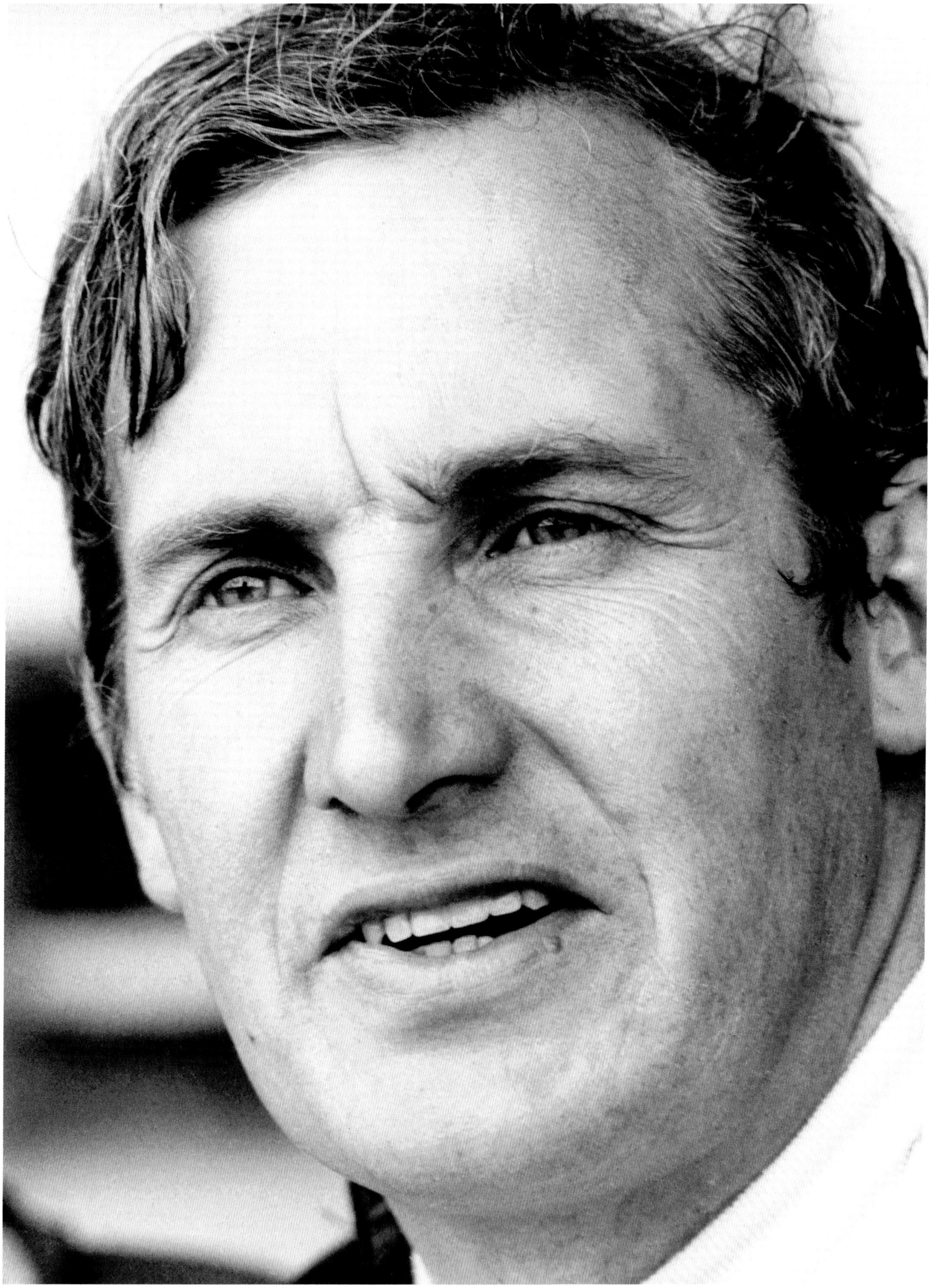

Alan Rees *1938

▶ The merits of Alan Rees, in respect of motor racing in general and Formula 1 in particular, undoubtedly can be found on this side of the pit wall to the track. Strictly speaking, his grand prix career lasted one weekend only, the 1967 British GP at Silverstone in a Cooper T81, a tired secondhand car.

But twice, in 1966 and '67, Rees' Brabhams were among the F2 cars filling the sparse field of grown-up GP single-seaters at the German GP, taking a second place in 1967, a high accolade indeed at the Nürburgring. In his five seasons from 1964, racing in Formula 2, then still a favourite playground of the F1 stars, Rees reliably ranked as one of the best. He was in the employ of Roy Winkelmann's utterly successful F2 outfit, as driver as well as team boss, quite an unusual combination – like a piano player who conducts the orchestra while also playing his instrument.

Thus Alan Rees belonged to the cadre when Max Mosley, along with his brilliant constructor, Robin Herd, brought the racing-car manufacturer March into being in 1969. In doing so, they applied a reverse domino effect, as it were. Herd recruited his schoolmate, Rees, who, in turn, brought in Graham Coaker, the fourth March musketeer. Together, they combined their initials into the company's name, with Rees contributing both of his to make the dynamic March logo possible, as narrated by Mosley in his autobiography, *Formula One and Beyond*.

Where Rees was concerned, Mosley appreciated not only his instinct for finding driving talent, but also the gift of talking Mozarts of the craft, like Ronnie Peterson, into joining March. Grief and frustration were enormous when, after three years with the Bicester company, the Swede succumbed to Colin Chapman's siren call and deserted to Lotus at the end of 1972. From 1973, Rees brought his experience as a team manager to bear in the novel Shadow team, then from 1977 in Arrows/Footwork, as a bedrock that seemed to be part and parcel of Formula 1 forever.

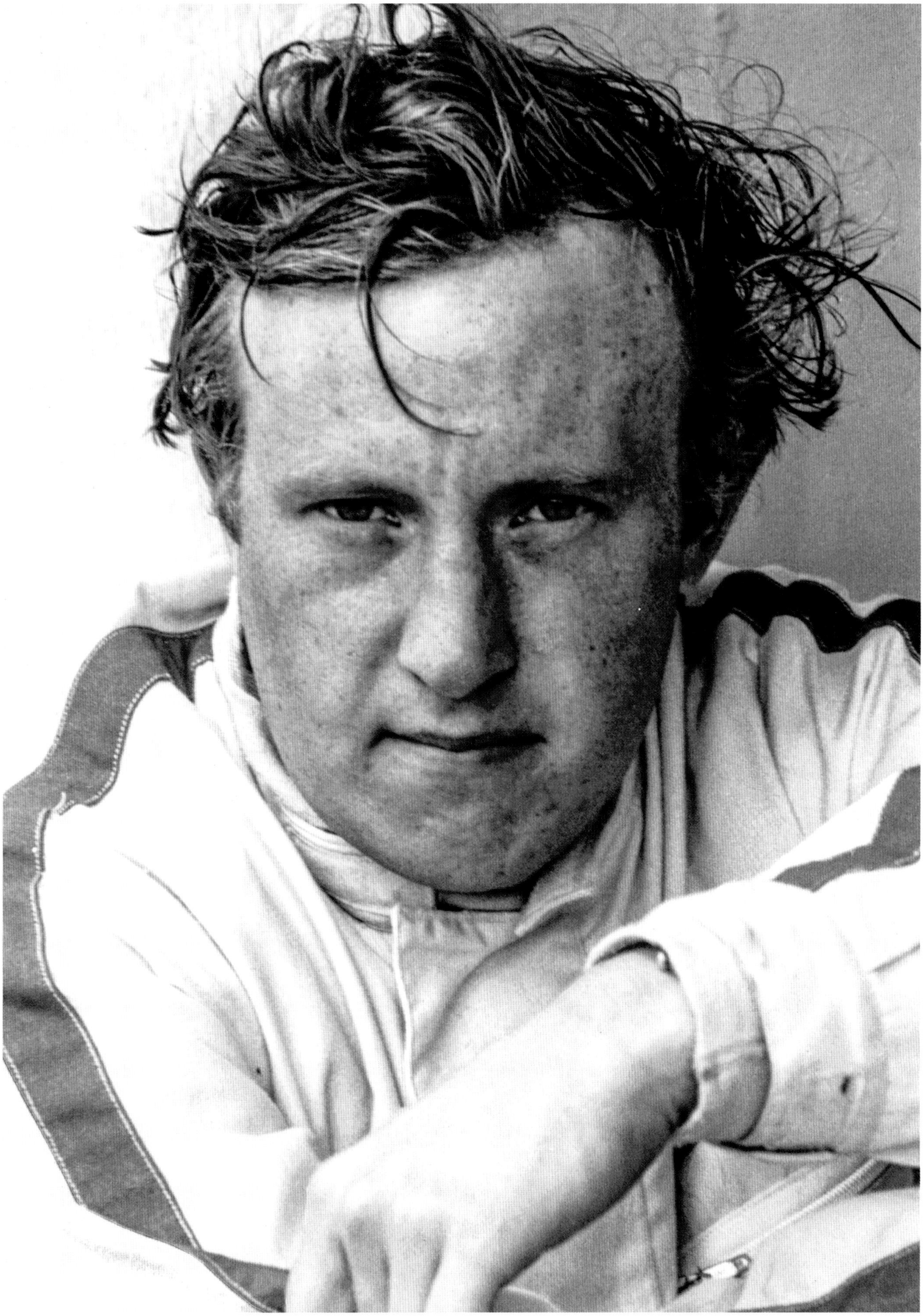

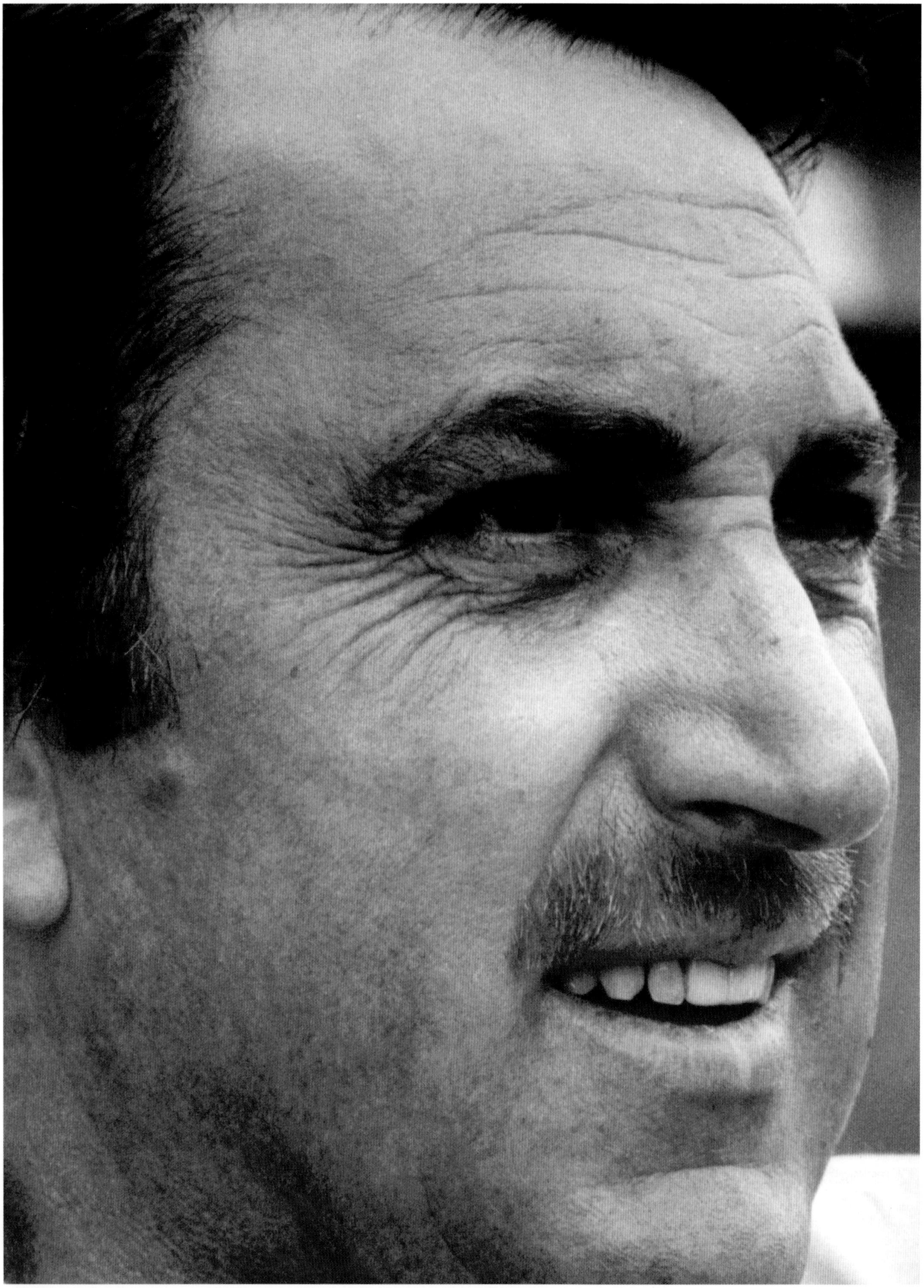

Jo Schlesser

* 1928 – † 1968

▶ The worst accidents in Formula 1 seldom happened when they seemed bound to occur, as for instance during the rainy races at the Nürburgring in 1968, at Monaco in 1984 or Estoril a year later. They came out of the blue, so to speak, as on that azure and gold October Sunday at Brands Hatch in 1971, when Jo Siffert died, or on that wonderful 1994 spring weekend at Imola, when Roland Ratzenberger and Ayrton Senna lost their lives.

For the 1968 French GP at Rouen, however, everything synchronised perfectly in fatal interplay – the forebodings, the horrible weather, Jo Schlesser's death. Race director 'Toto' Roche had waved the *tricolore* a quarter of an hour late, and not without his usual shenanigans and danger to life and limb. From lap three onwards, a portentous sky-high black cloud mushroomed over the fast right-hand corner before the Nouveau Monde hairpin and refused to disperse throughout the GP. It signalled Schlesser's death, amid the fiery magnesium hell of his Honda RA302. The brutal pictures even found their way on to the French newsreel, which I saw in Paris in the pre-programme of Steve McQueen's blockbuster Bullit. They haunt me to the present day.

Jo Schlesser was a strong personality. His roaring laughter – he laughed a lot and with gusto – could be heard all over the paddock. Vigorously supported by his wife, Annie, he had long since established himself in sports car racing, topped by his victory in the 1967 Reims 12 Hours, driving a Ford GT40 MkIIB, along with his buddy, Guy Ligier, and also an excellent second place in the 1968 Spa 1,000km with a works Porsche 907.

In Formula 1, though, his career never got going. Rouen 1968 war his first 'real' grand prix, with the air-cooled Honda, a speeding work in progress that nobody wanted to drive, least of all John Surtees, the number one in the team. Racing's top tier, then, was left with a macabre statistic – a driver who had to pay with his life for his only start.

Hubert Hahne   * 1935 – †2019

▶ The 1970 German GP, exiled to Hockenheim because of the drivers' boycott of the Nürburgring, was meant to be the high point of a career. It turned out to be an anti-climax.

Hubert Hahne, 1966 European Touring Car Challenge (Division 3) champion, with tight ties to BMW and runner-up in Europe's F2 series three years later, behind Johnny Servoz-Gavin, had purchased a silver-grey March 701 for 160,000 deutschmarks, with financial support from the Springer Verlagsgruppe, and entered it for his home GP. It was his first real F1 car, Hahne having taken part three times in the F2 section of the German GP at the Ring. The last of four non-qualifiers, he didn't even make it to the grid.

The Bicester racing car manufacturer, he dictated into the notepads of the baffled newsmen, had sold him a heap of junk. He wanted his cash back. The reaction of March musketeer Max Mosley was not long in coming. Hahne still owed him money, he retorted in fluent German. That was why the 701 had been delivered to him only just before the race. It was impossible to try to contest a grand prix with a car that was not fully sorted.

Legal action followed from both sides, but suddenly a strange hush prevailed. At Silverstone, March factory driver Ronnie Peterson posted competitive times aboard the controversial machine.

The Hockenheim farce sullied a racing CV that was on the decline anyway. What a pity – Hahne had indeed been world class in tin-tops, and his spectacular driving went down well with the spectators. He was the smiling king of opposite lock, with as many dead flies sticking to the side windows of his BMWs as to their windscreens. "Wasn't that a wonderful 11 minutes of gliding?" he once asked a terrified journalist who had had the pleasure of accompanying him around the Nordschleife.

He was thoroughly shaken, though, by the death of his friend, Jochen Rindt. Racing in the top tiers, he said, had long exceeded all limits of reason – the farewell of a German superstar.

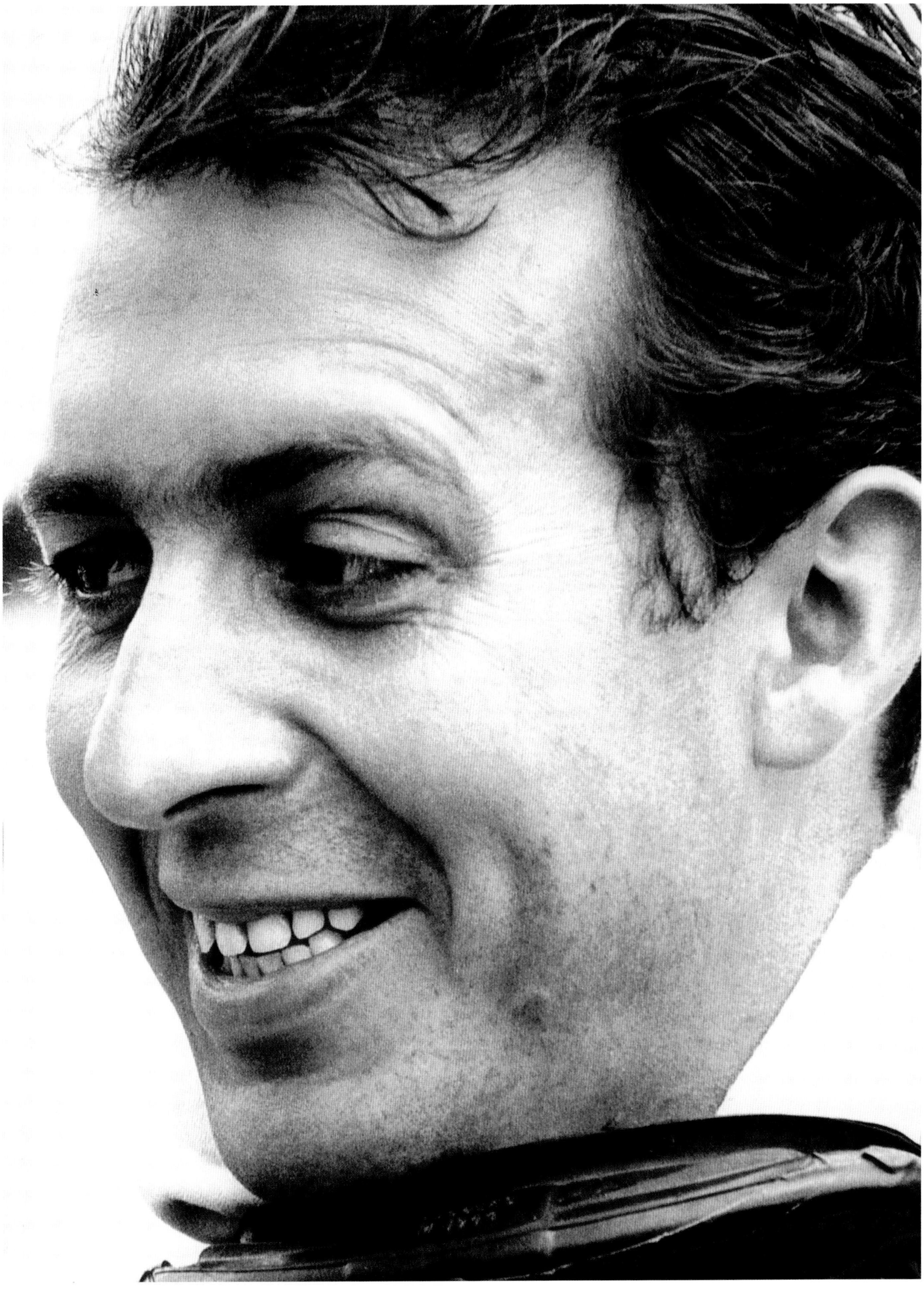

Jean-Pierre Beltoise

* 1937 – † 2015

▶ The weather conditions for the 30th Grand Prix de Monaco, on 14th May, 1972, were absolutely atrocious, perhaps the worst in the history of that blue-riband event until then. The Côte d'Azur was soaked.

Frenchman Jean-Pierre Beltoise, in his BRM 160B, with its attractive red-and-white Marlboro livery, had started from the second row. But, spurred on by tens of thousands of his sodden compatriots, the Parisian forced his car into an instant lead at the first corner and held that position to the end.

After four laps, he was more than five seconds ahead of second man Clay Regazzoni, in a Ferrari, and minutes later some 12 seconds in front of renowned rain-master Jacky Ickx, driving the other red 312B2. After two-and-a-half hours, the Belgian had to settle for second place, more than 38 seconds behind, while Beltoise never put a wheel wrong and further underlined his domination by setting the fastest lap. This was Beltoise's third grand prix for BRM, his only GP win, and the last for the long-established brand from Bourne after 17 years in the business, which by then had etched some rust and wrinkles into its once spotless reputation. Jean-Pierre himself badly needed this success. He definitely knew the hellish face of his profession, thoroughly shaken again and again by the fatalities of others, of which there were so many.

Doubtless, Monaco, 1972, was his greatest triumph, while his worst tragedy, in January, 1971, still haunted him. At the Buenos Aires 1,000km, he had run out of fuel and pushed his Matra MS660 prototype across the track in the direction of the pits, a hopeless and utterly perilous effort. Ignazio Giunti, arriving in full flight in his Ferrari 312PB, did not even see the blue car, hitting the Matra on its right side. An inferno followed. Giunti had no chance.

Beltoise is held in high regard, though. Had he not been hampered by arm injuries suffered at Reims in 1964, he might have been up there with the best.

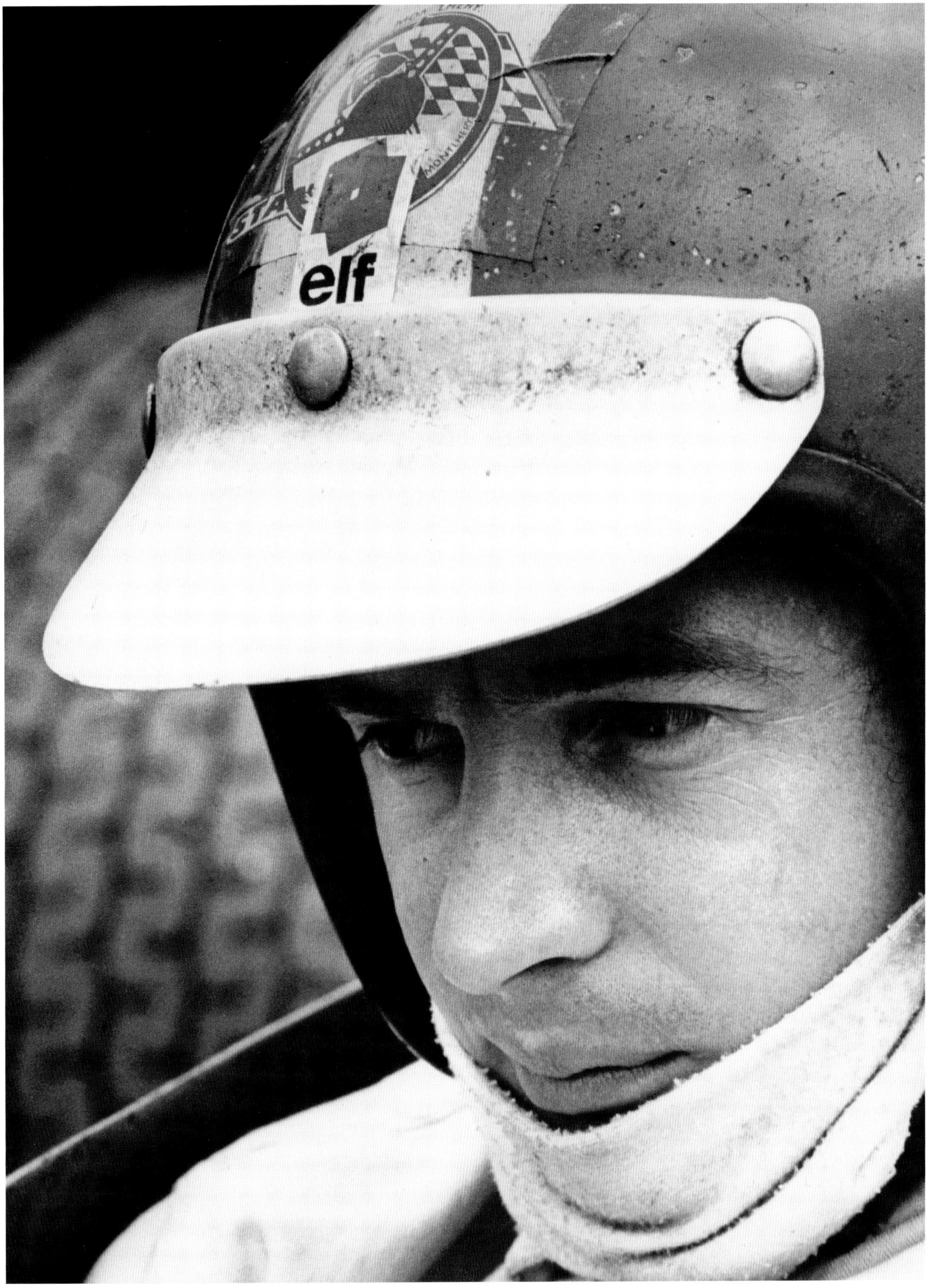
elf

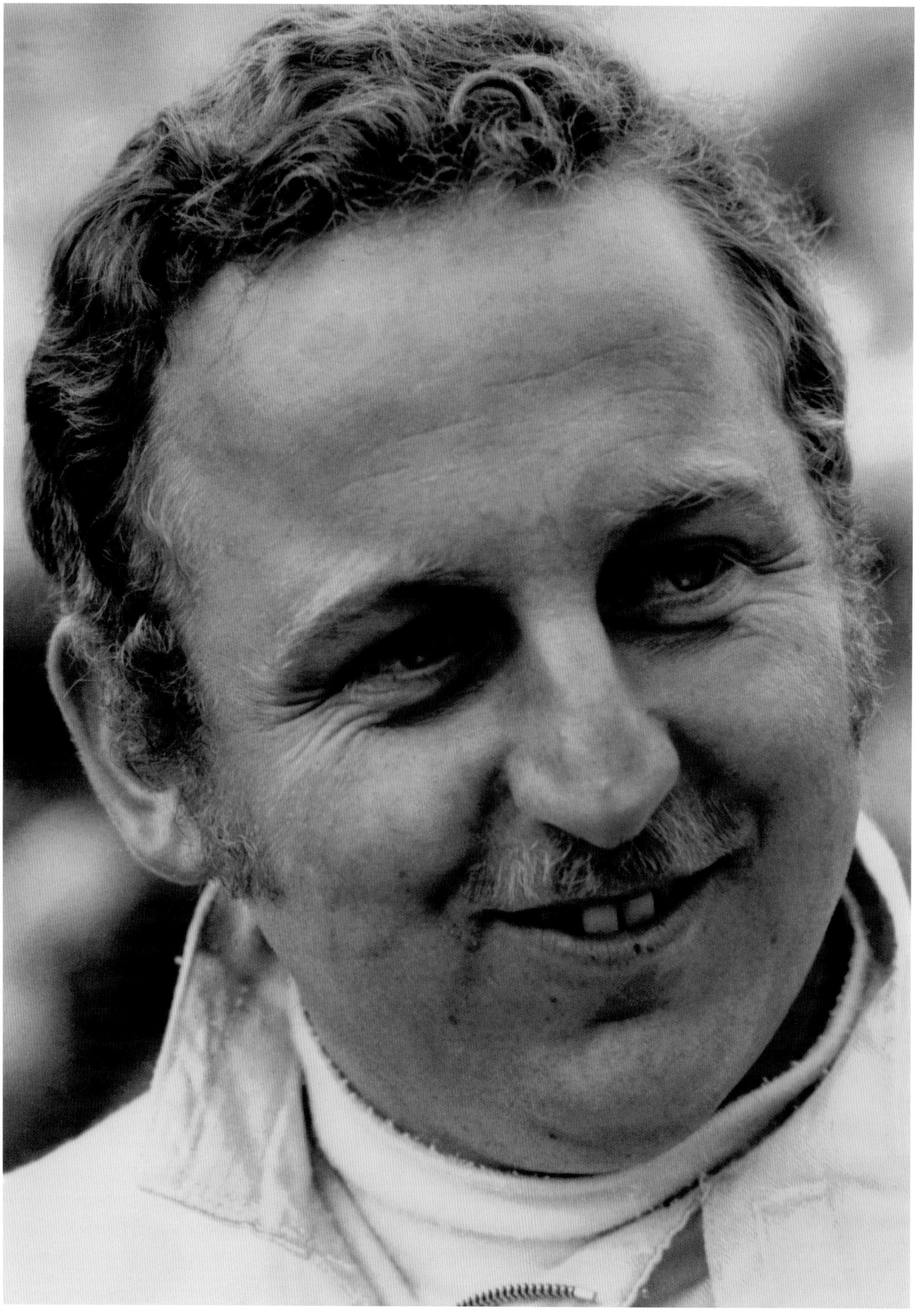

Kurt Ahrens *1940

▶ The single-seater career of Kurt Ahrens Jr, which lasted from 1958 until 1968, can be summed up in a nutshell: excellent results in the minor formulas, Junior, 3 and 2, with just one GP in a 'real' F1 car, the 1968 German Grand Prix at the Nürburgring, in the third Brabham in atrocious weather conditions. The result, against all high-flying expectations, was a poor 12th place, one lap behind winner Jackie Stewart. A bar of the rear wing of his BT24 had come loose and instead of the downforce so urgently needed, it had produced lift.

Ahrens was a ray of hope on the German motor sport scene of the sixties, though of rather limited popularity. An avowed family man, his modesty was proverbial and he hated all the ballyhoo that surrounded him. Like his father, who was also a well-known racer, he earned his bread and butter from a Braunschweig scrap-metal business, smiling at the attempts of the media to apply a linguistic upgrade to this modest source of income.

Kurt was well aware of the dangers of racing, but for many years, he tried to play them down, including his almighty aquaplaning crash at a horrendous 250km/h while evaluating a Porsche 917, in April, 1970, on the VW testing grounds at Ehra-Lessien. The Porsche was torn to smithereens by the Armco barriers, but a whole army of alert guardian angels seemed to take care of Ahrens himself.

The Ehra-Lessien miracle, Jim Clark's death at Hockenheim on 7th April, 1968, and all those other racing victims of the sixties were nails in the coffin of Kurt Ahrens' ambition. He had never been an extremist, anyway, blinkered to the world beyond his sport. In 1970, he said enough, like his good friend, Hans Herrmann, who had hung up his helmet after his Le Mans victory in that year. For some time, Herrmann had implored him, "Kurt, leave it. It is only a matter of time before it will be your turn."

Survive he did, and it's a pleasure to listen to him when he reaches into his treasure trove of juicy anecdotes.

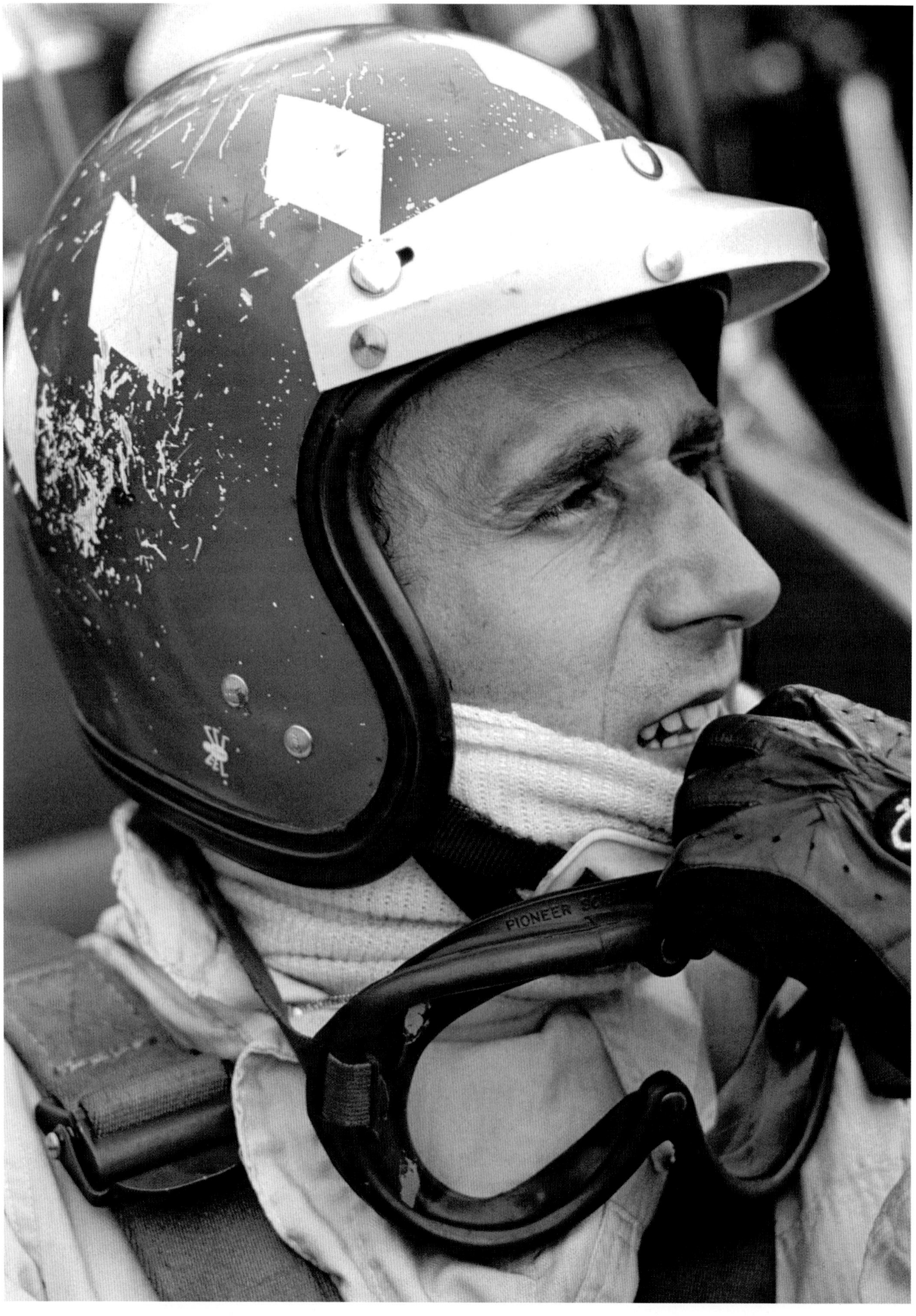
PIONEER

Silvio Moser   * 1941 – † 1974

▶ Swiss drivers have always been a rare breed in Formula 1, not least because the westernmost of the two alpine republics has dealt restrictively with motor sport ever since the black day of Le Mans in 1955, banning, for instance, all forms of circuit racing. The two Grands Prix de Suisse in 1975 and '82 were summarily exiled to the Circuit de Dijon-Prenois, in neighbouring Burgundy, France.

Only Jo Siffert (fourth in 1971) and Clay Regazzoni (third in 1970, second in 1974) managed to come within reach of the title. Their compatriot, Silvio Moser, however, had to content himself with the less attractive status of an also-ran. So, while the two superstars proudly sported the Swiss cross on their helmets and in their hearts, the little man from Lugano professed to racing instead for his home canton of Ticino, in whose blue-and-red colours his cars were painted. He boldly dreamt of establishing them among the familiar colour schemes of Formula 1.

Moser was a maniac, the world and its racetracks the playgrounds where he could give vent to his insatiable need for speed, frittering away his energies and means in the process. An early highlight: In March, 1964, he and his Brabham BT6 returned from the Temporada Argentina with wins in all four races, two of them in Buenos Aires, one each at Rosario and Córdoba.

He drove hillclimbs and circuit races, in saloons as well as in sports cars and single-seaters, but his Formula 1 career was frustrating. In only four of his 12 grands prix did he see the chequered flag, partly due to the exotic vehicles he opted for, such as a Cooper T77-ATS in 1967, and a Bellasi in 1970 and '71, a Swiss F1 project that was destined to founder from the outset.

Silvio Moser's restless, but happy life ended on 26th May, 1974. Four weeks earlier, on lap 144 of the Monza 1,000km, the suspension of his Lola had collapsed at the Ascari chicane, pitching the car into the March of a competitor, which had been parked there.

One of those racing incidents…

Piers Courage *1942 – †1970

▶ Courage came from the well-known beer-brewing dynasty, while racing-stable owner Rob Walker was a descendent of the renowned whisky empire, but neither was keen on the respective malt beverages. Walker once even told the author that never in his life had a drop of the stuff passed his lips.

There was also no parental assistance worth mentioning, with the possible exception of the Lotus Seven that dad Richard Courage had treated his son to at a young age, which was dropped off at the door in kit form, to be happily assembled in the garage. Piers earned his spurs in the mid-sixties as one of the wild Formula 3 mob who painted exotic places like Chimay, Opatija, Bauzen, Cascais and Cognac red – sometimes literally.

There was ample opportunity to do so. In 1965, for instance, the European F3 calendar comprised a hefty 82 events. It goes without saying that all of these racing nomads were world champions in the making. Mishaps would befall the others; immortality was part and parcel of the privilege of being so wonderfully young. Most of them were as poor as church mice.

Among the hardcore, swept along with immensely popular former Eton pupil Piers Courage were Charles Lucas and the two Williamses, Jonathan and Frank. In Frank's immaculately prepared Brabhams, Courage snatched his most cherished successes, first in F2, then with second places in the 1969 Monaco and United States Grands Prix in Formula 1. In 1970, Williams had entered his pal Piers in the De Tomaso 505, built by Dallara. The car was initially uncompetitive, but by Zandvoort he had qualified in middle of the field. In the race Piers was running in seventh place before disaster struck. A plume of smoke signalled a major accident out on the circuit where Courage was trapped beneath his burning car and beyond help.

Williams would never get over his death.

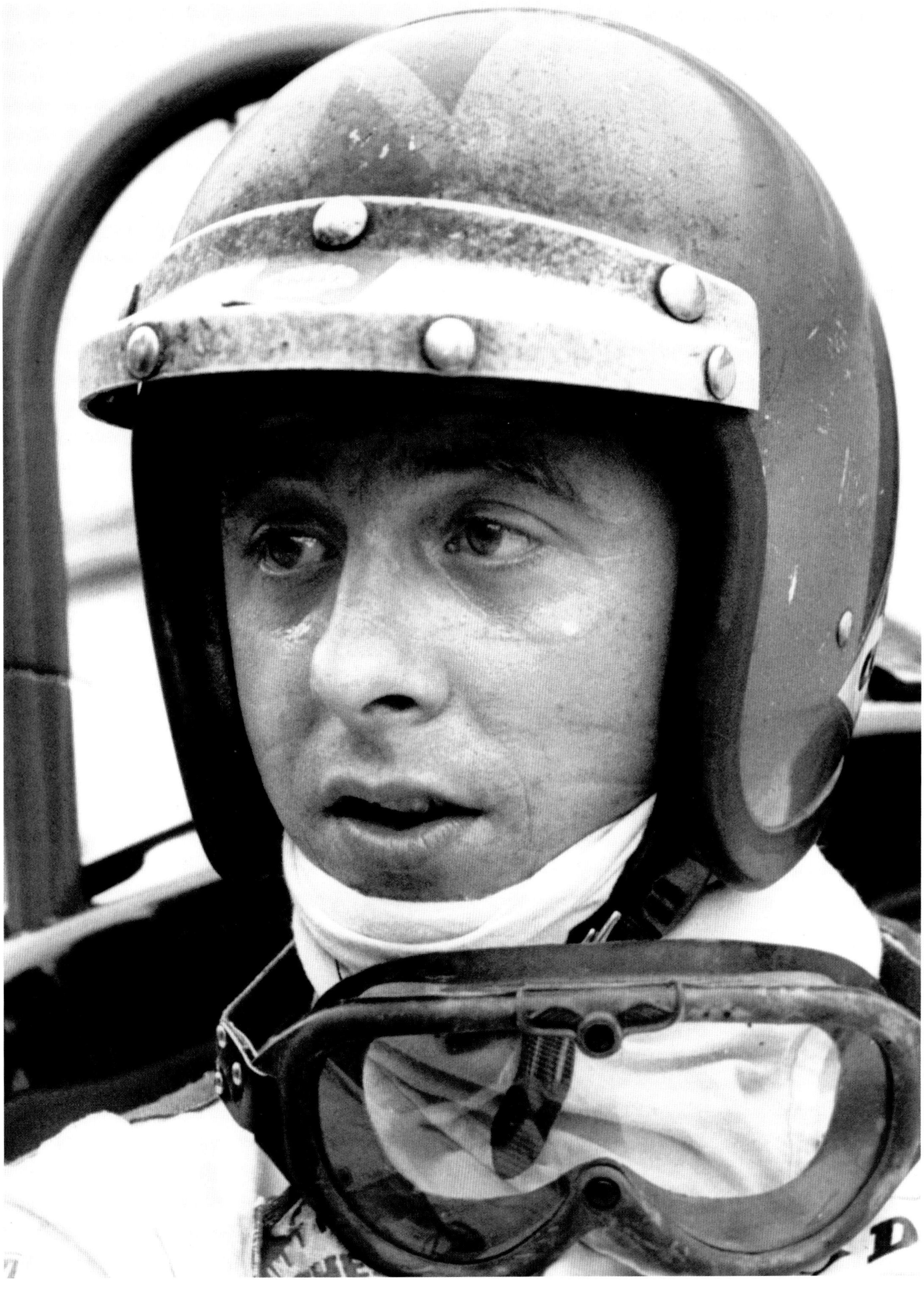

Jacky Ickx *1945

▶ In 1967, the second year of the 3-litre formula, fully-fledged Formula 1 cars were still somewhat of a rarity. On the 22.8km length of the Nürburgring, they would almost become lost, with only 17 of them competing.

That's why the organising Automobilclub von Deutschland, as in the preceding year, filled the sparse field of GP single-seaters with Formula 2 cars. On the starting grid, though, they had to line up in a second group behind the big ones. Young Belgian hero Jacky Ickx had achieved the third best practice time of them all in Ken Tyrrell's blue Matra MS7, a midget compared to, for instance, Jackie Stewart's BRM P115 H16. During lap six of the GP, Ickx appeared in fourth position. Then something broke.

To be quick on the Nordschleife in those years, you had to really make large jumps, 15 or so, some of them as much as 10m. Not only the pundits scented a sensation, a Mozart behind the wheel. That's where Ickx readily voices dissent. That notion was grossly misleading, he says, easy to see through. He had been in the right vehicle, in the right place, at the right time: "The Matra was so much lighter and nimbler than the F1 cars. And I knew the Ring like the back of my hand, from lots of private laps, as well as two 1,000km races and the German Grand Prix the year before."

Indeed, he had competed in the 1966 Grosser Preis, in the F2 division as well, driving the Matra MS5 of rugged British timber merchant Ken Tyrrell, retiring on lap one at Flugplatz after a collision with Briton John Taylor. What Ickx doesn't mention: Taylor suffered severe burns in the accident and died four weeks later. Jacky avoids talking about death, even though, or despite the fact, the Grim Reaper was his constant companion throughout his 32 years in motor sport.

Nevertheless, that Ring race in 1967 was a key event in his career and, he muses, "As a pupil, I kept dreaming out of the window. I didn't have the slightest inkling where to go. But from then onwards, I knew what destiny held in store for me."

And that was a lot, as we know.

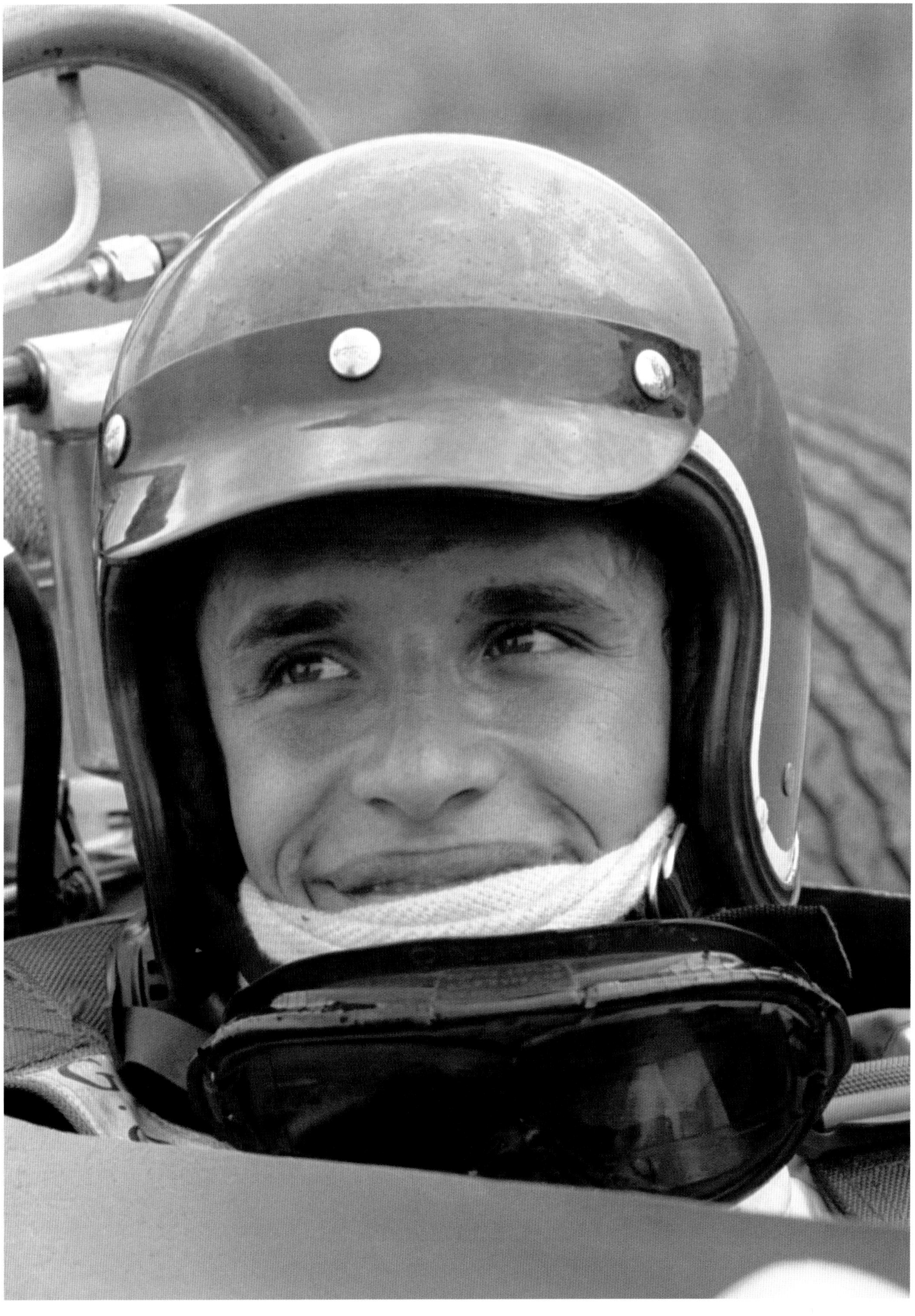

Johnny Servoz-Gavin

* 1942 – † 2006

▶ One man's meat is another man's poison. While Jochen Rindt, over the moon with his last-second victory at the 1970 Monaco Grand Prix, raised another bottle of beer to his lips in the famous Tip Top bar, following a time-honoured tradition of the house, one of his racing colleagues, aboard a yacht down in the Principality's harbour, announced that he would never again touch the steering wheel of a racing car. That was Georges Servoz-Gavin, universally known as 'Johnny' or just 'Servoz', and he was as good as his word.

The lightning career of the young Frenchman, just a dozen GPs old, somehow had taken a novelistic course, with an exciting entry, a dramatic turning point and then a finale with restitution of the established order. His spectacular start was a slot in the first row of the 1968 Grand Prix de Monaco, next to Graham Hill. It was his debut in racing's top tier. He led for three laps before damaging his Matra's suspension at the Chicane.

Superstar Jackie Stewart had injured his left wrist during an F2 race at Jarama in April. His boss, Ken Tyrrell, known for his fine instinct for slumbering talent, had accosted Servoz. Was he prepared to stand in for the Scot? Johnny never hesitated.

It all went wrong, however, most probably due to an incident in the winter of 1969/70. During a wild ride into the forest with an off-road vehicle, a branch hit him in the right eye. His peripheral vision, indispensable for a racing driver, was affected permanently.

For the GP year 1970, Tyrrell opted for the type 701 of new manufacturer March. Jackie Stewart and others demonstrated what was possible with the somewhat staid vehicle, but Servoz had lost his panache, even failing to qualify at Monaco. He didn't worry, though. As a character not unlike James Hunt, he returned to the good and sweet life he had led before racing took over, an avid sailor, polygamous darling of the Côte girls and, for quite a time, still a topic of debate in the tabloids.

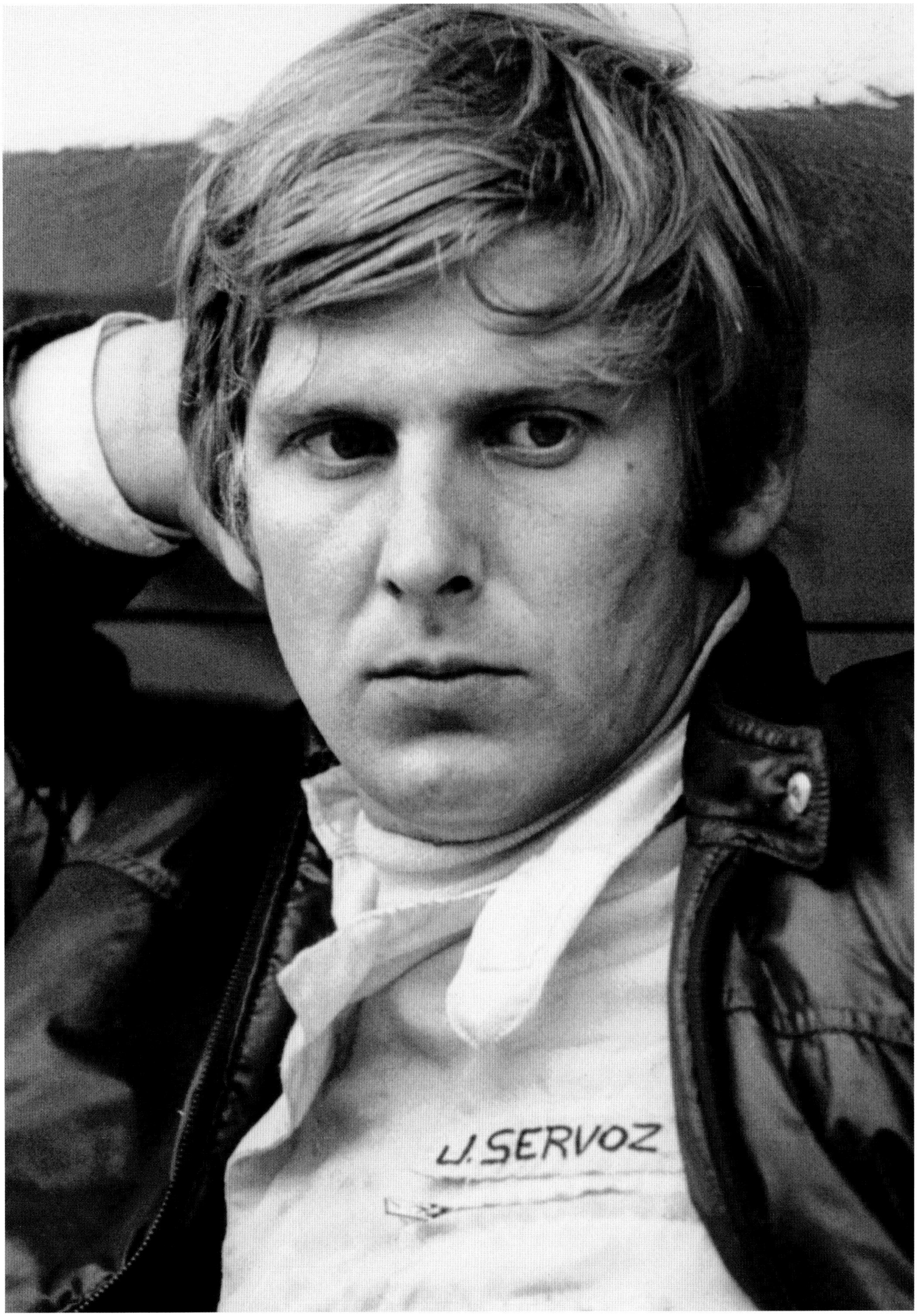
J.SERVOZ

David Hobbs *1939

▶ In the mid-sixties his "nom de guerre" was "The Brands Hatch Dicer" – the latest of the late brakers.

People knew what they were talking about. Particularly from the upper parts of the Kentish racetrack, one enjoys a splendid view of the entire kidney-shaped Brands Hatch Indy Circuit, and an enthusiastic crowd used to celebrate the bold actions of young David Hobbs.

Later, four things happened. 'The Dicer' morphed into 'Hobbo'. David smoothed away all drama from his driving style, an asset whenever arriving safely and reliably was at stake. For more than 30 years, he practised motor racing like a real profession, and did so all over the world in a plethora of vehicles, between Formula Junior and F1, NASCAR, Indy and CanAm, with titles in Formula A and TransAm to his credit. He drove 20 times at Le Mans and was part of the Championship of Makes human inventory for many years.

Never, by his own assessment, did he reach his potential in Formula 1, with seven starts between 1967 and '74. His modest best was seventh in the 1974 Austrian GP, driving a McLaren M23, when subbing for his mate, Mike Hailwood, who had injured himself severely at the Nürburgring that year. Standing in for somebody else, that's what 'Hobbo' often did.

In spite of an affinity for the limits, somehow he escaped major accidents. Apart from one. In his second race, at Oulton Park in 1959, aboard his father's Jaguar XK140 Drophead Coupé, he rolled on his last lap. When he rang his dad to inform him of the mishap, Hobbs Sr retorted, "I know, I saw it on TV. You broke it, you fix it."

David loves to tell this story, and his native English sometimes lapses into the unmistakable accent of his adopted home in Milwaukee. Together with his wife, Margaret, he has lived in the USA for 30 years now, enjoying life in his fine, rather British house overlooking Lake Michigan. Even more famous than 'Hobbo', the racer, he became David Hobbs, the TV commentator, not least because of his poignant comments regarding Formula 1.

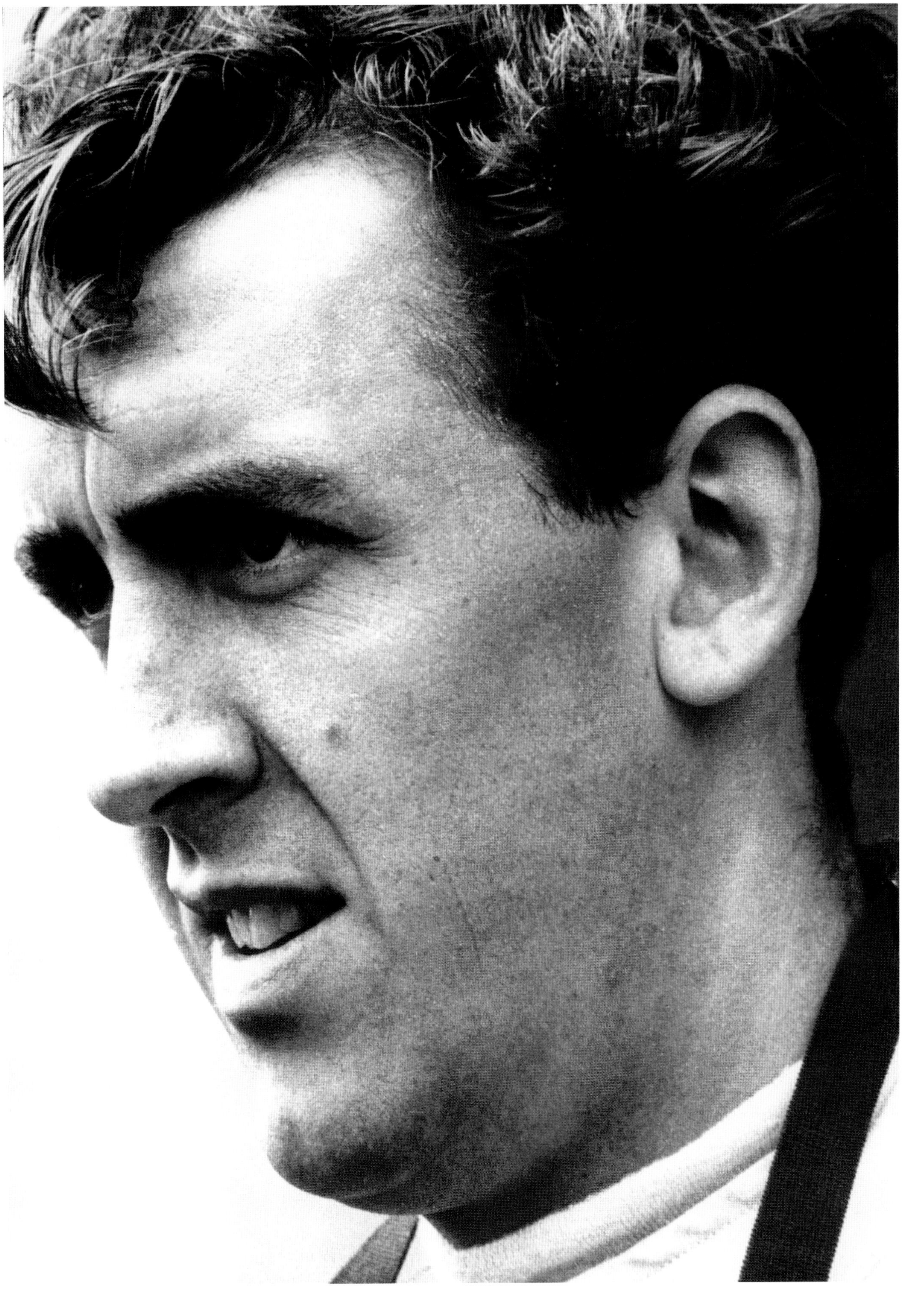

Jackie Oliver * 1942

▶ Jackie Oliver often likes to suggest that he is 'The Nearly Man'. Also, that he has always been convinced of his invulnerability, a 20th-century Siegfried, as it were, without the violable spot between his shoulders.

The second statement is definitely not in keeping with racing's reality, which demonstrably does not ensure that body and soul are bulletproof. When on the first lap of his very first GP, at Monaco in 1968, he shot out of the darkness of the tunnel into the bright daylight only to be confronted by Bruce McLaren's crippled McLaren, which had just lost a wheel against the Armco barrier, and Ludovico Scarfiotti's Cooper, slewing sideways to avoid the stricken car. Attempting to escape into a non-existent space, he lost two wheels of his Lotus 49, along with the frail benevolence of his new boss, Colin Chapman, who was not particularly known for the justness of his verdicts.

During practice for his fourth grand prix, at Rouen in the same year, the Lotus was torn in two after its delicate head-high rear wing collapsed. A bit shaken, but unhurt, Oliver gave interviews at the scene. In 1970, a collision between his BRM and the Ferrari of Ickx at Jarama triggered a fiery inferno. Oliver lifted himself, unhurt, from the fully-fuelled car.

His first insight is a fine example of British understatement, enriched with a hint of coquetry, unless you concur with the absolutist claim of many Formula 1 drivers that you have only reached your goal when you virtually annihilate all the others, like 'Schumi', the early Vettel or Lewis Hamilton. Certainly Oliver's 49 GP starts did not yield a single win, let alone the title. The same applies to the 382 races of the Arrows outfit that he called into being in 1982, ran for 21 years and then sold profitably, making him a wealthy man.

But anyone who, like Jackie Oliver, has won the prestigious CanAm series (1974), Le Mans (1969) and numerous 1,000km races, has certainly left his tyre tracks on the history of this sport.

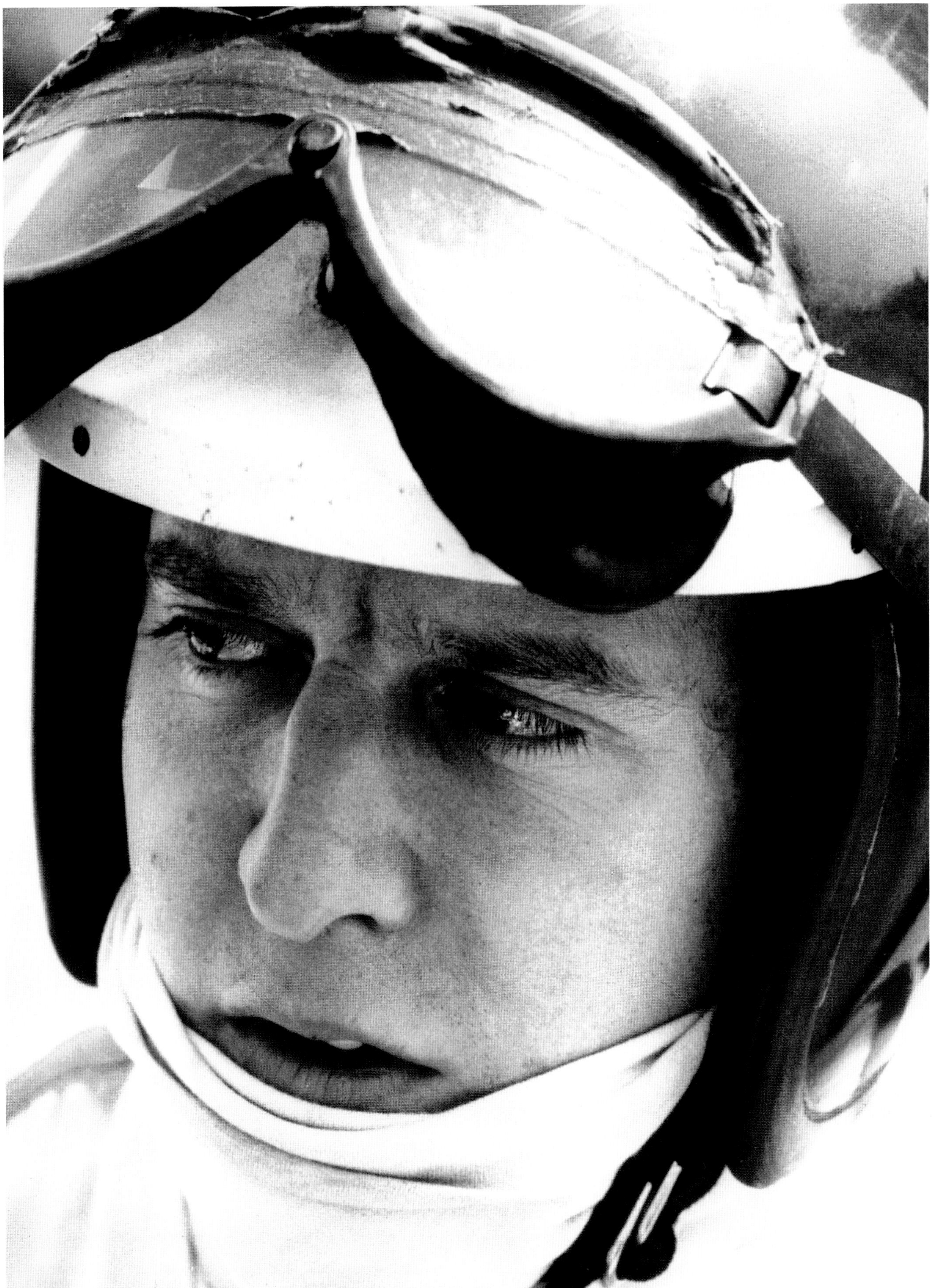

Brian Redman * 1937

▶ As is well known, modesty is not part of the basic psychological make-up of the grand prix driver. If there were a title for it, though, Brian Redman would certainly be the winner.

If you ask him why he became a racer, he will answer that that was all he knew how to do. Apart, perhaps, from delivering the products of his grandfather's mop business at high speeds to customers all over England in his Morris Minor Traveller estate car. He will shrug his shoulders apologetically if anyone reminds him that, in the Porsche 917 of John Wyer's famous sports car squad, he was often quicker than his more renowned team-mates, Jo Siffert and Pedro Rodrìguez.

Following his fifth place at Monaco in 1972, about halfway through his short and rather unspectacular career in Formula 1, he told me that, regrettably, he was not of the material from which great champions are made. Rather casually, I had asked him to outline his ambitions in motor racing's top tier. The pundits strongly disagree in that respect, confirmed by his three championships in North American F5000. In sports cars, he was world class, but he certainly knew how to handle a single-seater, as well.

He also didn't like all the hype and hullabaloo surrounding Formula 1. Redman drove for the fun of driving, not unlike his friends, David Hobbs and Derek Bell, who, like Brian himself, have long since set up home in the more beautiful parts of the United States, rather than in Britain. The premier league of this sport had welcomed him rather gruffly, though. In only his second GP, at Spa in 1968, Redman had almost lost an arm when a suspension element broke on braking for the fast Les Combes left-hander, his Cooper hitting the parked car of a marshal and exploding in flames.

Spa would be a trauma for him as well as a venue of triumph. On the triangle of ultra-fast country roads, Brian Redman grabbed four of his 21 victories in world championship sports car races – also victories over his anguish and sleepless nights.

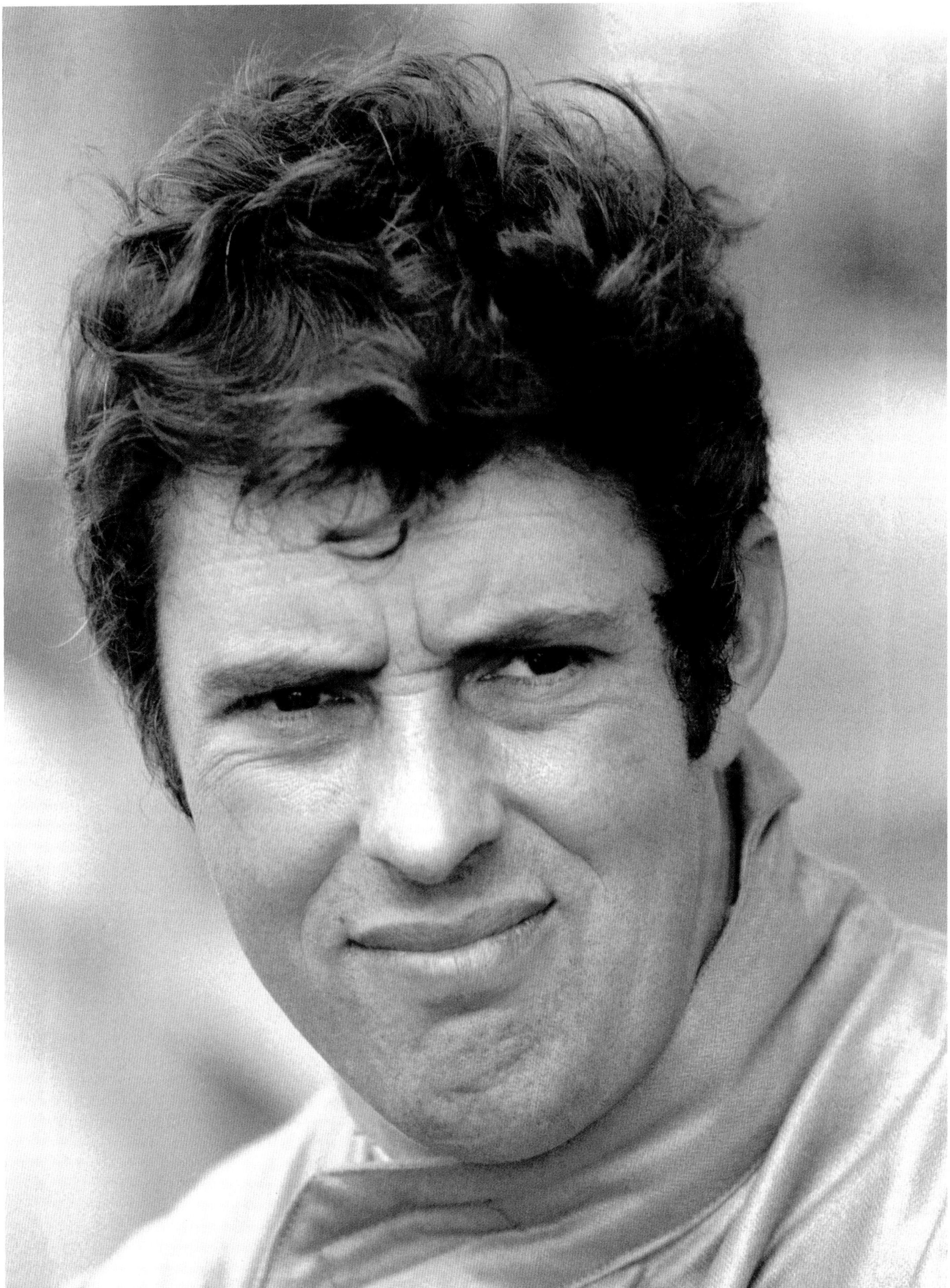

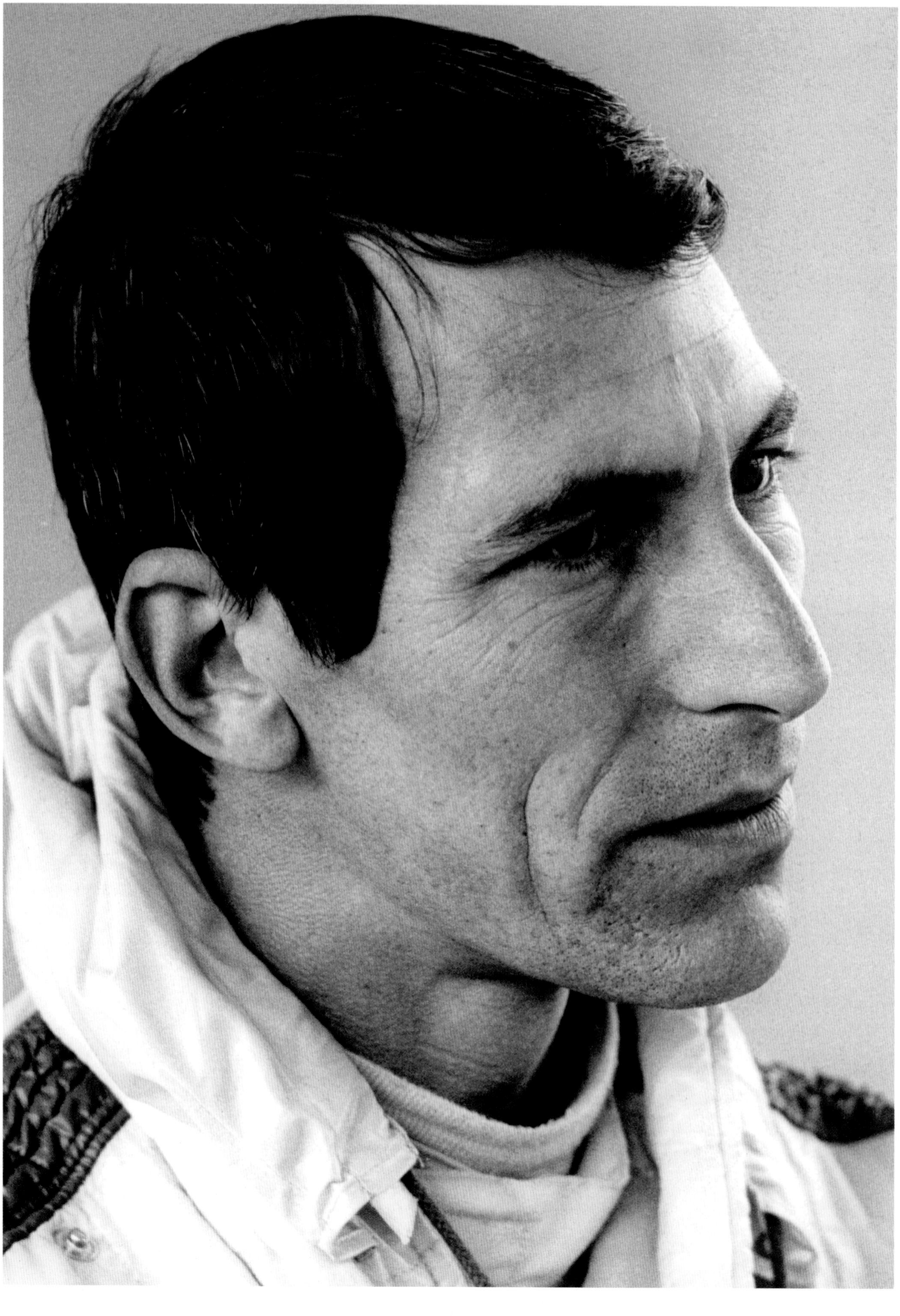

Vic Elford

*1935 – †2022

▶ They called him 'Quick Vic', but not just for the sake of the rhyme. Vic Elford was indeed ultra-fast, in all the motor racing categories in which he chose to drive, a jack-of-all-trades in what was a calling, rather than a profession. And, as betrayed by his name, a winner as well. Victories eluded him only in his 13 GP starts, a fourth place in his very first grand prix, in July, 1968, at Rouen, being his best result, on a circuit that was awash.

An excerpt from his racing diary in the first five months of that year says everything about Vic's phenomenal versatility: 26th January: deserved and highly-acclaimed win at the 37th edition of the Monte Carlo Rally in a Porsche 911 T. Nobody can hold a candle to Vic Elford, especially on the icy mountain sections.

4th February: Elford and a collective of four other drivers win the Daytona 24 Hours in a Porsche 907, five laps ahead of their team-mates in second place. The lion's share at the wheel is done by Vic. Until then, he has never seen the International Speedway. Long classified as a rally specialist, he had driven his first big international motor race nine months previously in the shape of the Targa Florio.

5th May: first at the Targa Florio, winning by almost three minutes. Initially, Elford loses a precious 16 minutes when his Porsche 907 limps back to the pits, hampered by a loose wheel and a puncture. But then the Londoner barrels through the Madonie roller coaster as though in a trance to catch up, annihilating the lap record.

A couple of days before the Grand Prix de France, on 7th July, John Cooper calls him. It will not have escaped Elford, he says, that the new boy in the team, Brian Redman, had had a huge accident at Spa. Is Vic ready to stand in, for £200? Although a pittance by today's standards, Elford agrees, revels in the atrocious conditions and even manoeuvres the unwieldy Cooper-BRM into the vicinity of a podium place.

There might have been more to his F1 career, say the experts.

Derek Bell * 1941

▶ Aged 80, and on the home straight of a rich and fulfilling life, you definitely have the right to repeat yourself. Derek Bell likes to make use of that privilege, not least at his many public appearances as an immensely popular ambassador of his sport. "What I have experienced," he will say in a humorous little speech, "was a wonderful mixture of hobby, career and business all rolled into one. I've travelled the world, met interesting people, driven wonderful cars, and have been paid decently to boot. Haven't I been lucky?" Time has shot by unbelievably quickly, he muses, addressing himself and his audience. It seems like only yesterday when he was setting out, full of optimism, to forge a grand prix career, and now he is standing in front of them, owing most of his success to two-seaters, predominantly in long-distance races.

Of course, his listeners know that. Derek's five Le Mans victories in 1975, '81, '82, '86 and '87, three firsts at Daytona Beach in 1986, '87 and '89, and two World Sports Car Championships in 1985 and '86 are common knowledge for a racing aficionado.

But something went wrong all the same, in spite of good results in F3 and F2, or the 'staircase of talent', as Jackie Stewart puts it. Formula 1 had been Bell's goal, after all. An interlude at Ferrari, between 1968 and the summer of 1969, failed to bear fruit, and somehow his GP career never got going, with just one point in nine starts until 1974.

Today, being long regarded as a living legend, he doesn't seem to mind, a contrast to the searing heat of ambition in his early years. It's fun to read about all that in his autobiography, *My Racing Life*, a delightfully colourful account of a colourful CV, which flew by far too quickly.

The cosmopolitan with the amicable, hawk-like face still doesn't contemplate a leisurely pensioner's life. Most of the time, he lives in Florida, spending his summers in his idyllic home on the English south coast.

But that's only a small detail from his agenda.

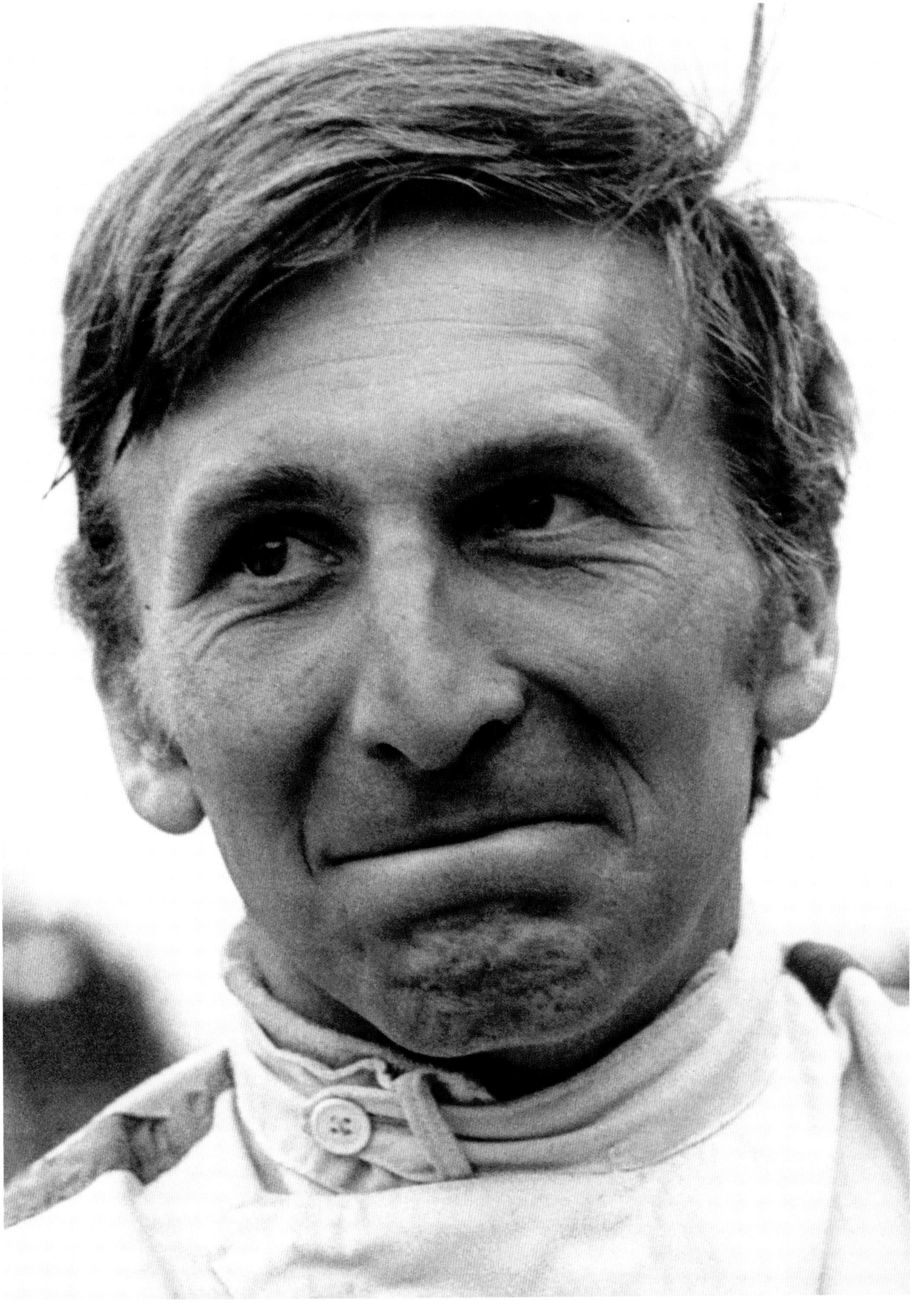

Henri Pescarolo * 1942

▶ The green helmet – once the central prop in the eponymous racing movie from 1961. It became famous in real life as the truly bilious-green head protection of bearded Frenchman Henri Pescarolo. In 1967, racing in F3, he had grabbed the title of his country, victories in ten of the 58 European races and, above all, the blue-riband event at Monaco, driving the swift and nimble little Matra MS5.

A win in the Principality used to be the equivalent of a free ticket to Formula 1. And indeed, Pescarolo sat in the screaming 12-cylinder MS11 of the state-owned French company in 1968. But the anticipated glory escaped him, apart from a poor dozen points between 1968 and '76, a third in the 1970 Monaco GP and fastest lap in the epic slipstreaming drama of the Gran Premio d'Italia a year later as minor consolation. To 'Pesca's' mind, he had fallen incomprehensibly from the grace of Matra boss Jean-Luc Lagardère, who had employed Chris Amon in Henri's stead to lead the team in 1971, alongside Jean-Pierre Beltoise. That had been like murder, he grumbled.

He made up for his F1 deficit elsewhere, unswerving in his quest to cover ever more distance in ever decreasing time, establishing a couple of records in the process. Henri Pescarolo at the wheel: four firsts in 33 Le Mans starts, 22 races won in the World Sports Car Championship and its variants, participation in the 1976 Bandana Rally in the Ivory Coast jungle, then the Chamonix 24 Hours ice race a year later. Again and again, he plunged into the desert marathon of the Paris-Dakar. Twice, his own team, Pescarolo Sports (2000–13) came close to winning Le Mans, but it was not to be.

Besides all that, Pescarolo set a Paris–London best flying a microlight aircraft, and also a New York–Paris best aboard a single-engine plane. Additionally, he circumnavigated the globe as a member of the crew flying a venerable Lockheed 18 Lodestar, taking fewer than 89 hours.

These are just excerpts from an existence that eschewed rest and repose.

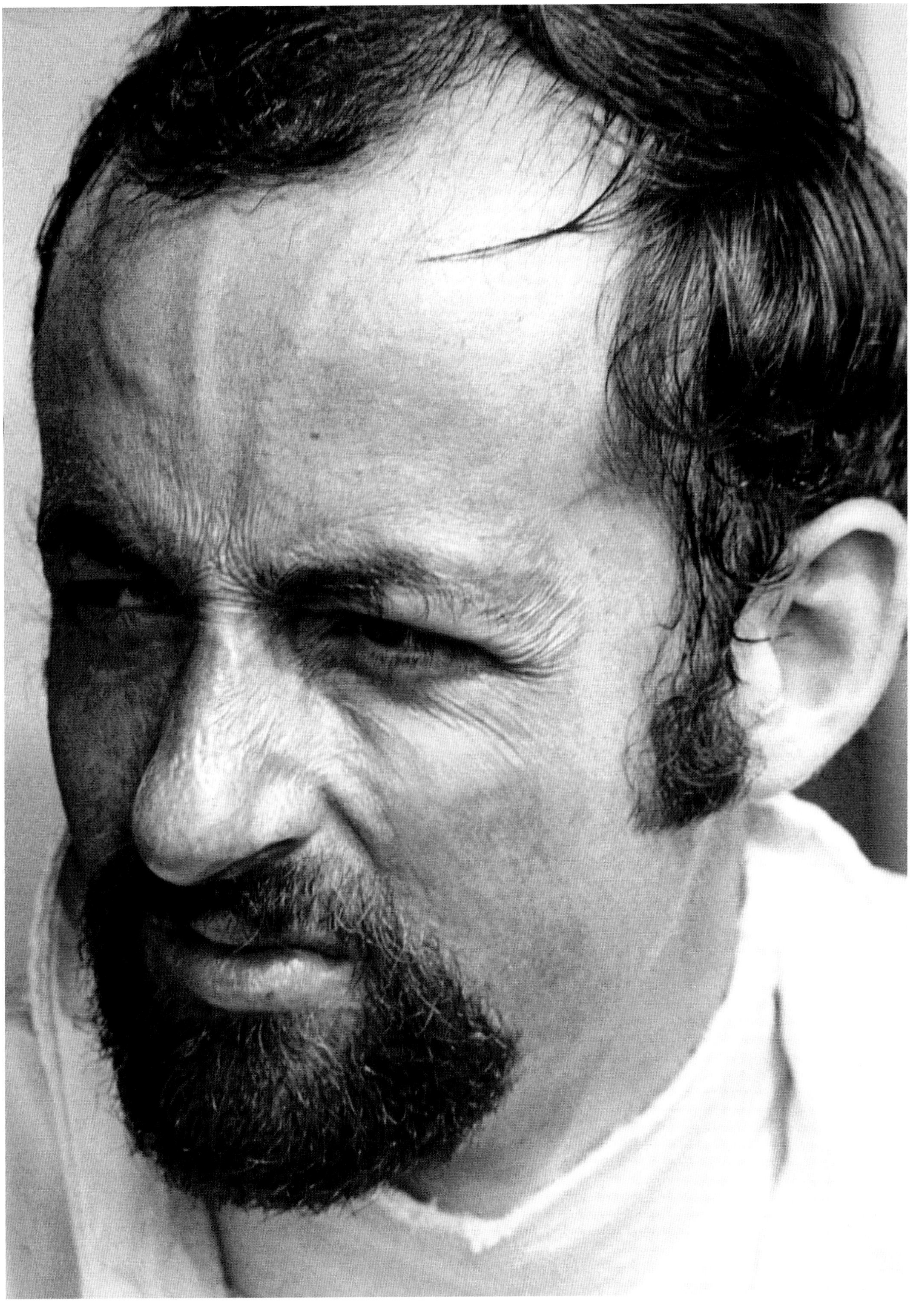

Mario Andretti * 1940

▶ Getting an autograph from Mario Andretti will almost always turn into a little gala. He will affably ask the name of the applicant, sign and add an encouraging short maxim, such as, "Always follow your dream".

This advice comes straight from the horse's mouth. Andretti has been a role model himself, with his unstoppable rise from an unknown and penniless Italian immigrant all the way to the status of a world icon of the sport. His medium to make the 'great American dream' reality was motor racing – in all its unique variety. For half a century, Mario Andretti was part and parcel of it: a winner in Formula 1, sports cars, Indycar and CanAm vehicles, on the NASCAR and IROC scenes, in Formula 5000, hill climbing into the clouds of Pikes Peak and dirt track racing, as well.

But somebody will always have a gripe. If Andretti had not dissipated his remarkable energy with that scattergun approach, they say, he could have been F1 world champion more than once, in a Lotus in 1978, and grabbed more titles in USAC and CART than just in 1965, '66, '69 and '84, as well as scoring more than just a single victory at Indy in 1969 and the Daytona 500 in 1967. But Mario couldn't care less. In 2010, he took part in a reunion of former F1 champions in Bahrain, on the occasion of the grand prix, all smiles and looking as fit as a fiddle. His doctors, he told me, had just informed him that he could do it all again, at the ripe old age of 70. And yes, he really felt like it.

He was always pleasant to talk to, even half an hour before the start, or at the Hunsrück wine festival he once visited with my friend, Jochen von Osterroth, much to the delight of the locals.

The motivation for this insatiable driver was his passion, he says, never the money. He had needed the cash to justify himself to his family and, above all, to his wife, Dee Ann, at home in Nazareth, for all the time he had been busy elsewhere around the globe and, of course, for the risks he had taken.

Happily, things turned out well, as if by magic, really.

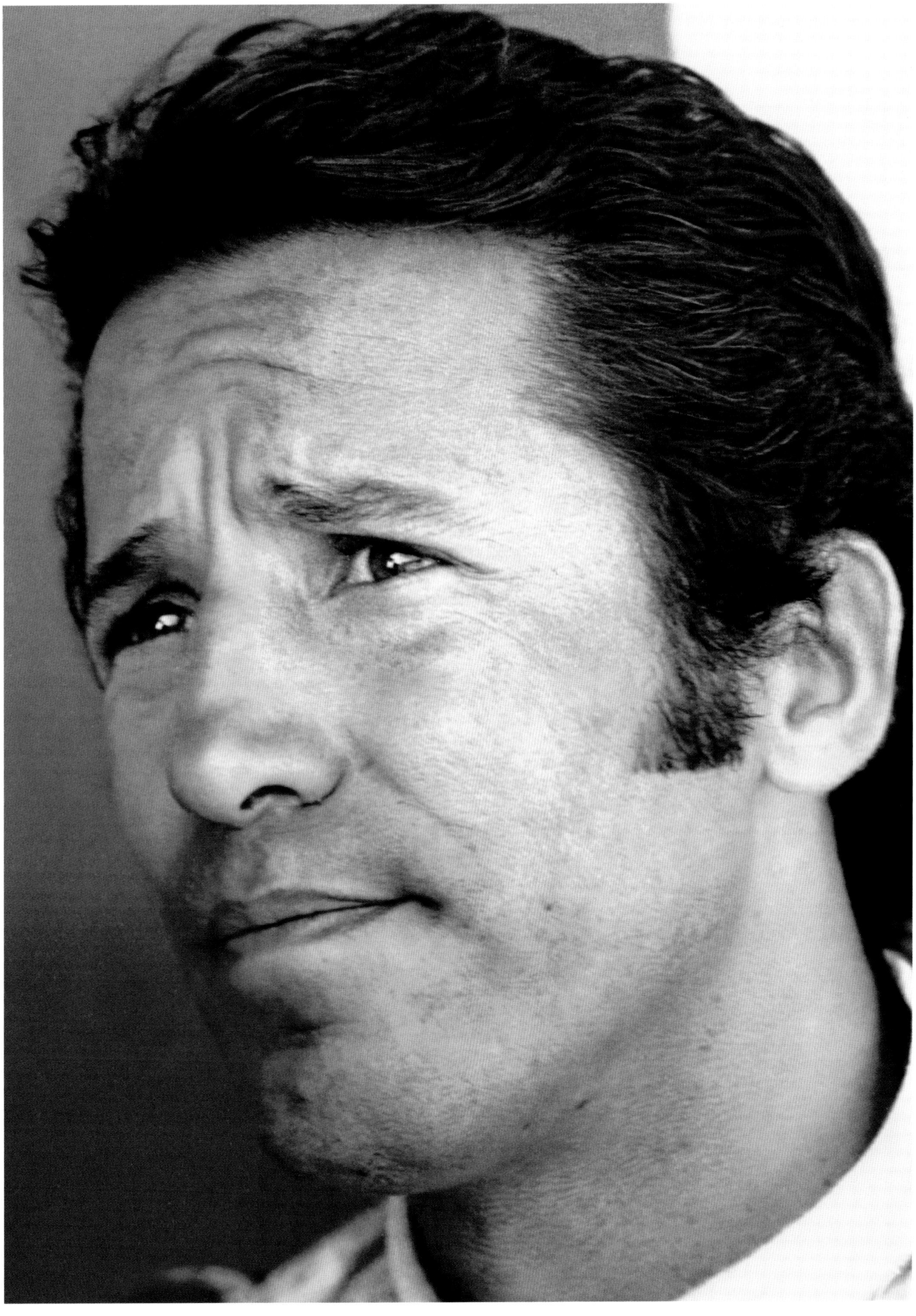

Credits

Photography: **Dr. Benno Müller/Archiv Födisch.**

Additional photography:
Grand Prix Photo (endpapers)
Chris Bayley (title page)
Paul-Henri Cahier (page 3)
Unternehmensarchiv Porsche AG (pages 10, 135, 180)
Autocourse Archive (pages 37, 82, 97, 111, 127, 131)
Peter Kurze (page 49)
Revs Institute (pages 67, 94)
Motorsport Images (page 99)
Stephen Latham (page 114)
Ulrich Schwab/Archiv Födisch (pages 148, 180)
Front cover image: Motorsport Images.
Rear cover images: Dr. Benno Müller/Archiv Födisch and Ulrich Schwab/Archiv Födisch.

Copyright: We have made every effort to trace and acknowledge copyright holders and we apologise in advance for any unintentional omission. We would be pleased to insert the appropriate acknowledgement in any subsequent edition.

FACES OF FORMULA 1/GESICHTER/DER FORMEL 1
by Hartmut Lehbrink/Jörg-Thomas Födisch
First published with German and English text
by Prova Edition in 2023
ISBN: 9783000-742729

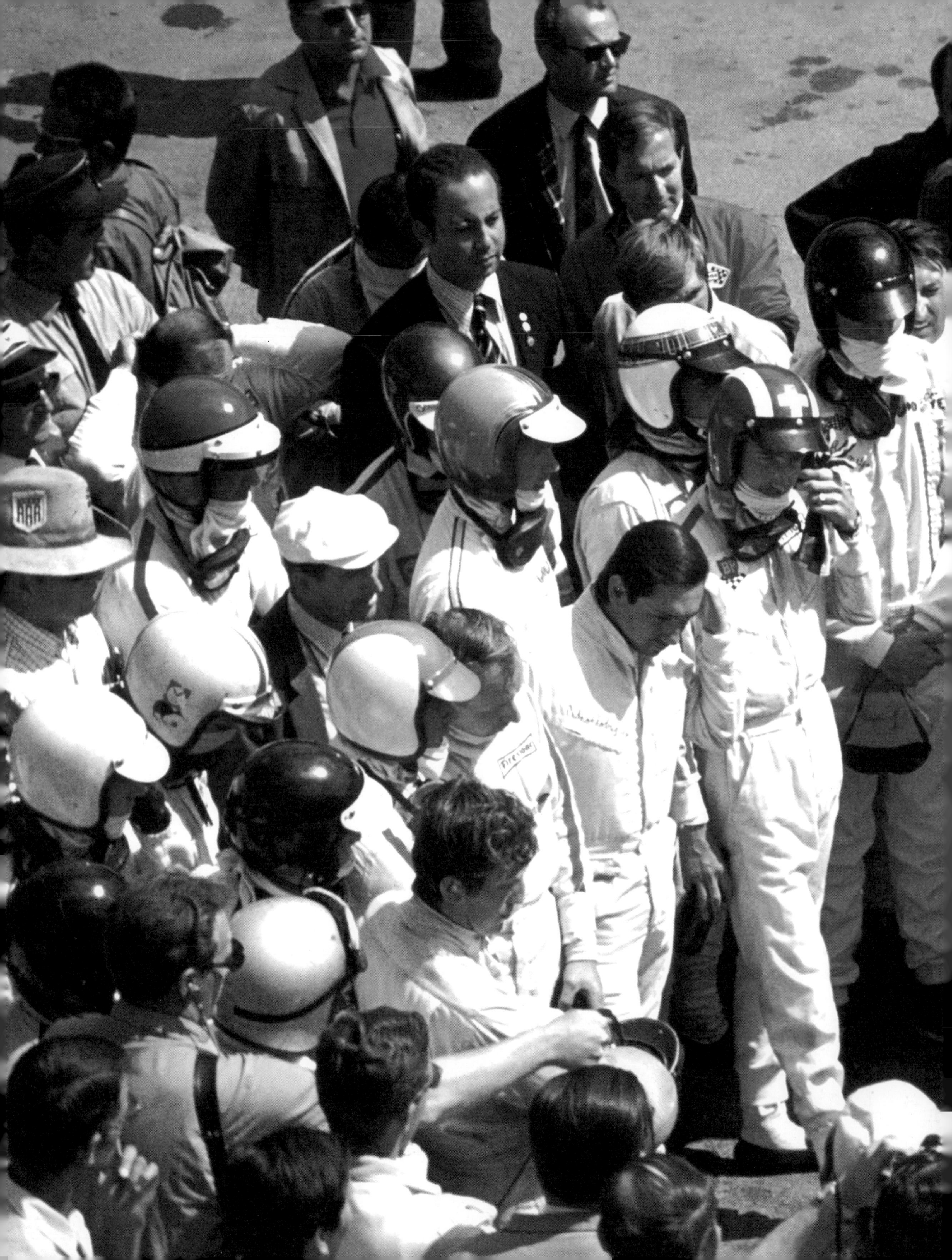
Firestone

UE

You must remember this...

Old favourites arranged for clarinet and piano

James Rae

Inhalt • Contents • Table des matières

Daisy Bell	2
As Time Goes By	4
La Paloma (The Dove)	6
Give My Regards to Broadway	8
Fascination	10
Bill Bailey, Won't You Please Come Home?	12
When Johnny Comes Marching Home	14
Over the Waves	15
Misty	18
Chicago	20
Préface	22

Preface

You Must Remember This… is a collection of ten of the world's most well-known and loved melodies arranged for clarinet and piano. They are all set in comfortable keys to enable the performer to concentrate on the melodic line. The piano accompaniments are very 'teacher friendly' and include chord symbols. The technical levels of these pieces range from easy to middle grade.

You Must Remember This… makes an ideal prequel to the well-established Universal Edition publications *Take Ten* (UE 19736) and *Take Another Ten* (UE 21169).

James Rae, June 2016

Vorwort

You Must Remember This… ist eine Zusammenstellung von zehn der beliebtesten Melodien, arrangiert für Klarinette und Klavier. Die Stücke stehen in bequemen Tonarten, um es Spielerinnen und Spielern zu ermöglichen, sich ganz auf den Melodieverlauf zu konzentrieren. Die Klavierbegleitungen sind „lehrerfreundlich" und mit Akkordsymbolen versehen. Die Stücke variieren im Schwierigkeitsgrad von leicht bis mittelschwer.

You Must Remember This… ist die ideale Fortsetzung der bekannten Universal Edition-Reihe *Take Ten* (UE 19736) und *Take Another Ten* (UE 21169).

James Rae, Juni 2016

Daisy Bell

Harry Dacre
(1857–1922)
arr. James Rae

Bright Waltz Tempo ♩ = 148

Clarinet in B♭ (concert pitch)

Piano

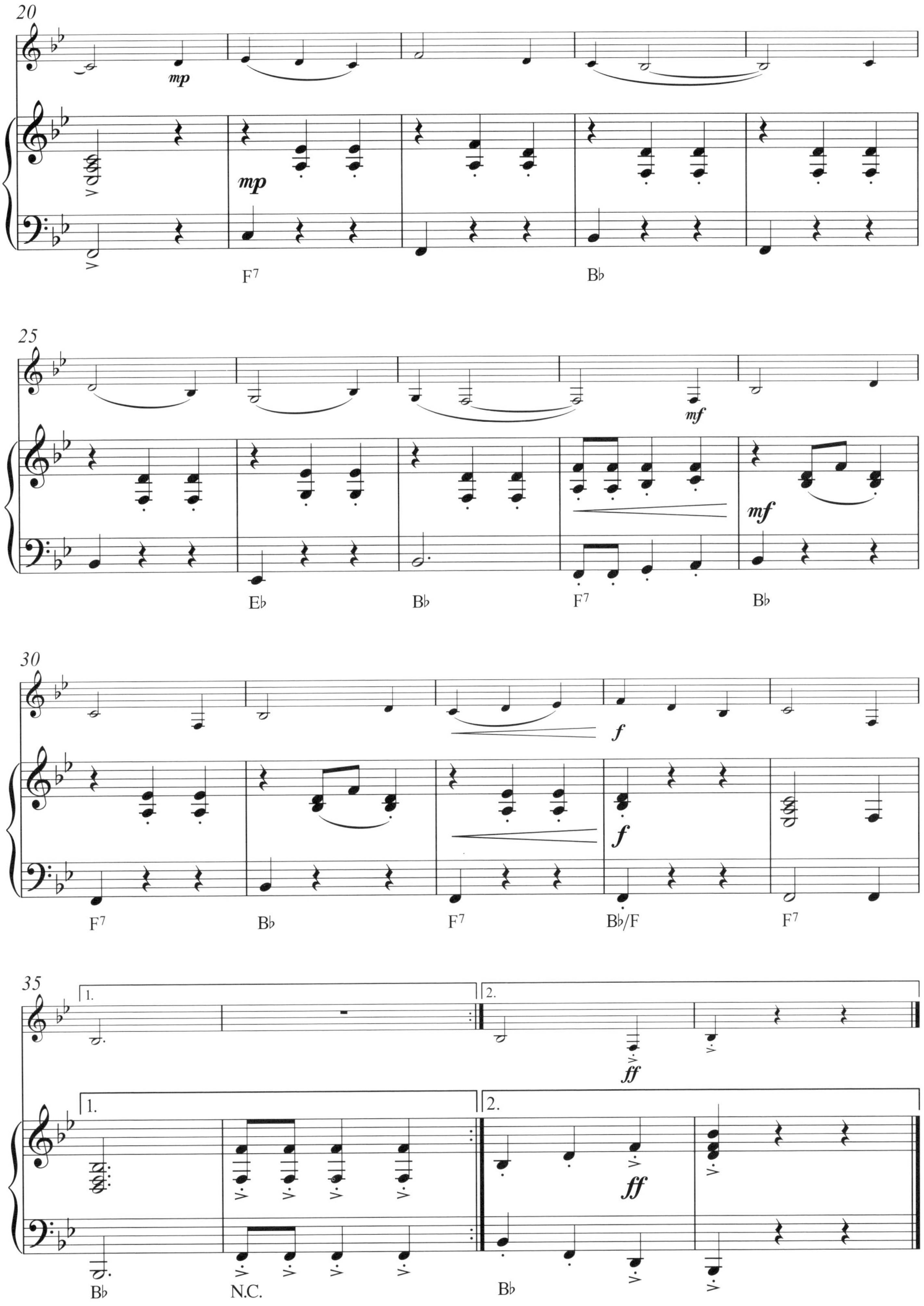
20
mp
mp
F7
B♭
25
mf
mf
E♭
B♭
F7
B♭
30
f
f
F7
B♭
F7
B♭/F
F7
35
1.
2.
ff
ff
B♭
N.C.
B♭

As Time Goes By

Herman Hupfeld
(1894–1951)
arr. James Rae

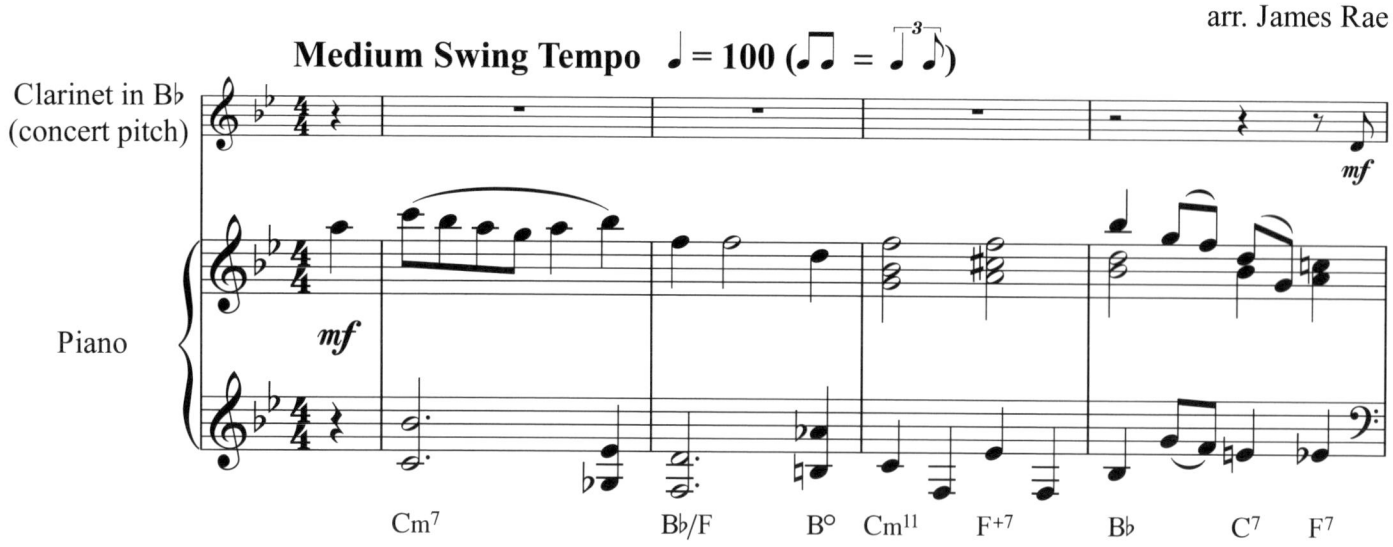

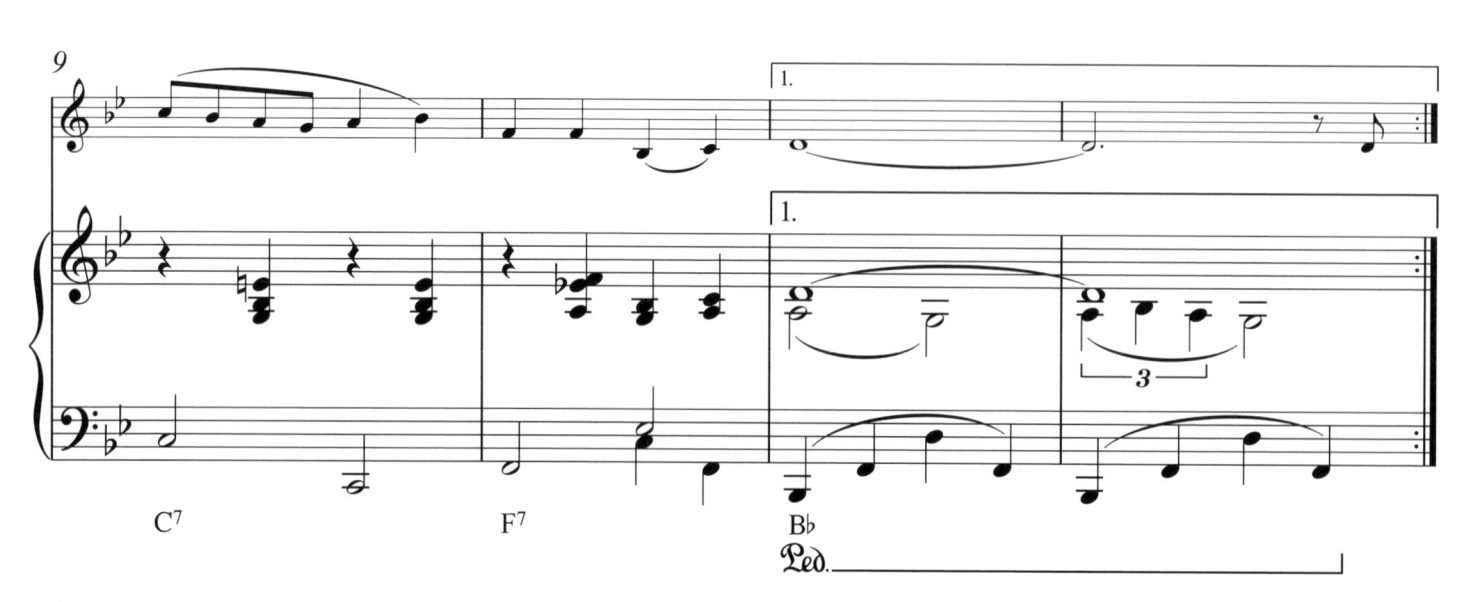

© 1931 (Renewed) Warner Bros. Inc., /Redwood Music Ltd. (100%)
All Rights Reserved – used by kind permission of REDWOOD MUSIC LTD (Carlin)
London NW1 8BD

UE 21 708

13
2.
mp
B♭ E♭ E♭m B♭ B♭7 E♭ G7 Cm
18
f
mf
E° Gm/D E♭7 C7 F7 B° F7
D.S. al Coda
Coda
23
rit.
3
C7 B♭/F B° Cm11 F7 B♭ A♭7 B♭
Ped.

La Paloma
(The Dove)

Sebastián de Yradier
(1809–1865)
arr. James Rae

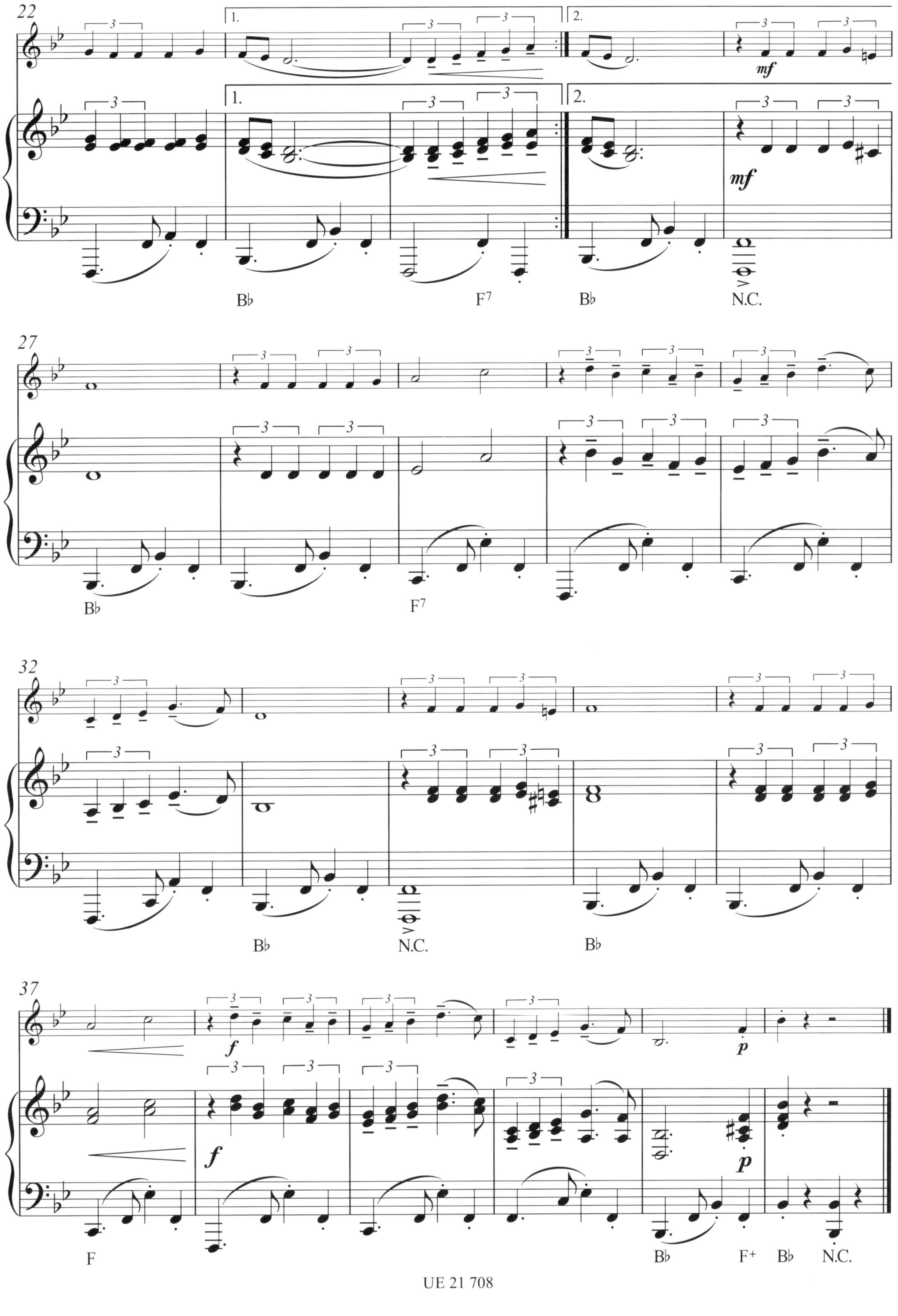
22
1.
2.
mf
B♭
F7
B♭
N.C.
27
B♭
F7
32
B♭
N.C.
B♭
37
f
p
F
B♭
F+
B♭
N.C.

Give My Regards to Broadway

George M. Cohan
(1878–1942)
arr. James Rae

21
f
mf
f
mf
Dm
G7
C7
F
26
B♭m6
C7
Gm7
C7
31
F
D7
Gm7
D7
36
ff
ff
Gm7
B♭m
F
Dm7
Gm7
C7
F

Fascination

Fermo Dante Marchetti
(1876–1940)
arr. James Rae

20
mp
mp
B♭
25
f
f
B♭/D
B♭°
Cm
N.C.
Cm
30
mf
mf
Cm7
F7
Cm
F7
35
1.
2.
1.
2.
mp
mp
B♭
N.C.
B♭
E♭m6
B♭
N.C.

Bill Bailey, Won't You Please Come Home?

Hughie Cannon
(1877–1912)
arr. James Rae

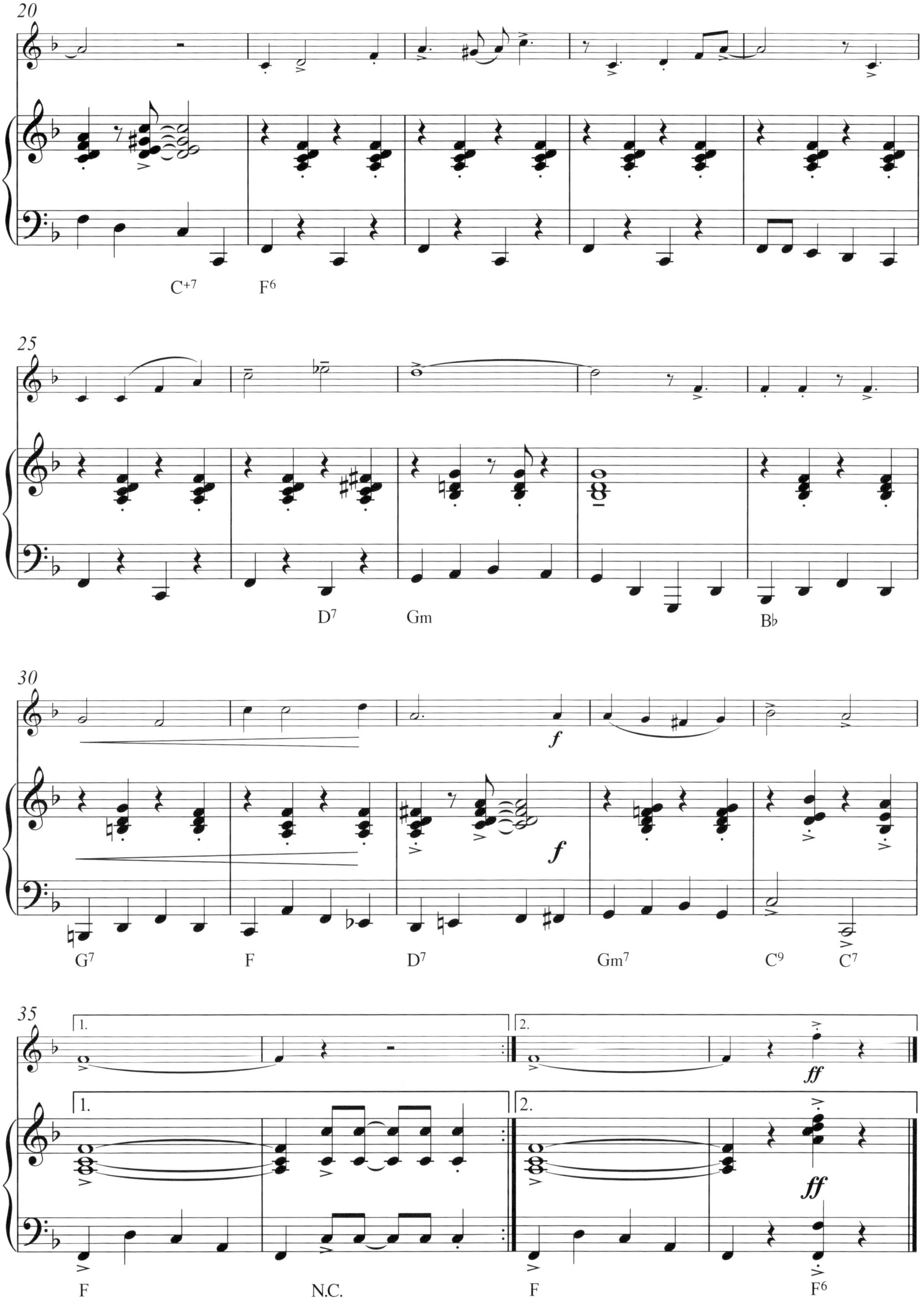
20
C+7 F6
25
D7 Gm Bb
30
f
G7 F D7 Gm7 C9 C7
35
1. 2.
ff
F N.C. F F6

When Johnny Comes Marching Home

Louis Lambert
(1829–1892)
arr. James Rae

Lively March ♩. = 120

Clarinet in B♭ (concert pitch)

Piano

Over The Waves

Juventino Rosas
(1868–1894)
arr. James Rae

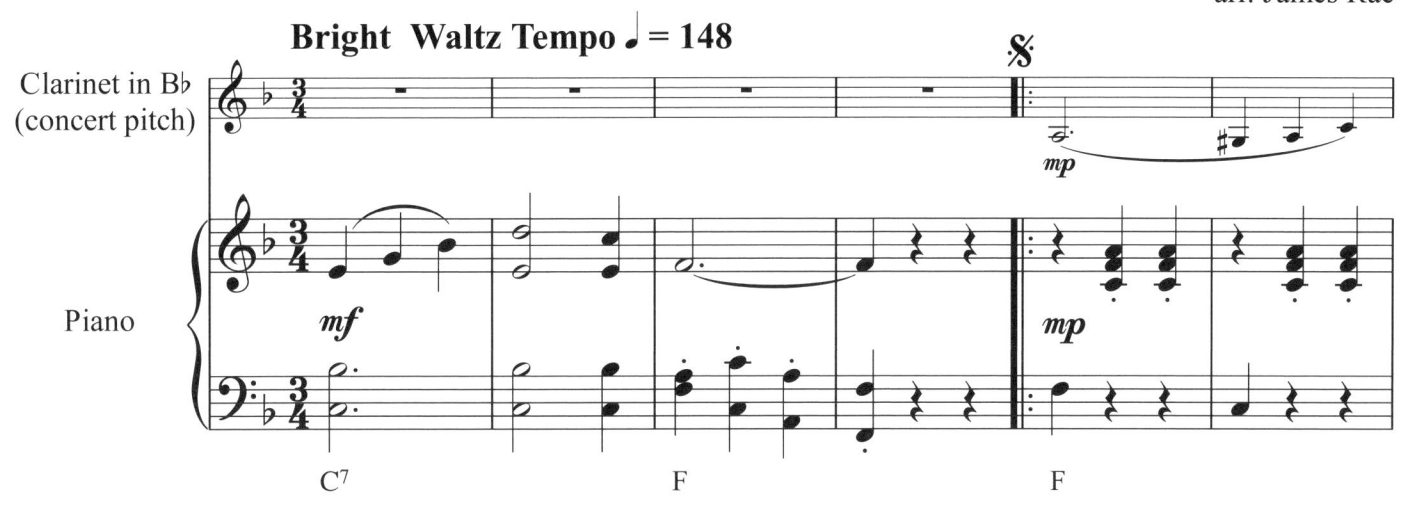

Bright Waltz Tempo ♩ = 148

16

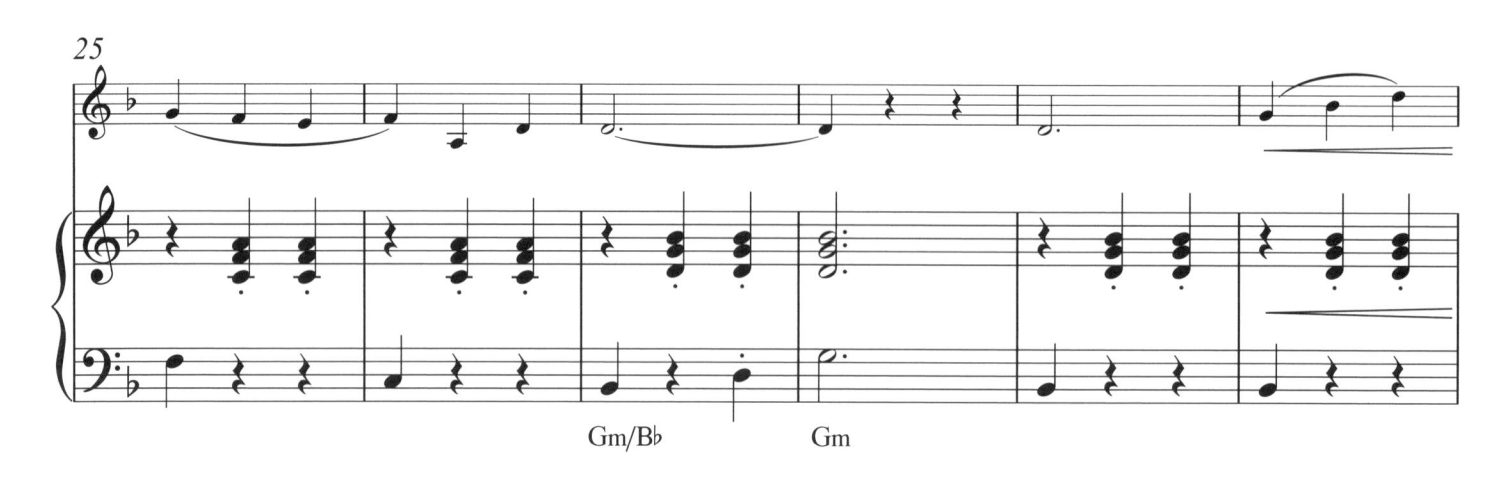

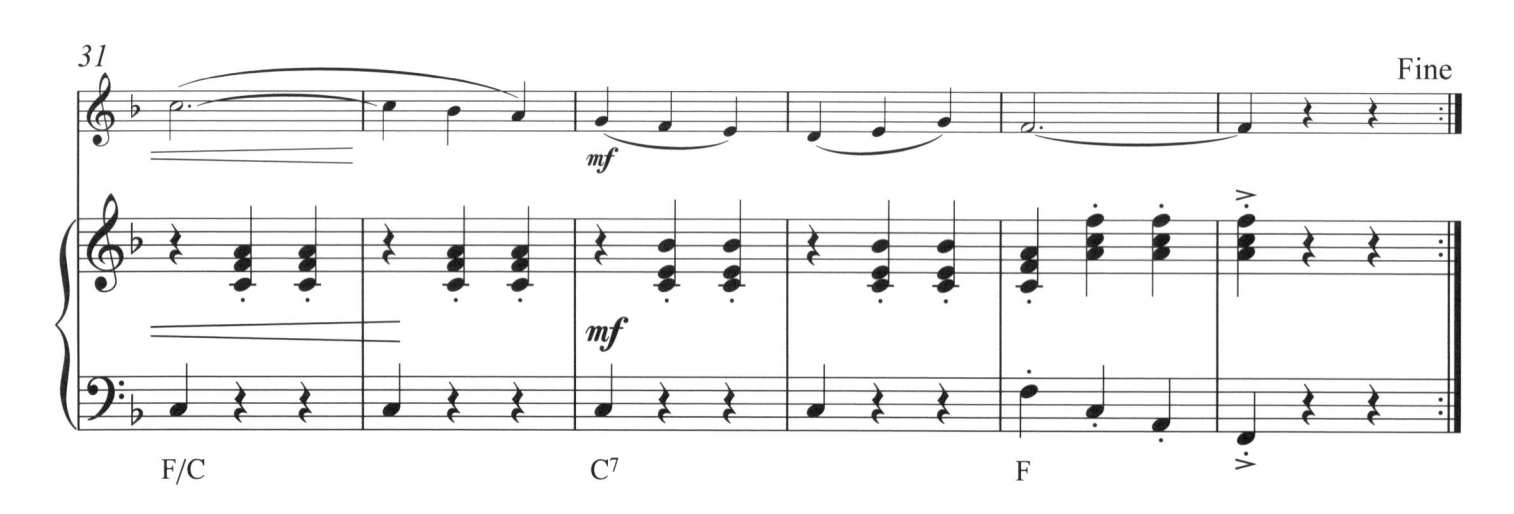

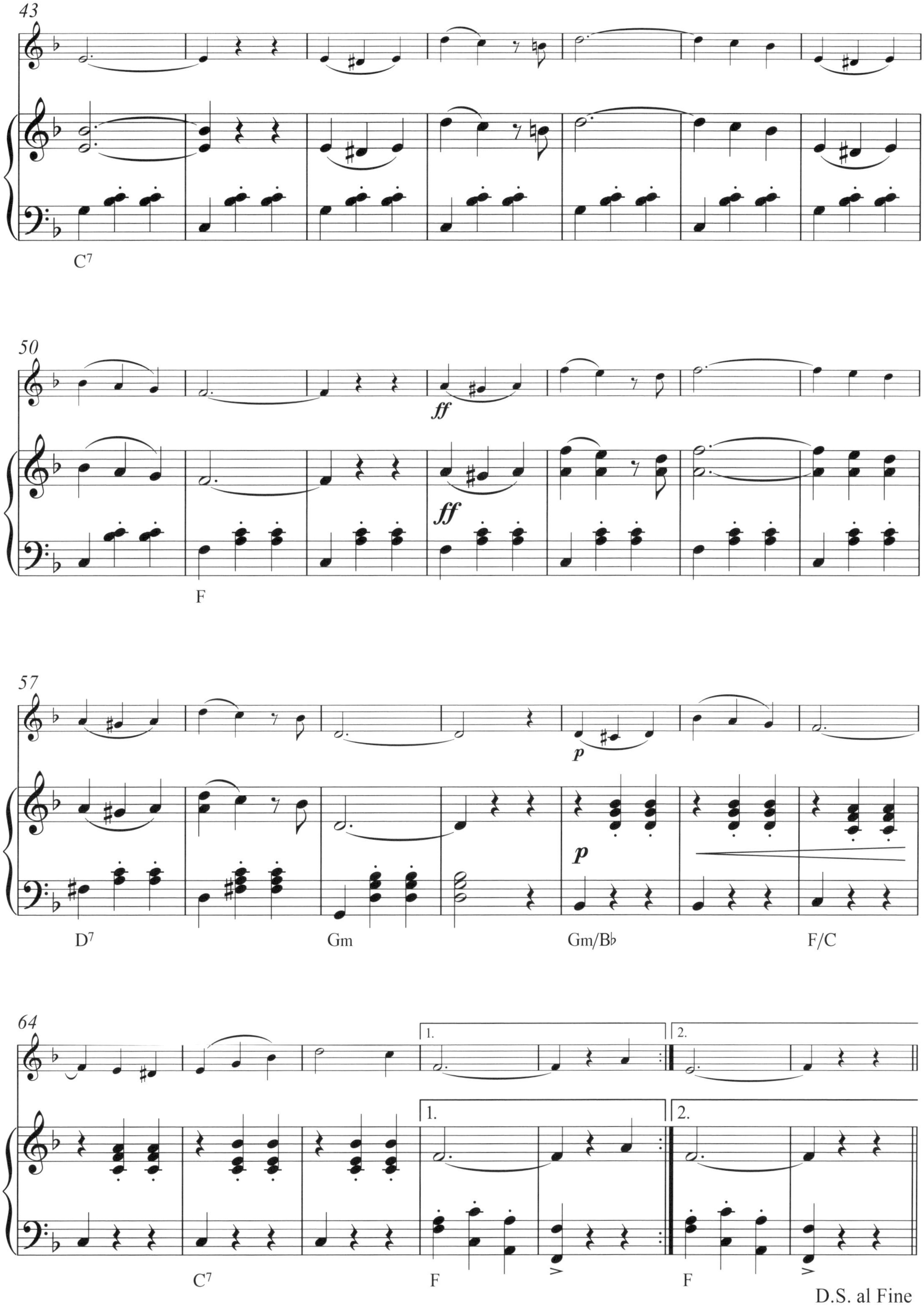
43
C7
50
ff
ff
F
57
p
p
D7
Gm
Gm/B♭
F/C
64
1.
2.
1.
2.
C7
F
F
D.S. al Fine

Misty

Erroll Garner
(1921–1977)
arr. James Rae

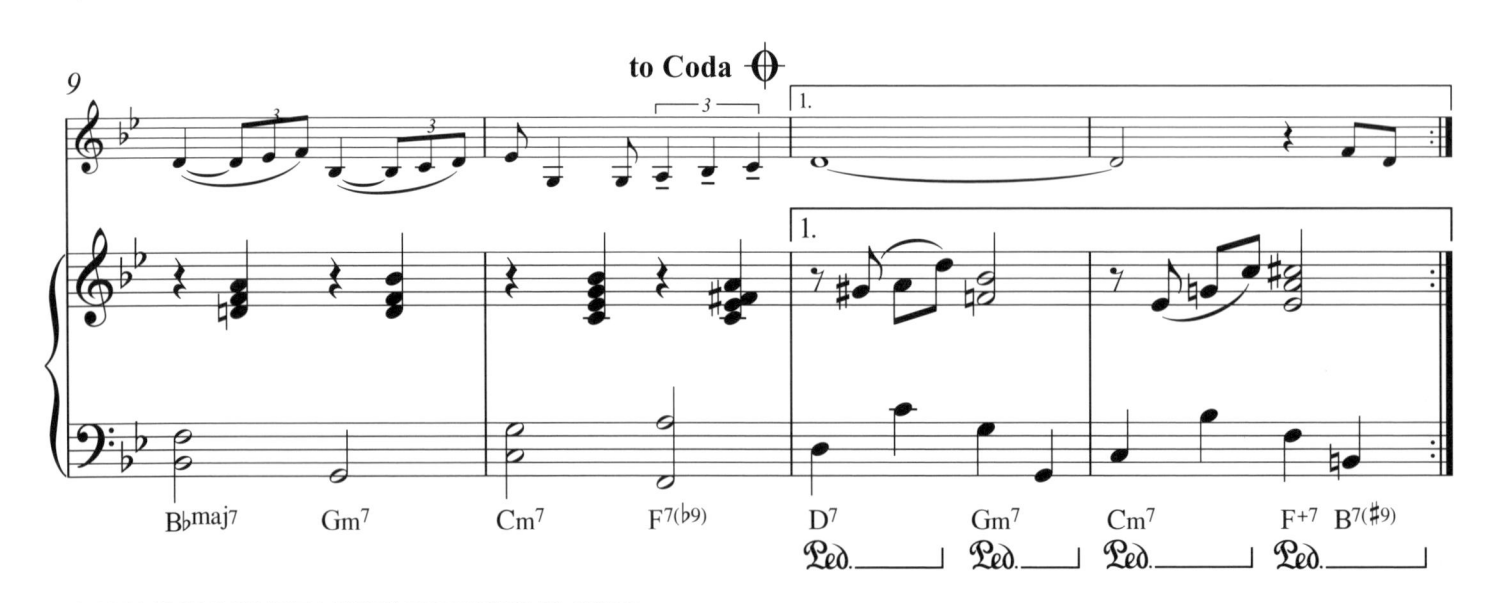

13
2.
mf
Bb Eb7 Ab7 Bb E° Fm7 Bb7(b9)
Ped.
17
Ebmaj7 Eb6 Em7 A7 Gm7 C7
21
f
mp
Dm7 G7 Cm7 F+7 B7(#9)
D.S. al Coda
Coda
rit.
Db7 Cm7 Bmaj7 Bbmaj7

Chicago

Fred Fisher
(1875–1942)
arr. James Rae

20
Dm9 G7 C6 Em7 A7 Dm7 G7 Dm7 G7
25
Dm9 G7 Bm7 E7 Am A7 Fmaj7
30
B♭9 C7 B7 B♭7 A7 A♭7 G7 F♯7 G7 Dm7
34
1.
2.
G7 C6 E♭° Dm7 G7 C6 G+7 C N.C.

Préface

You Must Remember This… rassemble dix arrangements pour clarinette et piano de mélodies parmi les plus célèbres et les plus appréciées du monde. Toutes sont écrites dans des tonalités confortables, pour permettre à l'interprète de se concentrer sur la ligne mélodique. Les accompagnements de piano sont « pensés pour le professeur » et comprennent des symboles d'accords. Les pièces sont d'un niveau technique allant de facile à moyen.

You Must Remember This… est le préalable idéal à d'autres publications bien connues d'Universal Edition : *Take Ten* (UE 19 et *Take Another Ten* (UE 21 169).

James Rae, juin 2016

You Must Remember This…
Old favourites arranged for clarinet and piano by James Rae

Cover design by Lynette Williamson

UE 21 708
ISMN 979-0-008-08760-8
UPC 8-03452-07142-6
ISBN 978-3-7024-7431-7

© Copyright 2016 by Universal Edition A.G., Wien

CLARINET

UE

You must remember this...

Old favourites arranged for clarinet and piano

James Rae

Daisy Bell

Harry Dacre
(1857–1922)
arr. James Rae

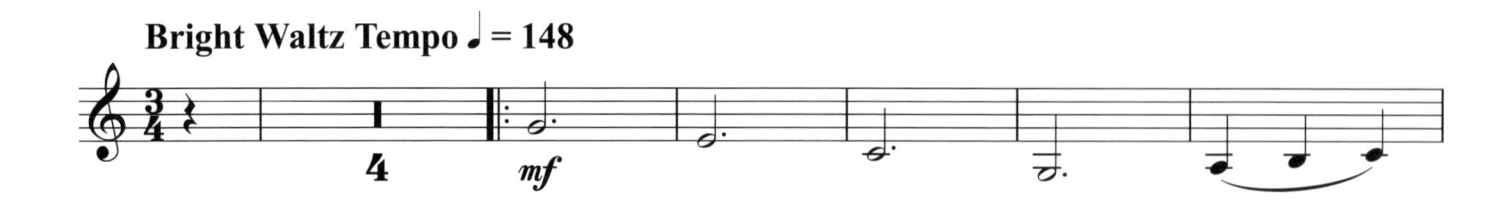

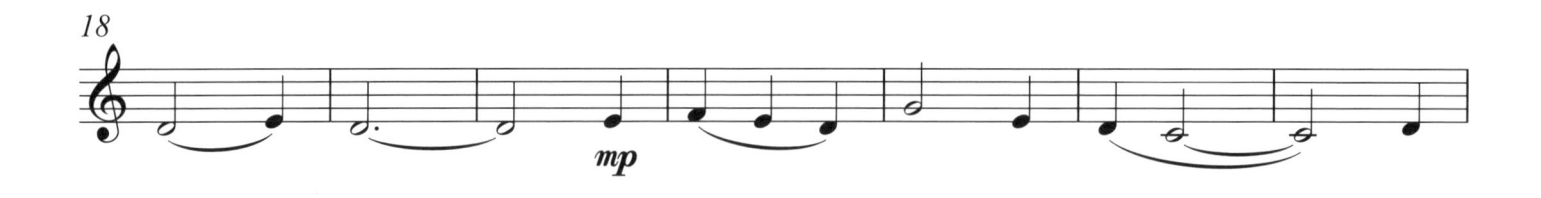

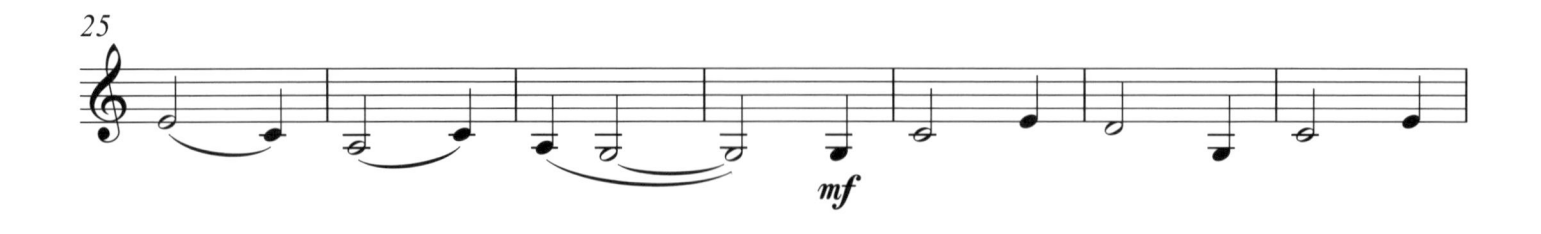

As Time Goes By

Herman Hupfeld
(1894–1951)
arr. James Rae

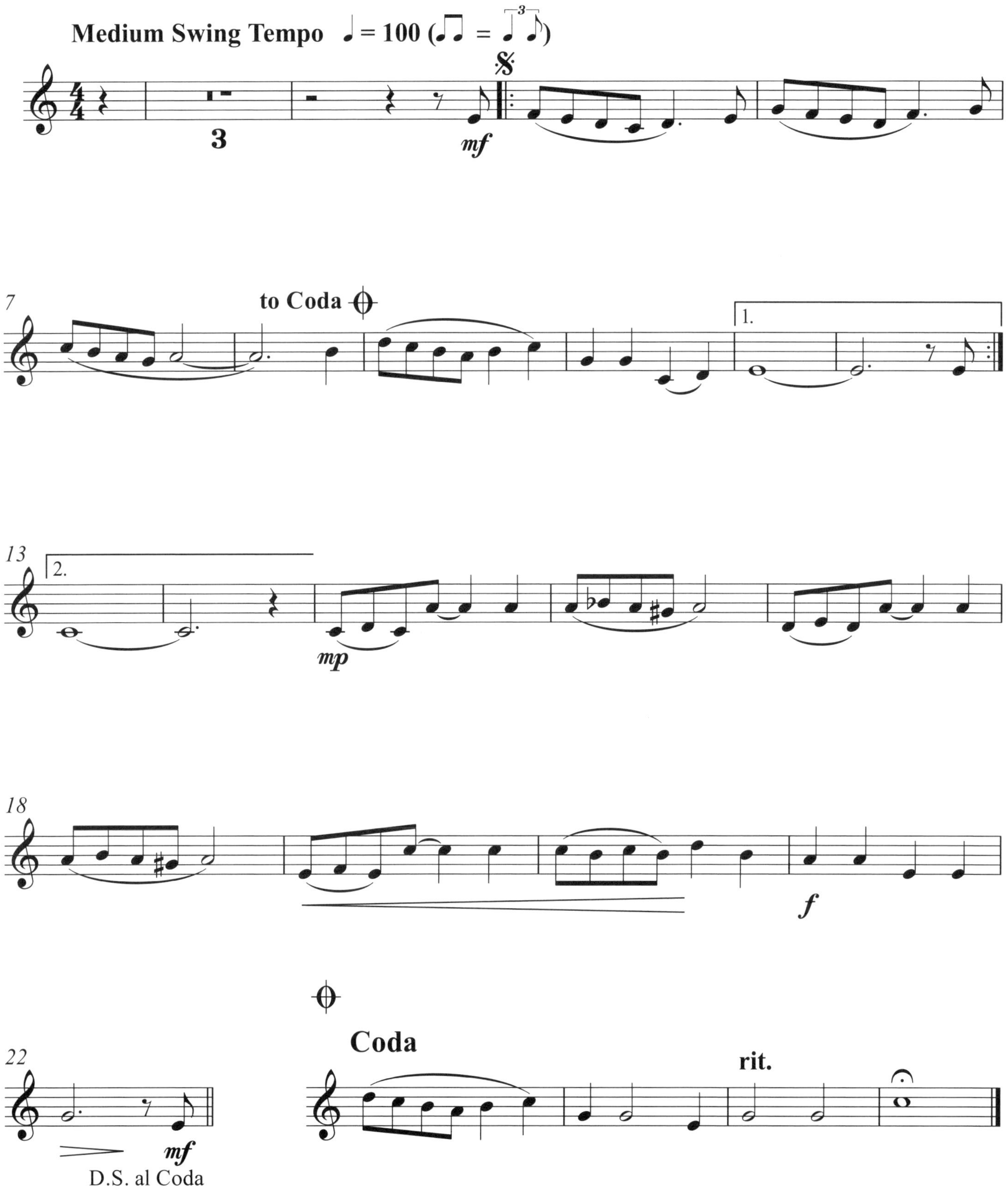

La Paloma
(The Dove)

Sebastián de Yradier
(1809–1865)
arr. James Rae

Give My Regards To Broadway

George M. Cohan
(1878–1942)
arr. James Rae

Fascination

Fermo Dante Marchetti
(1876–1940)
arr. James Rae

Bill Bailey, Won't You Please Come Home?

Hughie Cannon
(1877–1912)
arr. James Rae

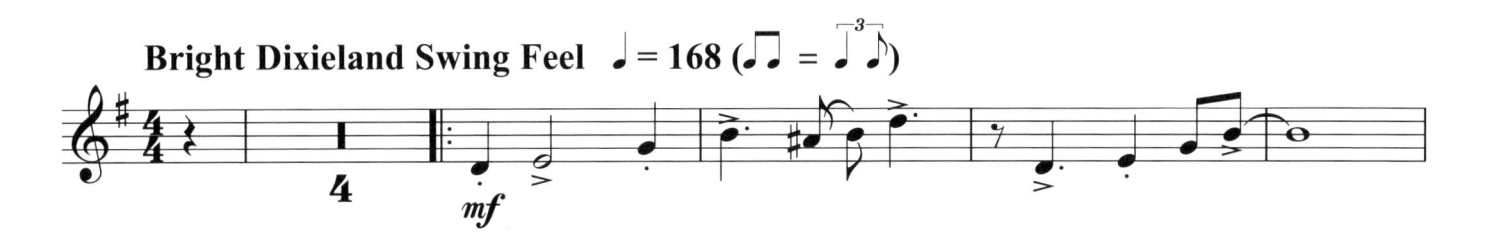

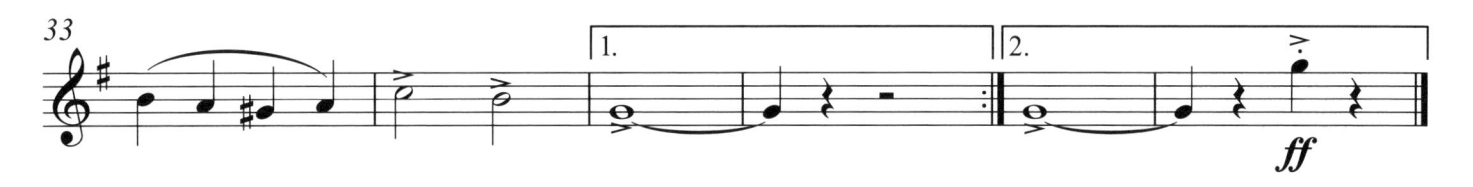

When Johnny Comes Marching Home

Louis Lambert
(1829–1892)
arr. James Rae

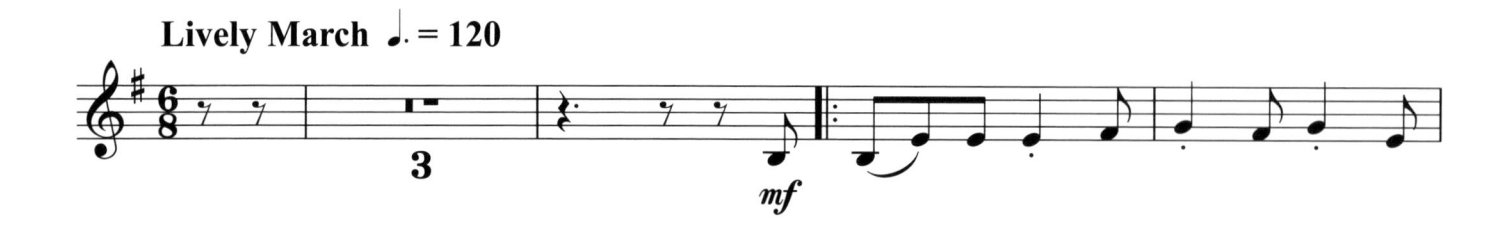

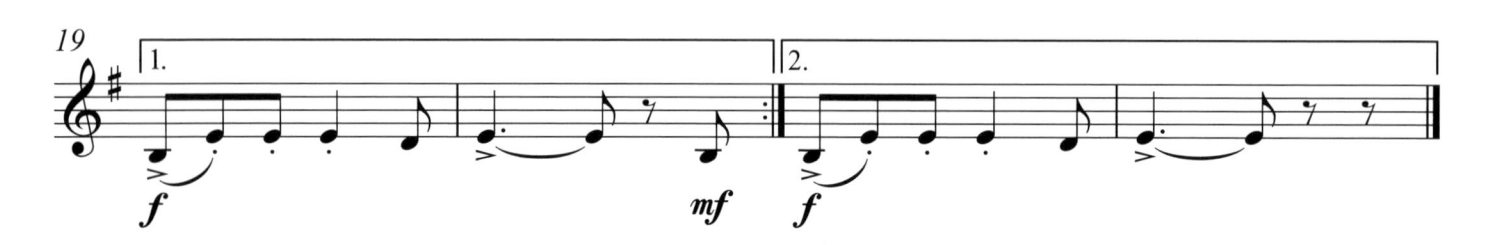

Over The Waves

Juventino Rosas
(1868–1894)
arr. James Rae

Bright Waltz Tempo ♩ = 148

D.S. al Fine

Misty

Erroll Garner
(1921–1977)
arr. James Rae

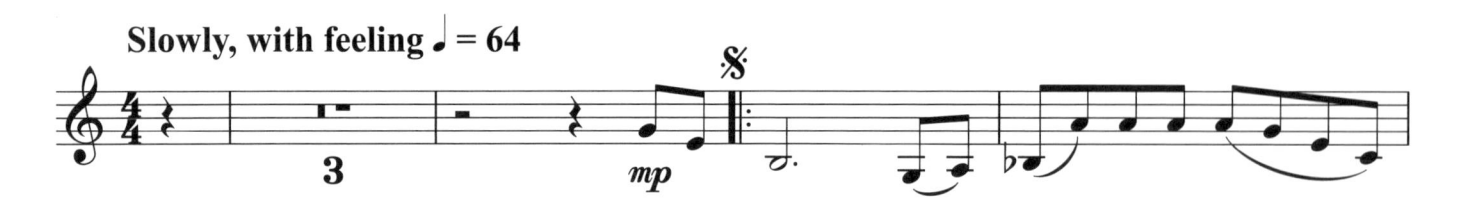

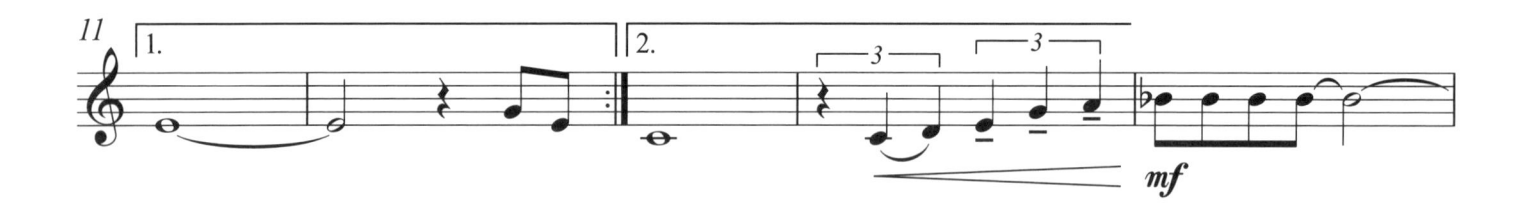

Chicago

Fred Fisher
(1875–1942)
arr. James Rae

Inhalt • Contents • Table des matières

Daisy Bell	2
As Time Goes By	3
La Paloma (The Dove)	4
Give My Regards to Broadway	5
Fascination	6
Bill Bailey, Won't You Please Come Home?	7
When Johnny Comes Marching Home	8
Over the Waves	9
Misty	10
Chicago	11